Including Everyone

Including Everyone

Creating Music Classrooms Where All Children Learn

Judith A. Jellison

OXFORD
UNIVERSITY PRESS

OXFORD
UNIVERSITY PRESS

Oxford University Press is a department of the University of Oxford. It furthers the University's objective of excellence in research, scholarship, and education by publishing worldwide.

Oxford New York
Auckland Cape Town Dar es Salaam Hong Kong Karachi
Kuala Lumpur Madrid Melbourne Mexico City Nairobi
New Delhi Shanghai Taipei Toronto

With offices in
Argentina Austria Brazil Chile Czech Republic France Greece
Guatemala Hungary Italy Japan Poland Portugal Singapore
South Korea Switzerland Thailand Turkey Ukraine Vietnam

Published in the United States of America by
Oxford University Press
198 Madison Avenue, New York, NY 10016

Library of Congress Cataloging-in-Publication Data
Jellison, Judith A. (Judith Anne), 1940-
Including everyone : creating music classrooms where all children learn / Judith A. Jellison.
pages cm
Includes bibliographical references and index. ISBN 978-0-19-935876-2 (hardcover : alk. paper) — ISBN 978-0-19-935877-9 (pbk. : alk. paper) 1. School music—Instruction and study. 2. Elementary school teaching. 3. Inclusive education. I. Title.
MT1.J35 2015
372.87—dc23
2014015979

CONTENTS

PREFACE

Major reforms in educational policies have deeply affected the lives of children who struggle academically and socially in school, and have likewise affected the roles of teachers in public education. Contemporary music classrooms include a beautiful mosaic of individual children from diverse backgrounds, children who vary considerably in their capabilities, interests, and levels of motivation, and who present a variety of challenges much greater than what teachers may have encountered as recently as a generation ago.

This book is not so much about how to teach as it is about how to *think* as a teacher confronting a variety of learning challenges. The principles of effective thinking that I outline are a path to effective teaching through the application of generalizable ideas that promote creativity and independence in music teachers, whose task is to provide appropriate educational opportunities for all children, experiences that prepare children to participate in music happily and successfully. The goal of joyful lifelong music involvement is central to the philosophical underpinnings of this book.

Much of what we understand about learning and teaching applies to children across the spectra of abilities and across grade levels and music settings (general music, band, choir, and orchestra). The principal features of learning experiences that effectively prepare children for meaningful musical lives beyond school are universal in the sense that they engage diverse groups of children in common experiences, experiences that are valued by their teachers, their parents, and the children themselves.

The unnecessary separation of students from one another limits opportunities for music achievement, positive peer interactions, and the development of self-determination. A universal approach to instruction, which serves as a guiding principle throughout the chapters that follow, is one in which teachers recognize the individual needs of students and design learning environments where all students participate in the same activities, experience personal success, and contribute to the success of their classmates. When a culture of inclusion is fostered, students develop musically, develop a sense of belonging, and feel good about their accomplishments and those of the children who share their experiences. This book is about making that happen.

ACKNOWLEDGMENTS

I have vivid memories of beautiful children who lived in restrictive, remote, confining institutions while other children experienced the world differently, living with their families, learning in neighborhood schools, and playing with their friends. I have vivid memories of beautiful children, many of whom struggled in school and yet showed me, a young music teacher, how important it is to have a place where you can feel safe, where you can try and fail, and where you can develop a sense of accomplishment and belonging. All of them taught me about the problems children encounter as a result of exclusion, when they are separated from the enriching experiences available to those deemed more capable. They also taught me to confront hard questions about education, to think about the realities of time in school, what should be taught, and why.

My knowing and working with such diversity of human potential led to the development of the ideas I explain in this book. In a very real sense, this book is about the children I have known. It is also about the thousands of other children whose lives are dependent on the decisions adults make for them, decisions that affect their educational opportunities in the present and their prospects for happiness in the future.

I didn't learn to think this way on my own, of course. I am deeply indebted to my former teachers who have become my dear friends: Cliff Madsen, for helping me learn to think deeply, question received wisdom, and ask penetrating questions about whether what we do accomplishes anything meaningful, beginning with my first lesson on "values and techniques." He showed me what it takes to be a scholar, a teacher, and a loving friend.

For fueling my passion and energizing my rebellious spirit, and ultimately for shaping my thinking about inclusion, I thank the tenacious, audacious, impatient Lou Brown, a force of nature who changed the way countless people have come to think about what it means to be a whole human being, irrespective of seemingly insurmountable limitations that fate may ordain. Inspired by notions of equity, access, and educational programming developed by Lou and his colleagues, I began publishing articles nearly 40 years ago that explained the application of these ideas in music education and music therapy practices. These early efforts toward making music experiences as inclusive as any others in children's lives led eventually to this book.

Cliff's and Lou's boundless generosity shaped who I became and allowed me to imagine that I too could help change the world for the children and adults who deserved to experience life to its fullest, disabilities be damned.

I have learned a great deal from my university students in Minnesota and Texas, to whom I assigned earlier drafts of this book, which they read and wrote about in ways that led to the improvement of my thinking, and from my generous friends, who graciously agreed to read what I wrote and offered the kind of pointed criticism that only really smart people who really care about you can deliver. All helped me to refine the written expression of ideas that seemed oh so clear inside my head before I attempted to write a book about them.

I continue to benefit from feedback from those closest to me, especially my dear friend and colleague Laurie Scott, one of the smartest people I know, and someone who understands intimately the challenges faced by the teachers and parents of children with disabilities. As I was writing this book, I experienced the joy of working with my now former doctoral students Laura Brown and Ellary Draper, who listened to my lectures, read my manuscripts, questioned my ideas, offered insightful comments, and worked along with me in helping to get my message across to our students at UT. Thanks also to the many others who read early versions of this book and offered feedback, especially our wonderful daughter Jeneen Irwin, and Marilyn Kostka and David Wolfe, people I love deeply and have known seemingly forever.

I am grateful to Norm Hirschy, the skillful and imaginative editor at Oxford University Press, New York, who believed in *Including Everyone* from the beginning and who provided invaluable guidance, the amazing staff at Oxford for their competence in production and editing, and the anonymous readers whose insightful suggestions made this a better book.

As most authors are wont to do, I conclude with thanks to those closest to me. I feel privileged to work with children, to teach in a great university, and to work with parents, teachers, and caregivers devoted to helping children lead rich and rewarding lives. But I am especially privileged to have a family who sees me as I am and loves me in ways that propel life forward, inspire me to go beyond what's easy, and remind me every day that the core of a meaningful life is the love of human beings who care about you as much as you care about them. Jeneen, Pete, Maggie, Ella, Gert, Mary and my extended family in Pennsylvania, and especially my husband Bob, who made this book possible: there are no words, but I know you know.

And to all of you patient enough to read acknowledgments, thank you as well. I hope that what I've written in the pages that follow will help you create something wonderful in the lives of the children with whom you work.

ABOUT THE COMPANION WEBSITE

www.oup.com/us/includingeveryone

The website contains resources, examples, and other supplementary materials that are referred to in the book. You will find examples of student profiles and assessments of teaching environments and activities for the development of strategies and activities, in addition to information about diverse populations and laws, including definitions and terminology.

You will also find useful information specific to music teaching and learning at cml.music.utexas.edu, the site for the Center for Music Learning (CML) at the Sarah and Ernest Butler School of Music at The University of Texas at Austin. For information specific to disabilities, go to the online resources page.

Including Everyone

CHAPTER 1
Who's Here?

OVERVIEW

It is your first observation of a new classroom full of unfamiliar children. You may be a student observer or may be meeting your own class on the first day of school. One child gets your attention. Is it the violinist who persists in his attempts to talk to his stand partner? Is it the singer on the back riser who nervously rubs his hands together during the entire choir rehearsal? Is it the percussionist who plays beautifully but consistently moves her head from side to side as she plays? Is it the girl seated in a wheelchair who smiles throughout the class but doesn't participate in any of the class activities? Is it the teenager who sings enthusiastically (loudly) but misses most of the pitches and many of the words? Or perhaps it is the young boy who physically rolls back and forth on the floor except when it is time to play mallet instruments, which he plays with perfect time. There are, of course, other children. Most seem very happy to be making music, a few seem lost when instructions are given, and one always seems to have her hand raised.

These are our children—children who are capable of showing surprise, happiness, pride, frustration, and a range of emotions and music capabilities. Our challenge as teachers is to find ways for this seemingly diverse group to participate happily and successfully in meaningful music experiences in school and throughout life. The long-term goal of lifelong music involvement—involvement that begins in a diverse learning environment—is central to the philosophical underpinnings of our work.

When you first saw the child who got your attention, what were you thinking? Most likely, you wondered why he or she would behave in such a way and perhaps then thought: disability or gifted or a "problem." You may have wondered about the child's future success in the class. Can you visualize this child participating happily and successfully in your classroom? Our expectations for children are based understandably on our past experiences, and they are often colored by a child's official or unofficial label. It is well known that teachers' expectations and attitudes have much to do with the successful learning of any child and that many labels can result in negative stereotyping and poor decision-making regarding the child's educational program. (One of my favorite organizations distributes T-shirts with the saying "Labels are for jars.")

You will read much about attitudes throughout this book. I will ask that you keep in mind that children who have been labeled by us or others will not behave just like other children with similar labels whom you may have observed, read about, or seen in videos. To overcome negative stereotyping associated with some labels, which can develop in spite of people's best intentions, it is important to observe as many positive examples as possible. Better yet, observe and interact with children from diverse populations in their music classes.

Most people have little difficulty accepting the notion that not all children are alike. The evidence for this is simply too compelling to ignore. But many people may not yet realize that not all children with a particular label are alike, either. Individuals classified as having autism or cerebral palsy or being "at-risk" are every bit as varied as children are generally. What this means is that knowing the label given to the child or the child's group membership based on ethnicity, culture, race, gender, native language, or any number of other factors provides precious little information about *that* child. We all seem to know this intellectually, but our personal histories and our experiences can get in the way of clear thinking.

Getting to know individual children reveals the personal characteristics that make them who they are. And children who are more understandable as individuals are more teachable as learners. Teachers who spend their days with very many children often tell me stories about one particular child, a child they would like to reach. Among all of the children they teach, *one* comes to mind. This is the child who gets and keeps their attention. More than being interested in general features that characterize various diverse groups of children, teachers want more help with the *one* child who is in their classroom *now*.

The uniqueness of individual children cannot be overstated. When children are grouped by any factor and become part of a statistic, there is a danger of forgetting our responsibilities to them—their names are unknown, as are their personalities and capabilities. More than 5.5 million children (ages six through twenty-one) are defined as having a disability,[1] and more than 20.9 million children (ages six though seventeen) live in low-income households.[2] All of these children have names, and most go to school.

This chapter focuses on ways to think about all children, their individual characteristics and capabilities, the support services some may need to be more successful and happy in school, and how their labels influence people's attitudes and actions toward them. Since my approach in this book is guided by the uniqueness of children and the principles that can positively affect their lives, extensive descriptions of children from diverse populations (e.g., at-risk, types of disabilities, groups representing different cultures) will not appear here.[3]

DESCRIBING, GROUPING, AND THE BELL CURVE

Good. Bad. Tall. Brown-eyed. Shy. How do we describe a child? What descriptors matter? What are the behavioral characteristics of a child with a specific learning disability? Intellectual disability? Autism spectrum disorder? And what is it about those labels that matter? How can I describe Peter to you? Sarah? Megan? How much more do I know about you now that I know you are an Aries? A Libra? A Texan? Do labels and group memberships matter? If so, when?

Think about a child you know. If you had to describe that child in one word or in one sentence, would you be satisfied with the description? Would others really know something significant about the child from one word or sentence? How would you describe yourself in a few words? Would you begin with the least disputable characteristics (height, gender, eye color, and so on) or with something more idiosyncratic? Would you begin with your deficits?

Try to describe one child you know well, including all of the child's physical and behavioral characteristics, capabilities, and educational needs. It's a difficult task. How would you describe two children with similar (not identical) physical and behavioral characteristics, capabilities, or educational needs? How are these two children the same or different? Move to describing three, ten, or more children. On what basis do you move a child out of one group and into another? How much of a difference is required to form another group?

Depending on the variables that you use to determine group placement, some decisions will seem easier than others (e.g., placement by height compared with placement by musical talent). The ease of making decisions about grouping and labeling is often determined by the manner in which individual characteristics are assessed (by using a tape measure, a panel of judges, or medical tests, for example). Stringent research requires that measurements be demonstrably valid and reliable. Measuring by inches is a valid and reliable way of reporting height, but at what point do you use the label "tall"? Or with other measures, use the label "at-risk" or "disability"?

Throughout this book, I use the term "typically developing" only because it is the one that appears most often in the work of professionals in psychology and special education to describe children who do not have a disability and are not at-risk. Remember the term "normal," a term loosely associated with the statistical bell curve? This term is no longer acceptable as a way to describe children. Other terms have evolved in our language, and even though we struggle to get free of many that have broad and confusing meanings, we are stuck with them . . . for the time. This is a good place to do a quick review of the bell curve and its properties. If you have a good understanding of how the bell curve is used to determine groupings, you will have a better understanding of how it can function to describe individuals and how those descriptions can be misinterpreted.

A normal distribution of a large number of instances of a given characteristic (such as IQ score or weight) in which the mode, median, and average are all identical is often referred to as a bell curve because of the shape that is created. You have seen many pictures, although you may want to refer to figure 1.1. As more and more individual measurements are included in a sample (e.g., height, intelligence, SAT scores), the histogram will begin to resemble a bell curve. Once the mean is known, the standard deviation (a score representing the average distance of individual scores from the mean) can be calculated to describe the extent of variation around the mean. When measurements are equally and normally distributed, 68 percent of the scores fall within 1 standard deviation above and

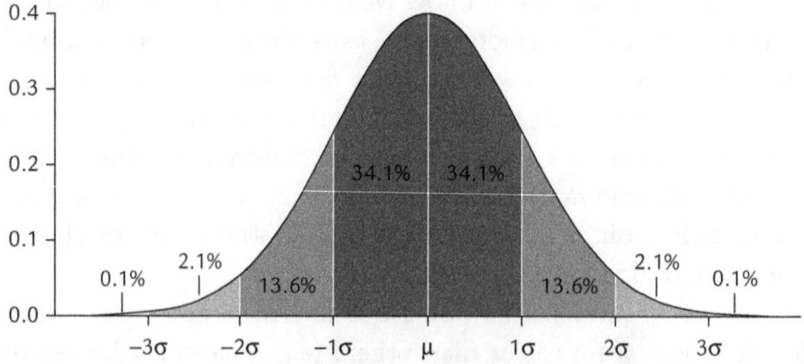

Figure 1.1 A graph of a normal distribution is often referred to as a bell curve because of the shape that is created when the mean, median, and mode of a normal distribution of data points are equal. About 68 percent of the data fall within 1 standard deviation of the mean, 95 percent within 2 standard deviations, and about 99.7 percent within 3 standard deviations.
Source: Wikimedia; figure by Mike Toews, Creative Commons license.

1 standard deviation below the mean, and about 95 percent of scores are within 2 standard deviations above and 2 standard deviations below the mean. That leaves only 2.5 percent at either end of the curve (beyond ± 2 standard deviations).

Let's consider musical talent as an example. If we had a valid measure of musical talent (no small task) and measured the musical talent of thousands of randomly selected individuals, we would expect a bell curve with the following: approximately 2.5 percent of the scores would be higher than 2 standard deviations above the mean (individuals with these scores might be labeled "talented" or even "gifted"), and 2.5 percent of the scores would be more than 2 standard deviations below the mean (these individuals might be labeled "untalented").

To pursue this further, let's separate the top 2.5 percent (the "gifted") from the previous distribution and make them into a separate group of "gifted, musically talented" individuals. When we look at the measurements of musical talent for this group, we would most likely recognize more clearly the variations within this elite group. Would we then look at their musical talent as "gifted gifted," "average gifted," and "untalented gifted"? If enough measurements of a variable are taken, and the instrument is a valid measure of the characteristic (don't forget that), it is likely that we will find some who do OK, others who are struggling, and still others who are flying along without any observable problems.[4] The same child may be labeled as having a disability according to one criterion, labeled typical according to another criterion, and even labeled gifted according to yet another criterion.

DEFINITIONS, ASSESSMENTS, AND ATTITUDES

Two of the terms that are probably used most often to identify children who may be in need of additional educational services are "disability" and "at-risk." The term "disability" is applied only when formal assessments have been conducted and professionals, using state and federal criteria, have classified the child as a child with a disability. Formal assessments may be conducted only with the approval of the parents or guardians. When, for whatever reason, a child is struggling academically and/or socially in school and this child has not been assessed as having a disability, the child may be identified as being "at-risk"—say, "at risk" of dropping out of school.[5] Some children identified as "at-risk" may also be suspected of having a disability and may be referred by teachers or parents for assessment. Others may receive other types of intervening services.

(Services for some children identified as at-risk will be discussed in the next section.)

The Individuals with Disabilities Education Act (IDEA) defines a "child with a disability" using a list of categorical labels (e.g., intellectual disability, speech or language impairments) and further defines a "child with a disability" as one who, as a result of his or her disability, requires *both* special education and related services (see note 1). Broad definitions of types of disabilities are included in federal and state laws but are also put forward by agencies and organizations such as the Learning Disabilities Association of America (LDAA) and the American Association of Intellectual and Developmental Disabilities (AAIDD). For example, AAIDD defines an intellectual disability as "a disability characterized by significant limitations both in intellectual functioning and in adaptive behavior, which covers many everyday social and practical skills. This disability originates before the age of 18."[6] But how are the various types of disabilities determined? The final determination rests with the results of evaluations of the child and the interpretations and decisions of knowledgeable professionals in schools and communities who then identify the disability, although it is important to note that the specific label or classification of the child's disability is not required before services can be provided. Some assessments may take several months. If there is general agreement that the child has a disability requiring special education and related services, the law allows for those provisions.

IDEA and disability organizations require nondiscriminatory and multifaceted evaluation and reevaluation procedures to determine a disability or type of disability, although evaluations also measure children's strengths and weaknesses. Evaluation procedures, however, are subject to change, as are the terminology and definitions in federal and state documents. Although terminology and definitions in state documents may differ from the exact language in IDEA, state categorical labels and definitions must closely follow the definition of "a child with a disability" put forward in IDEA, and states must rely on appropriate evaluation tools and procedures to determine those labels.

We have a history of trying to find words to describe "groups" of our citizens and the very groups to which we belong. What terms are now preferred by most individuals when defining their group membership by gender, ethnicity, race, or any other number of factors, and have those preferred terms changed throughout history?

The origin of the word "handicapped" has been traced to the phrase "hand in cap" used in a wagering game played in England sometime before the middle of the seventeenth century. Money forfeited was deposited in a cap. A century later, the term "handy-cap match" was used in horse racing, and it came to suggest a way to equalize chances for competitors who were at a disadvantage (meaning without advantage).[7] Consider the term "disability" (meaning without ability), which has gradually replaced "handicap." Will "disability" be viewed as a more pejorative term over time, and will we see it disappear or be replaced with another?

When the first school for individuals with intellectual disabilities was established in 1846, it was named "The Experimental School for Teaching and Training Idiotic Children," a perfectly awful name by today's standards. Of course, the selection of the name of this and other schools was not intentionally insensitive but rather reflected the language of the times. Throughout the twentieth century, labels such as "trainable mentally retarded" and "educable mentally retarded" were common; now they have all but disappeared. With the development of more exacting assessments, other categories have emerged. For example, autism was not identified as a separate disability category in IDEA until the 1990 reauthorization of the law. Children who now may be identified as having an autism spectrum disorder would have been identified earlier using other categories of that time, such as "behavior problems" or "emotionally disturbed."

Changes in terminology slowly continue. For example, the term "mental retardation" has been used for more than a century; it appeared in the amended version of IDEA in 2004, in many other federal and state laws, and in common vernacular. The term is being gradually replaced. "Intellectual disabilities" is now widely used by professionals in the names of their organizations and in their journals. The work of parents and advocates eventually led to the passage of "Rosa's Law" in 2010, which requires changes in the language of federal documents; "mental retardation" and "mentally retarded individual" have been changed to "intellectual disabilities" and "individual with an intellectual disability."[8]

In broader terms, individuals with disabilities have been referred to as "special learners," individuals with "special needs," or "challenged." I heard a person at a conference comment about a friend with a disability: "His needs aren't special to him, they're part of his life!" Individuals using these terms may have intentions of softening what they perceive to be negative associations with the word "disability," but we should take our lead about language from individuals with disabilities and their organizations. There are few professional organizations that still use terms such as "special learners," "special needs," or "challenged." That's a strong signal to me about the language I choose to use.

Segregation and institutionalization played a major role in the early formation of negative associations with the words "disability" and "handicapped." The selection of categories and the organization of any information are often determined on the basis of some salient characteristic. For people with disabilities, salient characteristics were physical, behavioral, and intellectual "handicaps." Through this process, the language used to describe groups of people with disabilities set up artificial limitations and contributed to discrimination and negative stereotyping in popular culture, including literature and movies.[9] The thinking of communities might have been something like the following: "Something must be wrong with these people, or they wouldn't be separated (by law, by society) from the rest of us." Similarities among people were all but ignored.

Historically, individuals with disabilities lived in institutions in isolated rural areas, far removed from the mainstream of life. People outside of the institutions had little or no opportunity to observe similarities between themselves and people living separate, isolated lives. Local, state, and federal laws spread fear and misinformation and thus sanctioned isolation. Sweeping generalizations led to false beliefs that (1) persons with the same disability label have the same characteristics in all dimensions of their lives, (2) people with disabilities have limited knowledge and/or skills with regard to all aspects of life, and (3) people with disabilities can't fit into society and therefore have to be separated from other members of the community. (For an interesting account of life in institutions, music education in institutions, and the deinstitutionalization movement, read the essay "From Exclusion to Inclusion" in appendix B.)

From research into attitude formation, we know that extremely frightening or pleasurable experiences and repeated exposure to situations, persons, words, and advertising can influence emotions, shape attitudes, and affect behaviors. Classmates, neighbors, teachers, and legislators have attitudes that were formed in these ways; unfortunately, some have attitudes that result in discriminatory and biased actions toward individuals they perceive to be different.

Biases and lack of knowledge about diverse populations are often revealed in our use of written and spoken language. To educate the public and to counter some of the negative stigmatizing effects of words, many organizations representing diverse groups (disabilities, ethnicity, culture) promote the use of terminology preferred by a majority of individuals in those groups. This is not an issue about semantics only and cannot be dismissed as simply being "politically correct." Words convey meaning at multiple levels. Words can harm. Words can hurt. And words can help.

They can help teachers build rapport with students and parents and can help create positive learning environments.

It is easier to observe changes in print than to observe changes in the way people speak. Numerous examples of ways to reduce bias in written language appear in professional journals, online, and in criteria for publication in professional journals (e.g., *Publication Manual of the American Psychological Association*).[10] One of the easiest changes to avoid labeling in spoken and written language is eliminating the use of the definite article "the" (e.g., the disadvantaged, the emotionally disturbed, the elderly, the disabled, the poor), which objectifies individuals. If a student's group membership is important to communicate (most often it is not), use commonly accepted designations, being sensitive to preferences of the student and parents (e.g., individual preferences for "black" or "African American"). For disabilities, simply put the person first in your sentence and then the disability or, in some cases, the services or equipment that the individual needs or uses. Here are some examples:

People *with* disabilities	(Handicapped people; special needs children)
With autism	(He's autistic)
Has a physical disability	(She is quadriplegic; is crippled)
Uses a wheelchair	(She is confined to a wheelchair; wheelchair-bound)
Receives special ed services	(Special ed kid)
Accessible parking	(Handicapped parking)

Modeling person-first language may not be enough to change the way children in schools and members of the community talk and write about disabilities. In classrooms, however, music teachers can model and teach children to use words that emphasize the worth of all individuals. It is obviously more difficult to suggest these changes to adults. Anyone feels uncomfortable when gently trying to teach the sales clerk or family member who says, "Sorry about that, I must be retarded" or "dyslexic" or whatever. But do try. The person may be taken aback somewhat, but a kind person may also begin to change the way he or she speaks and thinks about people with disabilities. This same person becomes a model and perhaps will also "teach" others.

Some of you may wonder, with all of the problems associated with negative stereotyping and labels, are there any benefits to having the label of "disability"? That's a good question. A child must be defined as having a disability according to definitions and criteria in IDEA in order to receive services and legal protections for which the child is eligible. Definitions of disability vary among agencies, although appropriate personnel (psychologists, medical doctors, etc.) must document the presence of a disability in all cases for a child to receive services under IDEA or Section 504 of the Rehabilitation Act of 1953.

Procedures to identify, assess, and categorize disabilities vary among countries, as do methodologies for collecting and reporting national statistics. In the United States, the numbers of children with disabilities are determined by counts of infants and toddlers (birth through age two), preschool children (ages three through five), and children and young adults (ages six through twenty-one) who receive services under IDEA (meaning they have been assessed and a disability has been documented by local and state education agencies).

According to the Office of Special Education Programs (OSEP), of the more than 5.5 million students who received services under IDEA in 2011, the highest percentage for ages six through twenty-one was for the category specific learning disabilities (40.7 percent). It is possible that this percentage would vary (be lower or higher) if tests, criteria, policies, and assessment procedures were different. It is therefore difficult to compare percentages of children with specific disabilities among countries and sometimes among states. For example, "learning disabilities" may be a preferred term in other countries when referring to individuals who in the United States would be identified as having "intellectual disabilities."

If measurements are accurate and reliable, we can statistically expect the percentages of disabilities to remain approximately the same in any normal distribution of school-age children. For example, in the report by OSEP, the percentages of different types of disabilities have remained relatively unchanged, with the exception of increases for two disabilities: other health impairments and autism. Although I have not found substantiated information for increases in other health impairments, among the reported explanations from states for increases in autism are improved identification procedures. As a result of improved assessment procedures and increased awareness, many children who were previously diagnosed with other disabilities (e.g., emotional disturbance, mental retardation) are now more accurately diagnosed as having an autism spectrum disorder. Professionals and the general public have been alarmed by this increase, and there has been an upsurge in research and publications on multiple causes and risk factors, signs and symptoms, and assessment.[11]

Professionals in testing and measurement spend their careers developing valid assessment procedures. There are, however, enormous complexities regarding assessment, particularly for children who are "borderline" cases or who have multiple disabilities. The introduction of assessment profiles and authentic assessments (how children behave and perform tasks in the actual environments in which they function) has led to assessments that not only identify the presence of disabilities but also suggest curricular goals and instructional practices.

Parents play critical roles in the assessment process, and through IDEA, they have the right to request or deny assessment. I know of one particular case in which parents refused assessment of their child who uses a wheelchair and an alternative communication system. The child has problems with mobility but can navigate in many situations and can communicate (although not in a typical way). She has no other particular medical or educational needs. Her school district requires children with physical disabilities to attend a separate school for children with physical disabilities, a school which could only be reached by a lengthy bus ride. Special education for children with physical disabilities in this district was a place and not a service. Thus, the child's opportunities would have been greatly limited had she officially been assessed as having a disability. By denying the schools the right to conduct an assessment, the parents ensured that their daughter was allowed to attend their neighborhood school with typical children. (Provisions were made by the parents for the child's travel and her other needs throughout the day.) Assessment and its intended and unintended consequences have received much attention in the literature and in IDEA, particularly as they relate to specific learning disabilities.[12]

SCHOOLWIDE SERVICES: AN OVERVIEW

Research in genetics, embryology, fetal development, and the birthing process unveils what can happen before, during, and shortly after birth that will put children at risk for disabilities. Also, environmental factors such as poor nutrition, substance abuse, disease and infection, and physical trauma can have dire consequences for the development of the brain and central nervous system, musculoskeletal and neuromuscular systems, organs, and sensory systems. The risk of disabilities or other physical, emotional, or behavioral problems can increase when social-emotional environments are unhealthy and traumatic. Any of these factors can result in children who struggle academically and/or socially in school and children who will need support services.

Remember the children you read about in the opening paragraph of this chapter? It is quite possible that they could all be receiving some type of support services to help them be more successful and happy in school. What interventions and resources do these children need? Do schools have procedures in place to develop effective interventions, and can they provide the necessary resources and supports? How can we make sure that no child who needs help "slips through the cracks"? What can you do to help?

Schools, as you can well imagine, differ in the ways they go about answering these questions. Funding for educational, psychological, and medical personnel (e.g., special education, resource teachers, music therapists, physical therapists, counselors) and resources (e.g., assistive technology, equipment) is available through IDEA and other sources; however, it often takes a schoolwide effort to put the funds to good use. Putting the issue of funding aside for now, think about a few of the decisions that must be made. Who identifies the child who needs help? Who makes decisions about what the child needs? Who will be responsible for implementing interventions, getting appropriate resources to the child, and assessing the child's progress? And how should all of these efforts be coordinated?

From decades of research, we know that educators must work as a team to keep children in school, to create positive learning environments for them, and to provide them with meaningful learning experiences. When the administrative leadership fosters positive environments for teachers and students, everyone benefits. You will want to be involved; you will want to be a part of any schoolwide effort to make sure that your students will benefit from all of the services, resources, and supports available to them. (Ideas for collaboration are presented in chapter 3.)

When IDEA was first passed in 1975, and for decades afterward, the focus of schools and teachers was not on services, resources, and supports *first* but on the placements of students, most often in special education classrooms where specialized services and resources were thought to be most available. Unfortunately, some of this thinking still prevails, even though IDEA has always required that children be educated in the least restrictive environment, meaning that to the maximum extent appropriate, children with disabilities are to be educated in regular classrooms with children without disabilities and can only be removed when the nature or severity of the disabilities is such that they are not being successful, even with the use of supplementary aids and services.[13]

As a result of amendments to IDEA, particularly those in 1997 and 2004, increased attention is now given to the provision of services that will help students with disabilities progress in the regular classroom and the general curriculum. Among the amendments are those that require (1) access to the general curriculum and extracurricular activities, (2) monitoring of student progress, (3) high-quality research-based instruction, (4) early-intervening services for students not identified as needing special education but who require academic or behavioral support, and (5) assessment of the students' responses to scientific, research-based intervention.[14] The provisions made for students with disabilities have greatly influenced the development of educational models that are proactive and will help identify students at risk for failure in school.

You will read about many different types of services throughout this book and about ways you can become involved in the development and implementation of appropriate interventions for students to accomplish music goals. I would, however, like you to have some idea of the breadth of services that are available to meet the needs of many different children, from those who are off-task frequently to those who have severe emotional, behavioral, cognitive, and physical needs.

Most often, a range of services is provided through two federal laws, IDEA[15] and Section 504 of the Rehabilitation Act of 1973,[16] and through a more recent educational model called Response to Intervention (RTI).[17] As you might imagine, the rules and regulations under the laws are quite complex and written in excruciating detail, as are some of the procedures for RTI. You will read more about these services in other sections of the book. Here I provide only brief summaries, with additional information in the notes.

IDEA

- A federal education law that defines necessary *services only for children who have been assessed and identified as having disabilities*; assessments are to be conducted only with parental consent.
- Requires access to the general curriculum and education in the regular classroom, to the extent possible, with special education, related services, and supplementary aids and services as needed.
- Requires a team of individuals (parents, teachers, administrators, other professionals, and the student as appropriate) to develop a written Individualized Education Program (IEP) for each child identified as having a disability; the plan is a legal document and must have signed parental consent before implementation.
- Requires annual meetings of the IEP team to determine curricular goals for general education and special education settings, related services (e.g., physical therapy, music therapy), and other supplementary aids and services (e.g., assistive technology). The team decides where services will be provided, who will provide them, how progress will be

assessed, specific types of accommodations and/or modifications, and other details regarding the student's IEP.

- Requires a transition plan to be developed by the IEP team for the student no later than age fourteen (the plan focuses on the academic and functional achievement of the student and educational goals) and, no later than age sixteen, transitions statements are to be *in effect*, and with a plan for coordinated services and resources that will facilitate the student's movement from school to postschool employment, residential living, and recreation.
- Requires public agencies to make the IEP accessible to each regular education teacher, special education teacher, related services provider, and any other service provider who is responsible for its implementation, and to inform them of specific responsibilities related to implementing the child's IEP and the specific accommodations, modifications, and supports that must be provided for the child.

Section 504

- A federal civil rights law that *protects children from discrimination for reasons related to their disability, and other children who may not need special education, but who have been assessed as having an "impairment" that "substantially limits" one or more major life activities*. Major life activities in school are often identified as reading, writing, and doing math; students with substantial limits may have accommodations or additional instruction by a specialist. As a civil rights act, Section 504 also protects these children and others with disabilities from discrimination such as harassment, bullying, exclusion from school activities, or unnecessary separation from peers.
- Most often, teachers consult with the principal and parents if they suspect that a child could benefit from support services through Section 504. Appropriate assessments are necessary to determine eligibility for services; these assessments are usually conducted by physicians, psychologists, psychiatrists, or educational specialists and in consultation with parents.
- Services such as accommodations, modifications, and additional instruction are determined in consultation with parents and other professionals; the schoolwide team may develop individual 504 plans.
- Unlike with IDEA, there are no legal mandates for a team to meet to develop a plan, for a plan to be written, for written parental consent, or for assessment of students' progress under the plan. Schools may vary

in their procedures for the development of 504 plans and assessments of students' progress.

RTI

- A multitiered instructional model that relies on *schoolwide and grade-level teamwork to proactively identify students who are struggling in school and to address their needs as early as possible. All students who need additional support to make adequate progress in school receive individualized support services and interventions.* Children who receive services through Section 504 or IDEA would also be eligible for a comprehensive RTI plan to maximize their participation and success in inclusive settings.
- Organizational frameworks can vary across schools and school districts but usually include the following components:
  - High-quality, scientifically based classroom instruction.
  - Universal screening conducted at least three times a year (team reviews tests and other assessments) to identify students who are struggling academically; frequent assessment of students' academic and behavioral progress.
  - Three tiers of instructional interventions that vary in intensity and are developed to meet students' individual needs; most students identified for support after universal screening are at Tier 1, with more intensive interventions at Tier 3; all decisions are data-based; team recommendations may be made for a comprehensive evaluation to determine if a student would be eligible for services under Section 504 or IDEA; parental consent is required for evaluations.
  - To the degree possible, interventions implemented schoolwide by appropriate school personnel, teachers, and service providers.
  - Frequent communication with parents regarding their children's progress, goals, interventions, and service providers; parents may request formal evaluations of their children to determine eligibility for special education services.

From these brief descriptions, you can see the range of services available for students and the value of coordinated efforts to help them succeed in school. Some students will have frequent absences, will not complete assignments, will fall asleep frequently in class, or will show aggression toward other students. Others may struggle to communicate, to move, to smile, to learn. You can become involved in the development and implementation of IEP, 504, and RTI plans and in spotting problems and intervening before problems worsen. For example, for a student who frequently is confrontational with you or his peers, a school team may recommend a schoolwide intervention plan, which may require consultation with other professionals and the development of a formal Behavioral Intervention Plan (BIP). Every teacher would know the environmental cues and actions that could trigger an emotional response from the student, how to minimize these cues, how to talk to the student, and what to do if the situation escalates. School for this student would be a place where adults are consistent in their expectations and in their responses, and school for teachers would be a place where they feel supported by their colleagues and experience success—a good place for any child or teacher to be.

MUSIC CAPABILITIES

We've all seen children who have had problems in school, and yet they do well in music. Sometimes we are surprised by their musical capabilities because we've expected less of them based on their school record or disability label. We've all heard stories of students who are motivated to attend school simply because of their music classes and children with disabilities who experience success and feel good about themselves and their musical achievements because they have been given appropriate instructional support. Shouldn't all children have these experiences?

Children can be limited in their musical development by low expectations associated with their labels, particularly labels associated with intellectual disabilities. However, extended, direct, face-to-face interactions positively influence attitudes toward individuals from diverse populations (e.g., disabilities, race, gender, culture) and may raise expectations for teachers and classmates regarding students' music learning and capabilities.[18] The musical development of almost all students, regardless of labels assigned to them or their group membership, is dependent on their experiences in music classrooms.

For students with disabilities, with the exception of the very few identified as musical savants, or those who appear to have highly developed music skills (e.g., many children with Williams syndrome and some with an autism spectrum disorder), their musical development has received little attention in the research literature. In reviews of music research involving children with disabilities, in only a few cases were music learning outcomes measured.[19] In some studies, however, music capabilities were shown to be similar, and sometimes superior, to those of typically developing peers. With the exception of comparative studies between groups of children with and without disabilities, the data reported were most often for therapeutic outcomes (e.g., engaging in music activities to improve academic or social skills or listening to music as a reward after successfully completing an academic task or for appropriate social behavior).

Although there is insufficient empirical evidence to inform us fully about specific instructional strategies for teaching music to children from diverse populations, there is a wealth of knowledge on human learning. It is the purpose of this book to bring you as much of this knowledge as possible so that you may use it to improve the musical lives of all of your students.

CHAPTER 2
What's the Point?

OVERVIEW

You are by now familiar with the underlying premise of this book: All children, with few exceptions, belong in regular (neighborhood) schools and music classrooms with competent teachers who prepare them for a meaningful life with music. Sensitive teachers want all children to have a sense of belonging when it comes to their schools, classrooms, and ensembles. Regardless of students' varied abilities and disabilities, all can learn to participate in music classrooms in meaningful ways.

Although instruction can be individualized, there is a sameness in the way children learn, and there is a sameness in the ways we should go about preparing a meaningful curriculum for them. Recognizing similarities among seemingly diverse children is an important step toward understanding how to make educationally sound decisions for each child's musical life. But before we go about making practices "the same" for seemingly diverse children, shouldn't we first think about what and how we are teaching now? Are we teaching knowledge and skills that are central to a musical life, and are we using effective techniques to do so? Asking questions begins the important process of evaluating our actions.

The question of *why* forces us to reexamine our curricular and instructional decisions. For example, should typical middle school students know the first fifteen amendments to the US Constitution? Why? If yes, and an important justification can be found for this objective, then would modifications be made for some students who could not learn that many? I know of a student who was just assigned the thirteenth, fourteenth, and fifteenth amendments. But why these? And should most elementary students learn the lines and spaces in the grand staff while a few students have a less difficult task and learn only the names of spaces in the treble staff? Why? And when most students are moving at a rapid pace in their books, is it only one child who will require repetition and review of fundamental playing or singing skills? Other questions arise. Should *any* middle school student learn all fifteen amendments or *any* elementary student learn the lines and spaces of the grand staff? Teaching children with varied abilities and disabilities provides opportunities to rethink traditional practices ("business as usual") in music teaching and learning. Busy teachers, particularly new teachers, may find themselves relying on extant curricula (national, state, methods books) for decisions about what and how to teach. These are helpful resources, some better than others, but none is foolproof. Teachers will still need to question the importance of *what* to teach, *why* they are teaching it, *when* it should be taught, and the *context* in which it should be taught. I'm reminded of the parent who was tenacious about his child leaving school with skills and knowledge that would allow the child to be more independent as an adult, to live and work in the community, and to have a network of friends. The parent pleaded with the special education teacher to "stop teaching dumb stuff." He was making an important point worth remembering. We all need to, use precious teaching time wisely, and stop teaching dumb stuff. How should teachers go about developing a *meaningful* music program for all children, one that will lead to students' musical success in school and throughout adult life?

It is difficult to change traditions in education, even in the face of compelling empirical data that support change. When enough individuals become dissatisfied with conditions, a movement begins, and change happens. We've seen this in the field of special education. The quality of people's lives changed dramatically because parents, teachers, and advocates questioned where children received an education, in addition to what and how they were taught.

All students benefit when teachers ask hard questions about their music programs, consider new ideas, take some chances, create and implement new plans, and assess outcomes. In this chapter, you will read about instructional practices with which you are most familiar and which have been supported in the research for decades. You will also read about ideas for change, ideas supported by data. I hope to make strong enough arguments to lead you to consider a different approach to music education, particularly in elementary music education, an area that provides the foundation for a musical life. I hope to engage you in this topic to the point that you will share my concerns and in such a way that you will work to bring about what I believe are much-needed changes in music education practices.[1]

THE "TRADITIONAL" MUSIC PROGRAM: WHO DECIDES WHAT AND HOW TO TEACH?

There are many ways to think about the components of teaching—what's important to teach and how to teach. You can think of the *what* as the curriculum and the *how* as instruction. For example, in any given lesson, a teacher usually decides what's important to teach, the sequence of learning activities for the lesson, and the teaching strategies that will lead to students' having success at each step in the sequence.

The *what* and *how* of teaching and learning are integrated into traditional lesson plans. Undergraduates learn to write elaborate plans consisting of objectives, sequences of instruction, assessments, materials, and arrangements of the physical environment. With experience, teachers write plans that consist of a few words or sentences showing what students will do and how objectives will be met. When implementing plans, experienced, competent teachers think, often at lightning speed, of changes necessary for successful outcomes. They demonstrate flexibility.

Many good minds have come together to try to answer the question of what's important to teach. At district, state, and national meetings of curricular committees and task forces, individuals work to come to a consensus about what is important to teach, to whom, and when. In addition to curricula developed by these committees, teachers have access to basal series books and other method books. As a way of organizing curricula, developers often present ideas in domains (categories or strands of activities) and standards (what students should know and do). In same cases, districts and states require teachers to follow their respective curricula, although national standards have thus far remained "voluntary."

Domains have been identified using various music elements (e.g., rhythm, melody, form) and activities (e.g., singing, creating, movement). Traditionally, components of the curricula are presented specific to grade levels. The organization of curricula, however, can take many different forms. Duke uses as the basis of his curriculum "what intelligent musicians do." He organizes curricular components, which he refers to as "component skills of intelligent musicianship," within the broad areas of performance, knowledge of subject matter, and music appreciation but does not confine these skills to specific grade levels. He points out that these skills "can be performed by musicians at all levels of experience and expertise" and explains that differences among levels are a result of technical demands of the contexts in which each skill is demonstrated.[2]

The idea of domains and strands seems to be a popular method for organizing objectives for different grade levels in music basal series. *Standards*, the more lofty term, came into its own in the mid-1990s and often serves as the framework for state and national curricula. You may be familiar with the National Standards for Music, which presents music content through nine standards, and the more recent National Core Music Standards (NCMS), which presents content through what have been identified as four artistic processes: creating, performance/producing/presenting, responding, and connecting.[3] These processes were influenced by the framework used by the National Assessment of Education Progress (NAEP) to assess arts learning. (You will read more about the results of the NAEP for music in upcoming sections.)

There are many ways to cut and name pieces of the pie known as a curriculum. Which organizational framework will result in children participating happily and successfully now and throughout their adult lives? You may have a favorite. Regarding national standards, the new music standards may be an improvement over those published in 1994, in that the artistic processes (e.g., creating, performing) may focus teachers' thinking on higher-level outcomes and how classroom activities can be structured to enhance those processes. Also, philosophical foundations and lifelong goals were used as a basis for the new standards, and the inclusion of lifelong goals for "artistically literate citizens" may contribute to teachers' thinking about their students' musical lives beyond school.

Many disagreements, sometimes heated, can occur among members of curricular committees when they try to determine objectives for music programs; far fewer occur in discussions of long-term musical goals for our citizenry. The importance of the long view is articulated by Duke, who suggests that teachers have a "vision of students as accomplished learners." He writes: "The more vividly we can envision an exemplary student who has successfully accomplished the goals we set out, the more intelligently we can organize our instructional time and activities to facilitate the accomplishment of those goals by all of our students."[4] It follows that the more vividly we can visualize a goal of meaningful music participation throughout life for our students, the more intelligently we can organize a music program to accomplish this goal.

With meaningful long-term goals and objectives for the music program, most experts would agree that teachers must then maintain students' attention; give individualized contingent feedback to groups and individuals; move efficiently and effectively through a carefully designed sequence of instruction; model and prompt when appropriate; teach for transfer of students' knowledge and skills; assess when learning has occurred; maintain flexibility; and, throughout, demonstrate good musicianship, tenacity, sensitivity, appropriate seriousness, and humor. *Whew.* Not easy.

Although much of what we know about human learning can be empirically verified, there are myriad decisions throughout instruction that must be made by the teacher (e.g., number of repetitions in rehearsal, where to begin teaching in the song or piece, what questions to ask). Knowing what to ask students to do at any given time in instruction is perhaps one of the most important and difficult aspects of teaching. An instructional sequence consists of activities for students, and depending on the outcome (successful or unsuccessful), we may give feedback and ask them to do more of the same (repeat), do something related (e.g., repeat in a different context, perform a less complex task), or do something entirely different. Of course, the art and skill of teaching lie in asking students to do things for which they are prepared.

Curriculum, objectives, and assessment are more similar, rather than different, in practice. The teacher decides what is important for the student to learn (specific behaviors identified as goals, objectives, tasks, or whatever you want to call them) and assesses these same behaviors to determine whether the student's behavior changed in the way the teacher had intended. If it did, learning happened.

We have an extensive database that describes behaviors of expert teachers in many fields and at all grade levels. Although personal characteristics vary among these teachers and some teachers may not be able to describe their own actions precisely, expert teachers are strikingly similar. They effectively establish successful learning environments for children because they know what is important to teach and how to reach curricular goals using well-established teaching principles. In the classrooms of expert teachers, all children progress, and all children learn.

Many competent teachers, however, are confronted with an insurmountable problem: trying to teach too much content in a limited amount of time to far too many children and with limited resources. This problem exists at all levels but perhaps more so at the elementary level, traditionally described as "general" music curriculum, which could be interpreted as a curriculum emphasizing no particular domain (e.g., singing, playing instruments, listening to music, reading and writing music) over another. The solution is not simply in a new curricular framework using "traditional" curricular domains or different instructional strategies. The solution requires a rethinking of what we are teaching and how we are teaching in light of facts about whether students are learning what we intend to teach them, their music participation as adults, and the status of school music programs, resources, and instructional time.

FACING THE GOOD AND NOT SO GOOD FACTS

In suggesting that we think about changes for the way we think about teaching music and for the music education program in general, I want to clarify that my concern is not about the quality of teachers, most of whom work very hard to bring meaningful music experiences to children, or about the national or state music standards or extant published curricula, all of which can serve as useful resources for teachers. My thinking about this issue is a direct result of collecting and reviewing years of descriptive and experiential information about music participation and achievement in our country and the realities of the music teacher's school life.

Throughout my lifetime, it seems that almost all music professionals have expressed the concern that active music participation and music skills in children and adults are not what they should be. Unfortunately, the persistence of this concern may have desensitized us to the issue. Less-than-positive outcomes are often attributed to factors outside the control of music education professionals: usually, instructional time, money, and other resources. Teachers, however, still have control of some of the most powerful and influential variables influencing educational outcomes: what to teach and how to teach.

I value the privilege to exercise this freedom in my classroom. Most often, we have many opportunities to make changes in music classes and in the way we prepare music teachers. There are some good reasons to think about further changes, which I hope you will consider. There are data, hard and soft, that support instituting changes in music programs and in the way we go about preparing teachers and teaching children.

These data indicate unhappy truths that we have known for some time. Children in music classrooms often do not learn what we intended to teach them. There are, of course, reasonable cautions to be considered in interpreting these data, but the results cannot be ignored. The data I'm about to summarize, along with years of observations of music classrooms, have convinced me that the way we think about music education must change. After reading this chapter, I hope that you will agree. I encourage you to challenge traditional practices that simply are not working and implement those that will increase the likelihood of successful music learning for all children.

In the field of education, the experiences, knowledge, and skills that are defined as meaningful are assessed in order to evaluate whether what was taught was actually learned. National large-scale surveys of adult music participation, preferences, attitudes, and experiences, in addition to assessments of students' skills and knowledge, provide some information to answer two important questions: Are individuals participating in meaningful music experiences that are valued by many music educators? And are students learning skills and knowledge that will contribute to their meaningful participation now and in the future?

Surveys and assessments are naturally limited in their scope; however, in many cases, the experiences, skills, and knowledge measured in these assessments have been defined by music educators as meaningful (e.g., listening to live and recorded performances of music, playing instruments, singing), thus making the data relevant to issues of music teaching and learning. Some of these surveys were conducted several years ago, but I'll summarize results from national surveys that are most current, beginning with the music participation of adults.

Adult Participation and Attitudes

The most current national surveys regarding adult music participation were completed in the late 1990s,[5] although it is unlikely that there are more positive results today, considering current economic conditions in the nation. Given priorities in state and federal agencies, we will most likely see few such surveys in the near future, although there is much to ponder from early surveys.

From these surveys, we have learned that a large percentage of all adults have positive attitudes about music and believe that music should be part of a well-rounded education; they believe that the state should mandate music education in schools; they believe that playing a musical instrument can be fun; and a very high percentage believe that playing an instrument can provide lifelong enjoyment. Yet, perhaps paradoxically, many adults believe that it isn't worthwhile to invest in an instrument unless a child has some degree of talent. This response came from approximately equal percentages of adults who played instruments and those who were former players. What factors would lead to such a response?

We also know that even though a large majority of adults have positive attitudes about music, music making, and music education, more than half who once played instruments stopped playing before their late teens. The percentage of individuals who stop playing continues to increase, with almost three-fourths of all players becoming "former players" by the time they reach their thirties. A large majority of current and former players report that they began to study because of parental encouragement or their own interest; a much smaller percentage credit encouragement from a teacher. Most of these adults, with or without ensemble experiences in schools, do not join community choirs, bands, or orchestras, and we find that adult attendance at live performances of music continues to decline, even among older adult populations with higher incomes. In addition to results from surveys, all of us have heard and read news reports about declining audiences and the economic struggles of professional music organizations.

Can we attribute any of these situations to the quality of music education programs and the lack of adults' participation as students in those programs? Although there are data showing positive relationships between early success in school and success in life, we have no data to support the idea that there are similar positive relationships between quality music education programs and continued music participation in school and throughout adult life. Many, however, would agree that this seems a reasonable hypothesis and have examined the current state of affairs of our music programs to assess their quality specific to availability of music instruction and program characteristics.

Status of Music Education

Much of what we know about the status of music education in public schools comes from data collected by the National Center for Education Statistics (NCES) for the years 1994–1995, 1999–2000, and 2009–2010.[6] The most recent report for the 2009–2010 school year compared data for two school years (1999–2000 and 2009–2010) and showed percentages for schools by concentration of poverty (ranges of students eligible for free or reduced-priced lunch from between 0 and 25 percent to 76 percent or more). Data were collected from school principals and music specialists at elementary and secondary school levels. I want you to have some of the results from these surveys so you can see several issues of concern.

For elementary schools in 2009–2010, music was available in 94 percent of the schools (low-poverty schools, 97 percent; high-poverty schools, 89 percent). Most often, music instruction was offered at least once a week by music specialists, although it was offered throughout the entire school year in 93 percent of schools in low-poverty areas compared with 89 percent in high-poverty areas. Interestingly, more specialists in low-poverty schools taught at more than one school (54 percent) compared with specialists in high-poverty schools (47 percent). Regardless of level of poverty concentrations, specialists spent an average of twenty-two hours teaching and had an average of twenty-five different classes of students per week; class size averaged eighteen students.

For secondary schools for the year 2008–2009 (most data are from 2009–2010 with this exception), music instruction was most often provided by music specialists and was available in 91 percent of schools (low-poverty schools, 94 percent; high-poverty schools, 86 percent). Of the secondary schools that offered music instruction, an average of 46 percent offered five or more courses (low-poverty schools, 62 percent; high-poverty schools, 35 percent), and 91 percent offered instruction in dedicated rooms with special equipment for classes taught (low-poverty schools, 94 percent; high-poverty schools, 86 percent). Similarly to those in elementary schools, regardless of level of poverty concentrations, specialists spent an average of twenty-two hours teaching though only teaching seven to nine classes per week; class size averaged twenty-three to twenty-five students.

The high percentage of schools offering music instruction is good news; however, from this report, we don't know the numbers of students who were participating in music or the ways in which participating students reflected diverse populations (e.g., gender, race, ethnicity, or disability). Also, the lack of courses and resources for high-poverty secondary schools is of concern, as is the lack of adequate instructional time, particularly at the elementary level.

Consider the data for instructional time more closely. Music was offered at least once a week in a large majority of elementary schools, although teachers reported an average of only twenty-two hours of instruction across twenty-five different classes per week, and about half of them taught at more than one school. With an average of eighteen students per class, teachers would see an average of 450 students per week. If we assume that elementary classes are less than one hour, given a typical forty-week school yearweek, that would mean each class of students (each individual student in each class) would receive less than forty hours of instruction per year. This was less instruction time than was reported for the 1999–2000 school year, which shows an average of forty-six hours of music instruction per year. Secondary teachers also reported twenty-two hours of instruction per week but for an average of seven to nine classes per week. Although other factors influence student participation in music at the secondary levels and adult music participation, the issues of time and quality of elementary instruction for those forty hours are most likely influential factors.

Student Participation and Achievement

It is well known that music is often a required subject in many elementary schools and is an elective in many middle and high schools. In this section, we will consider students' participation at secondary levels and how well students perform on national assessments of music achievement. I'll discuss findings from a few sources that report participation at a national level, although most information regarding music achievement at the national level comes from middle school students who were participants in the National Assessment of Educational Progress (NAEP).

NAEP conducted assessments of nationally representative samples of eighth-grade public- and private-school students in 1997 and 2008.[7] When the results of the first assessment were published, they generated a great deal of discussion among researchers and teachers in music education. The second assessment was on a smaller scale and therefore has not gotten the same attention, since few comparisons can be made with the 1997 data. Overall, results from both assessments are disappointing.

Among the few comparisons that can be made, we learn that there was an increase in the percentages of eighth-graders who were receiving instruction three to four times a week (43 percent in 1997 and 57 percent in 2008), although the percentage is still low. For 1997 compared with 2008, participation was as follows: band, 18 percent and 16 percent; orchestra, 3 percent and 5 percent; choir, 22 percent and 17 percent, respectively. Why are these percentages so low? Is it that students don't have the skills and attitudes that would lead them to choose to participate in ensembles in schools, or are there other factors such as scheduling or a lack of electives, or do both contribute to these disappointing percentages? According to the 2008 data, most students were not choosing to participate in ensembles outside of school, either.

No data were shown for school ensemble participation by students representing diverse populations; however, for multiple-choice and constructed-response questions, the score gap between students with disabilities who could be assessed and students without disabilities was 39 points. The overall average for all typical students was a disappointing 150 out of a possible 300 points.[8] The larger 1997 assessment provides other results that should be of concern to all of us. Students performed poorly on all components of the assessment: creating, performing, and responding.

Additional information about diverse populations in high school performing ensembles is provided by Elpus and Abril at a national level.[9] These researchers found that 21 percent of American high school seniors participated in band, choir, and/or orchestra in 2004, with 61 percent female and race/ethnicity as follows: white, 65.7 percent; black, 15.2 percent; Hispanic, 10.2 percent; all others, less than 5 percent. For more than 90 percent of the students, English was their primary native language. Most (79.4 percent) came from two-parent/guardian homes, with 60 percent in the highest and third quartile for socioeconomic status (SES). Students in the highest SES quartile (32.2 percent) were significantly overrepresented, and those in the lowest SES quartile (17 percent) were underrepresented. Overall evidence shows significant associations between music ensemble participation and variables including gender, race/ethnicity, SES, native language, parents' education, standardized test scores, and GPA. Higher percentages of participation were found for students who were female, were white, had high SES, were English native speakers, had high test scores and GPAs, and had parents with more years of formal education. Many of these findings are substantiated in other reports with respect to individual states.

In addition to this information from surveys and assessments, we all have experiences with student performances that are charming but musically mediocre, teachers who are dedicated but exhausted, and adults who, by their own self-reports, love music but confess to being terrible singers and consider themselves not musically "talented," never having played an instrument and never having a music class beyond fifth grade. And variables such as SES, race, and ethnicity can make the picture more bleak for some students and adults. Even though a large majority of students leave school with positive attitudes about music (perhaps as a result of participation in elementary music classes), it appears that many have not internalized the values, knowledge, and skills taught in music classes and that many are not motivated to learn to develop their skills and knowledge regardless of the efforts of hardworking teachers.

Given the seriousness of challenges in education caused by population growth, teacher shortages, and dwindling budgets for children's educational and health programs, arguments in favor of promoting and improving the quality of music education and music teaching conditions can understandably appear of little importance to those outside our discipline. In the past, music educators, concerned members of communities, music education organizations, and advocacy groups have rallied, sometimes successfully, to preserve music opportunities for children. Fortified with the results of systematic research, the philosophies that seek to describe a meaningful life, and an inherent belief in the goodness of music and the benefits of music learning for everyone, the arguments are timeless.

Until these arguments are more successful in increasing instructional time and resources, training and hiring more skillful music teachers, and bringing additional weight to the merits of music instruction in school, teachers will continue to face tremendous challenges in bringing high-quality, meaningful music experiences to children in their classrooms. I remain optimistic that teachers can accomplish something meaningful in those precious, fleeting hours of instructional time.

Although the future may see new surveys and systematic assessments, after decades of discouraging news, I'm of the opinion that we now have sufficient information to act—to change the way we think about music education for all children—so that more and more children move through the system of school music and new generations of adults leave school with the knowledge, skills, and attitudes that we care so deeply about imparting.

RETHINKING ISSUES OF "STUFF" AND TIME

Almost all curricula, either explicitly or implicitly, present a multitude of skills that students must know and do. The more recent National Core Music Standards may help teachers think more deeply about the artistic processes as goals for their students, but ultimately, teachers will need to decide on specific classroom activities to enhance those processes, which will require time and resources. The problem of an overcrowded music curriculum is probably most egregious at the elementary level.

From survey results, we know that it is not uncommon for a child's elementary music experiences to be provided by a single music teacher who sees at least 450 students a week (or more) and who may travel between schools, valiantly trying to teach singing; playing instruments; improvising melodies, variations, and accompaniments; composing and arranging; reading and notating music; listening to, analyzing, and describing music; and more. How does someone do all of that in forty to forty-six hours a year?

Based on the facts we have for all levels of music instruction, our current practices do not predict a new generation of musical adults who provide musical homes for their children, who advocate for quality school music programs for all students, and who support the art music community. There is simply not enough instructional time to accomplish all of the many tasks with which teachers are charged, especially at the elementary level, when content areas are thought of as separate compartments, each of which needs "a lesson on it," and secondary levels, when there is little time for the development of musical independence.

Given the fact that small percentages of students continue with music at the secondary levels, I'd like to focus first on the idea of rethinking the notion of a elementary music curriculum as it is traditionally practiced. Again, my concerns are not with the teachers, the national or state standards, or extant published curricular materials but more with the interpretation that content areas are separate and that each is deserving of equal time.

One way to resolve the problem of an overcrowded curriculum in elementary music education is to give teachers better resources, more money, and more time. Teachers should have more time, but they don't. Yet despite the reality of limited instructional time and resources, the elementary curriculum over a period of decades has expanded to a point that I describe as "supersized," with all of the consequences that come from having too much of a good thing.

This is not to ignore that there are exemplary programs that subscribe to what many refer to as the traditional general music curriculum. In many cases, these programs are deemed exemplary based on highly visible music performances by the children who participate. But I wonder how "general" these programs are. We should applaud successful programs, of course. But my concerns are more for the vast majority of schools where teachers are trying to distribute teaching time across a general music curriculum for hundreds of students whom they may see for less than an hour each week.

Learning matters. Music learning matters. We cannot continue to use precious instructional time to do more of the same. Change can begin by recognizing transfer of learning as an essential part of education and facing the reality that teaching for transfer requires a great deal of instructional time.

From a substantial base of research in human learning, we know that the probability of transfer will increase when instructional time is used to create frequent opportunities for students to learn skills and knowledge deeply and thoroughly, practice the same skills and knowledge in a variety of contexts and with numerous and varied examples, and learn meaningful principles rather than only isolated facts and skills. Whether at the elementary or secondary level, teaching a music curriculum as we currently define it violates many of these principles. In upcoming sections, you will read more about transfer principles, how they apply to teaching at all levels, and how they relate to the underlying principle of transition and music participation in adult life.

Although teaching principles can be learned and practiced in teacher preparation programs and in classrooms, the disparities between traditional curricular expectations and the real-world pressures of a full-time position in a traditional general music program can send even the best teachers reeling. Trying to do it all often results in children's demonstrating poor to mediocre performing skills and encountering bits of knowledge that are fleeting and ultimately meaningless. Children who have no interest in learning to play an instrument and children who are, and who know they are, unsuccessful singers, when given a choice, most likely will not choose music in middle school.

Competent teachers can become disillusioned while trying to meet the demands of a general curriculum within the strictures of limited time. They may lower their expectations, limit performances, avoid assessment of their students, and perhaps eventually burn out. Or worse, teachers may simply resort to frivolous activities as a way to fill class time.

When instructional time is divided across a variety of separate activities, there is no time for children's music skills to be refined and no time for a deeper understanding of music. Making music should then be the core of the elementary curriculum, since expressive, technically accurate performance incorporates skills and knowledge from many other curricular areas. Learning to perform with competence and confidence, whether in formal or informal settings, can be central to a musical life.

Time and good instruction are required if we are to expect children not only to learn to perform but also to perform beautifully and with confidence. Teachers must go beyond simply introducing new music to sing or play—to *refining* the quality of children's performance skills.

For the vast majority of children who will not experience private lessons, their only opportunity to learn to sing or play instruments is in school. If children are not musically competent and confident when they leave elementary school, for many, their music education is essentially over.

The performance program I visualize for the elementary grades is vastly different from the narrow focus of some secondary programs, where all efforts are on public performances and contests, where students have few opportunities to gain a deep understanding of music and learn musical independence.

I have in mind an elementary performance curriculum where children have frequent opportunities to learn a varied repertoire of music and have frequent opportunities to sing and play instruments expressively and with technical accuracy, alone and with classmates, in large and small ensembles, in informal settings with audiences of classmates, teachers, parents, and administrators. Where children develop skills of reading and interpreting music through singing and playing instruments. Where they become discriminating listeners and have frequent opportunities to make independent musical decisions and evaluations of their own performances along with the live and recorded performances of others. Where they practice using the language of music to express preferences and describe and analyze music they perform. Where they have successful experiences leading to feelings of self-efficacy and where they come to develop personal values and attitudes about the importance of music in their lives. These goals are attainable if teachers make appropriate decisions about music literature, tasks, and contexts.

MAKING CHANGES WITH IDEAS THAT WORK

Assume that changes are made in elementary music education programs and precious instructional time is used to teach and refine important music performing skills and that children become confident and competent singers who can also play classroom instruments musically in a variety of engaging classroom activities. This is a great beginning! Now what? We can predict that many of these children will be interested in joining secondary performing groups and continuing their music study. Then what? If these same students enter music courses at the secondary levels, will they continue to participate for the remainder of their school years? What can be said about their participation outside of school and beyond school?

An overall plan must be designed that prepares students for transition to secondary music programs and adult musical lives. Transition to adulthood was the very idea that revolutionized special education practice, which, by law, must now include transition plans and services that focus on postsecondary outcomes for each student with a disability. In special education, transition services include a coordinated set of activities designed to be within a results-oriented process, focused on improving the student's academic and functional achievement, and designed to facilitate the student's movement from school to postschool activities.[10] The requirement for a transition plan and services for children with disabilities came about because the adult data were so disheartening; adults with disabilities had not learned what we had intended to teach. Now, make the transfer: visualize a music curriculum as a coordinated set of activities designed by music teachers at all levels to be within a results-oriented process, focused on improving students' musical achievement, and designed to facilitate students' movement from school music activities to postschool music activities. Now, that would be something! The reality is not beyond reach.

Principles of Transition and Transfer

Transition as a guiding principle for music teaching has wide-ranging applicability for people of all ages, people with a wide range of abilities and disabilities, and people from all ethnic populations, cultures, and backgrounds. It can also apply to a wide range of contexts within music programs—contexts that involve a variety of experiences, knowledge, and skills. Although specific examples and data in this chapter may become outdated, the overarching principles will not. The idea of transition as a guiding principle is supported by a substantial base of research on transfer learning. You read earlier that change can begin with recognition of transfer of learning as an essential part of education and that teaching for transfer requires almost all instructional time. From research in human learning, we know that the probability of transfer will increase when students (1) learn skills and knowledge deeply and thoroughly, (2) learn how to apply the same skills and knowledge using numerous and varied examples across multiple contexts, and (3) learn meaningful principles rather than only isolated facts and skills. You will read more about these three principles of transfer later in this section.

Much of the transfer research focuses on two elements: student tasks and contexts. *Tasks* (such as classroom activities, student behaviors, skills, knowledge) can refer to what we can observe the student do in the classroom (e.g., compose a short piece using nontraditional sound sources, read a simple melody, sing a song with expressiveness and technical accuracy, improvise an accompaniment, and demonstrate knowledge of the technical vocabulary of music in discussion with peers). *Contexts* can refer to various learning settings (e.g., classroom, community, home), including the physical properties that may be in those settings (e.g., lighting, seating, sound systems); people in settings (e.g., peers, parents, teachers); and materials and equipment that are part of the tasks (e.g., music literature for performance or listening, instruments, audio equipment).

Tasks naturally occur in contexts (e.g., a student plays a simple three-chord guitar accompaniment for peers singing "On Top of Old Smokey" in general music class). Consider the task (playing a simple three-chord accompaniment) and the context (peers singing "On Top of Old Smokey"). Now, consider the same student playing the same accompaniment for a middle school chorus performance. The guitar accompaniment remains the same, although the context is quite different from the classroom setting (different students, an audience). In other situations, contexts may remain somewhat the same (regular classes with same peers and teacher), although tasks may be very different (e.g., playing a more complex accompaniment for "Smokey," playing *and* singing "Smokey," or playing the same three chords to accompany a different song). You get the idea.

What we seem to be good at doing in school is teaching students knowledge and skills (e.g., sing a song, play a technical exercise, name the instruments in the brass family) and prerequisite skills (e.g., perform rhythm patterns with a steady pulse, start or stop singing or playing on cue) but without much attention to context and contextual variety. Although students may learn what is taught in one particular situation, with those materials and under those conditions, real learning requires transfer, and transfer requires contextual variety. There are any number of differences between school music experiences and those of independent adults in their homes and communities, so the task for the music teacher is to minimize those differences, to the extent possible, by teaching for transfer. The more school music experiences (tasks and contexts) are similar to music experiences that are valued for adult life, the higher the probability of transfer and the more successful the transition.

You can see the relevance of these ideas to that of transition and students' postschool music participation. Students are prepared to participate successfully in a variety of adult music experiences when they have had frequent opportunities to participate in school experiences that provide multiple contexts similar to those experienced by adults. Consider the example of students continuing to participate in music ensembles outside of school contexts. School experiences for students are more similar to the experiences of adults who perform in community organizations when students regularly participate in organizations' activities and have frequent positive interactions with members of the organizations—performing alongside members, successfully singing or playing appropriate parts or literature in rehearsals and in performances for audiences in their own school venue and other community venues.

At this point, you may be thinking about numerous prerequisites that are taught in school that are rarely, if ever, performed by adults. School experiences should be similar to valued adult experiences, but functional prerequisites required for those experiences must still be taught. Transfer also requires that students learn skills deeply and that they learn meaningful principles. Although there are many instances in music education when learning one skill is a necessary prerequisite for learning another (holding the instrument properly and forming the correct embouchure before performing a sound with good tone), many prerequisites are not functionally related to the desired learning outcome. With unnecessary prerequisites, precious teaching and learning time may be wasted, and students may become frustrated, their enthusiasm for making music lost in the tedium. In the process of determining what students will know and do, and in what contexts, so-called prerequisites should be questioned, since they may place an unnecessary delay on the students' learning and dampen student motivation. Some prerequisites may be functionally related to another skill in the hierarchy and to the ultimate goal, but many prerequisites have been erroneously established over generations of teachers and music texts. You will read more about the ubiquitous problem of unnecessary prerequisites for children with disabilities in the next chapter.

To further emphasize the importance of transfer to learning, I've summarized below the principles I discussed earlier. Each of the principles increases the likelihood of learning transferring to new situations. You'll see overlap across these examples, particularly in the way different types and degrees of contextual change can influence transfer.

Principle 1. Learn skills and knowledge deeply and thoroughly

This is probably one of the most understandable yet often overlooked principles for transfer; it concerns how well something is learned. Many individuals have memories of doing poorly on a particular piece they performed at a concert or recital because they did not practice the piece enough. How deeply and thoroughly was the piece learned? Using another simple example, for those of you who play clarinet, how efficiently can you assemble your instrument? Then watch the sweet young beginning student who is doing it for the first time. For those of you who sing, how in tune can you sing intervals? Then listen to young children working to acquire this skill. How many times have you assembled your instrument or sung intervals in your lifetime? Learning something thoroughly most often means repeated practice of the same skills over weeks, months, and years, to the point of automaticity or habit. (Of course, there must be assessment and feedback from a competent teacher along the way.)

It should be noted that learning to perform, discuss, or analyze only a few pieces is not the same as learning a skill or applying knowledge. In some situations, students practice and learn a limited repertoire throughout the school year (e.g., for infrequently occurring recitals, contests, programs) or can discuss and analyze only a few pieces heard in class. Learning to perform and talk about particular pieces well can be important at times, but meaningful skills and knowledge will be acquired only when students have frequent opportunities to practice, when practice is efficient, and when practice involves numerous and varied examples in a motivating environment.

Principle 2. Learn how to apply the same skills and knowledge using numerous and varied examples in multiple contexts

This principle considers the degree to which original learning is applied to a number of tasks or contexts, or the generality of the transfer. Reading music is one example of a skill that applies to various pieces of music and can occur in many contexts. Singing or playing music with a beautiful tone, regardless of the piece, is another. How do people who are good sight-readers get to be that way? They do it a lot, with lots of different music, and they often sight-read with other people. There is no magic to the reasons behind why some individuals excel at what they do.

When a student applies original learning about practice strategies while studying piano to practicing other instruments, transfer has occurred across a number of tasks. When students who learn to sing in tune with a pleasing tone use these singing skills while singing a variety of songs in their classrooms, in community groups, and at home with family and friends, they have transferred their original learning to a number of tasks and contexts.

The extent to which original learning transfers to other contexts is affected by the frequency and variety of practice opportunities. Students who sing the same repertoire expressively and with technical accuracy in small groups or with their class, for students in other classrooms, and in the principal's office will most likely transfer those well-learned skills to singing beautifully at the PTA meeting. Students who have frequent opportunities to perform particular rhythm or melody patterns in many pieces may independently transfer those skills to new literature. Students who use appropriate music terminology to describe numerous and varied examples of music in the classroom will not only increase the depth of their knowledge of the class examples but may also transfer this knowledge and skill to describing music heard outside of class. Discussing a variety of music in different contexts, with small groups of peers outside the classroom, with the teacher, or at home with parents, increases the probability of transfer further. It is not surprising that students who reported that they were asked to play instruments or sing, notate music, or make up their own music almost every day had the highest average scores on performing and creating in the NAEP assessment.

Principle 3. Learn meaningful principles rather than only isolated facts and skills

Sometimes learning something well requires drill and practice, although when repeated practice is combined with a student's understanding of underlying principles for the skill or knowledge, the learning situation is made more meaningful, and the extent of transfer is greater. Students can follow a cue and learn where to breathe when singing or playing a particular piece, or they can learn how to use their breath to perform expressively or adjust the pitch of a particular note. When students learn principles that explain why and how the breath affects performance, they are better prepared to make appropriate adjustments and decisions independently. Students can learn to identify the forms and periods of particular pieces, although when they learn and understand principles of composition evident in music of different periods, they are better prepared to apply the principles when identifying and talking about an unfamiliar piece of music. Knowledgeable teachers understand how to make learning situations meaningful, and they allot enough time for their students to learn principles of music making thoroughly and deeply and to apply them frequently with numerous and varied examples.

All three transfer principles require that teachers accept the idea that "less is more." Deciding what is meaningful and teaching fewer (highly valued) things allows time to teach those things more deeply and thoroughly, thus providing a greater opportunity for transfer of learning to occur. When deciding what to teach more deeply, examine the contexts for transfer. In future school or out-of-school contexts, how many music experiences require this knowledge or these skills, and how frequently will they be required? For most students, opportunities for transfer to new situations are more frequent for some music skills and knowledge (performing from notation, performing with expression and technical accuracy, sight-reading, talking intelligently about stylistic features of a piece of music, demonstrating audience behavior appropriate for recitals and concerts of classical music) than for others (reading alto clef, naming all the instruments in the symphony orchestra, writing note names, playing scales, identifying by name whole, half, quarter, and eighth notes).

Teaching for transfer is an essential part of education. When adults who have attended many years of school cannot apply their classroom learning to situations outside of the classroom, the educational system has failed them. The success of education is measured by the number of adults who are gainfully employed, who live independently, who participate as good citizens in society (parents, neighbors), and who participate in pleasurable and beneficial (to mental and physical health) recreational and leisure activities. Shouldn't we measure the success of a music education by the same standard, adults' successful application of music classroom learning to situations outside of school and the numbers who participate in pleasurable music activities? How can we use principles of transfer more effectively and ensure a successful transition of students to an adult musical life? Consider some of the possible outcomes for the following situations.

For some teachers, playing the recorder is considered a "pre-band" experience, an early experience in playing music from notation and one that may motivate students to play an instrument in succeeding grade levels. For other teachers, recorders also offer unique opportunities for students to acquire music knowledge and performance skills. These purposes may be admirable, but it is unlikely that traditional classroom recorder practices will result in these intended outcomes. In reality, the elementary teacher, pressed to include everything in the curriculum, often limits students' recorder experiences to a module of several weeks in the fourth grade and limits the repertoire to ubiquitous B-A-G songs. After the recorder module, do students continue to play their recorders at home for family and friends or play with others in ensembles? How many actually study another instrument, in school or as adults, as a result of classroom recorder experiences? Will adults join the Recorder Society and perform in the community or play at informal gatherings with friends? Do we see playing the recorder as a skill that is just "good for students," hoping that the experience will transfer to other types of music learning and participation in instrumental ensembles? What are realistic expectations for students as a result of several weeks of playing a limited repertoire?

If recorder playing were a highly valued adult music experience and transition were the basis for curricular and instructional decisions, many school recorder experiences would be different. Students would be regularly engaged in activities that were similar to the musical activities of the members of the community Recorder Society (playing arrangements of Renaissance tunes with tambourines and drums, sight-reading simple tunes, discussing music literature, listening to performances by well-known artists and ensembles). Think about possible outcomes if students collaborated with members of the local Recorder Society throughout their years in the upper elementary grades and middle school, playing with adult mentors and performing quality ensemble music with peers. Would these types of school experiences make a difference in students' attitudes and depth of knowledge and skills and thus increase the probability of their participation as adults listening to and performing recorder music alone or in ensembles?

Consider a situation that involves adults' singing. If singing (accurately and expressively) for others (children, other adults) is a highly valued music experience, and transition is the basis for decision making, then school experiences must involve more than those related to traditional concerts. Of course, students must be engaged in enjoyable singing experiences frequently and learn to sing accurately and expressively, but singing for others should occur as an integral part of those experiences. Perhaps, as an ongoing part of the music program, older students could learn to select and perform a repertoire of songs appropriate for younger students in the same school. The older students would actually learn to choose the music and sing the songs for the younger children on many occasions, in informal settings, and either in small groups or one-on-one. Given frequent experiences of this kind, would students have more positive attitudes about singing, would they sing better, would they serve as positive role models and mentors for younger children, would they want to continue to sing for others, would they recruit lower-grade-level students into choir, and would they sing for and with their younger siblings or their own children as parents?

In yet another situation involving community ensembles, what would happen if, on a regular basis, students in middle school and secondary school served as public liaisons and advocates for community performing groups and collaborated, interacted, or performed with the adult members of community groups? Several colleagues and former students who are particularly interested in adult learners and community music have told me about their exciting work bringing student and adult groups together for music making, tutoring, and so on—a wonderfully positive experience for everyone. Would school experiences similar to those of adults who are members of community organizations lead to an increase in the number of students who participated in community performing organizations or attended the concerts of these groups? When these students were independent adults, would more of them contribute their time and money to benefit community (including school) music organizations?

If students, as a part of most classes, reviewed program guides for their local classical radio station and selected dates and times for listening, would they, as adults, be more likely to listen to that station and lend financial support? What effects would we see if, beginning with kindergarten and continuing throughout the elementary grade levels, students shared responsibilities for turning on the radio and finding the public radio station so that their classmates could listen to beautiful music for a few minutes at the end of class.

If students left elementary school and middle school having had a choir (or band or orchestra) big brother or big sister for several years and had, on several occasions each year, performed with the older students, would they be more likely to join and stay in their ensembles? If elementary students spent most of their class time actually learning to sing a repertoire of songs in tune and singing for others, would our adult survey and NAEP data look more positive? Would we informally observe more friends and members of the community participating in music activities? And would we hear more guest speakers at music conferences talk about their successes in making music, instead of those half-apologetic statements about their poor singing or playing and how they weren't really talented? Why do vast numbers of adults apologize for their lack of music skills, knowledge, and participation?

Steps for Designing Meaningful Music Programs

Teachers in schools, colleges, and universities can immediately incorporate a principle of transition into classrooms and rehearsals and into the course content of teacher preparation programs. The principle of transition will be most effective in music programs when:

There is a general consensus among music teachers at all levels regarding the long-term goals that are meaningful for most students.

Students are given frequent opportunities to participate successfully in appropriate related school music experiences at each grade level.

Students learn to make appropriate transfers of skills and knowledge within and across grade levels.

Music teachers initiate collaborations with members of the community (teachers, artists, music organizations, parents, businesses, and other supportive individuals and organizations) to support transition program goals and educational experiences for students.

Many music teachers have sources of support in the community, skills to teach for transfer, and the freedom to develop music experiences for the same students across several years. One teacher can influence the extent of transition made by many students.

Procedures for designing music programs focus around a few key ideas. Simply stated, once it is decided which music experiences are valued for adulthood, similar school experiences need to be developed for each grade level, experiences that will then be defined and offered as a frequent and regular part of classes and rehearsals. Frequency is a critical consideration for each step in the process.

Transition requires frequent opportunities for students to practice skills and knowledge in context. Although several school experiences appear similar to adult experiences (e.g., performing for others in ensembles, attending concerts of classical music), these types of activities are often infrequent occurrences in the lives of students (e.g., performances may occur only in formal school concerts, and field trips to concerts may occur once every few years). Although they may be valued school experiences, they cannot substitute for frequent, regular instruction and practice. Competent instruction and frequent opportunities for contextual practice will increase the probability that students will learn the skills, knowledge, and attitudes to participate successfully in a wide range of music activities. You can approach transition planning in different ways, but almost all approaches will cover three basic steps, as presented in box 2.1.

Box 2.1

STEPS FOR DESIGNING MUSIC PROGRAMS BASED ON A PRINCIPLE OF TRANSITION

Step 1. Decide what music experiences are valued for students' adult lives and the general contexts in which these experiences occur.

Step 2. Analyze each adult music experience in context:
- Identify related activities (people, places, materials, etc.).
- Identify functional prerequisites.

Step 3. Develop a hierarchy of realistic age-appropriate experiences for students at each grade level. Each experience should meet the following criteria:
- Is as similar as possible to the adult experience, related activities, and contexts.
- Occurs frequently throughout the school year.
- Is practiced frequently using contextual variety.

Step 1. Decide what music experiences are meaningful for adulthood and the general contexts in which these experiences occur

Redesigning music classrooms and rehearsals does not require abandonment or revision of current district or state curricula or the national standards. It does, however, require teachers to begin by identifying music experiences for students that will be valued in adulthood and by giving priority to these experiences. This step is difficult for everyone, because it requires making hard choices. It is a critical first step, however, if teachers are to have the time to teach fewer things more deeply and thoroughly. All current school activities must be evaluated, and some activities will have to be eliminated or at least reduced to less instructional time (or effort or money).

One way to approach this decision is to choose music experiences that include skills and knowledge that will occur in many other music experiences, now and in the future. The experiences can be alone or with others; they may be in the home or in the community (including public schools); and they may range across many dimensions of music performance, listening, composing, thinking and talking about music, and music advocacy.

Teachers can also generate ideas by thinking of a young child they care about and then thinking about the kinds of music activities they would like this child to experience as an adult. What do music teachers value for the future adulthood of someone they really care about? Among the valued music experiences, music teachers may want this young child as an adult to sing songs to her own children, sing or play holiday songs with family and friends, play an instrument or sing in a community organization, read music well enough to select and play new music for pleasure at home, attend school board meetings when music is discussed, encourage her children to study music, contribute to music organizations or do volunteer work, and attend concerts in the community and in public schools, even when her own children are not performing. You will not see these experiences listed as goals in any organized curricula, yet they are valued by many music teachers.

If you read these adult goals again, you will see that they require the kinds of skills and knowledge that are a part of traditional curricula; however, they go beyond the tasks (what adults are doing) and include contexts (people, places, materials, etc.). Transfer requires attention to both.

Our hope has been that through the traditional curricular program, skills and knowledge will transfer to contexts outside of school. We know from the data that for a large majority of adults, they do not. As a wise colleague of mine tells his students, "Hope is not an instructional strategy."

Box 2.2

SCHOOL MUSIC EXPERIENCES BASED ON A PRINCIPLE OF TRANSITION: SMALL ENSEMBLES

ADULT EXPERIENCE: PERFORM MUSIC FOR AND WITH OTHERS IN A SMALL ENSEMBLE

Related activities in contexts and functional prerequisites (examples):

Select appropriate music and programming.
Rehearse with repetitions for accuracy and expressiveness.
Develop written or spoken descriptions of the music to be performed.
Perform for different audiences (concert venues, family concerts in the park, friends in informal settings, or groups of elementary-age students).

Functional prerequisites (examples):

Sing or play with technical accuracy, expressively, and with a good tone.
Sight-read ensemble music alone and with others.
Maintain a steady tempo while performing with others.
Demonstrate good practice skills when working on ensemble music.

Similar, age-appropriate experiences for older and younger students (examples):

Small select or small mixed-ability groups and appropriate parts can be assigned by the teacher.

Older Students

Groups of students from the high school large ensembles are selected to play in small ensembles for students in lower grade levels. Groups choose appropriate selections from current repertoire and prepare comments or program notes about the music for their mini-performance.

Students in the small ensemble make decisions regarding rehearsal schedule, repertoire to perform, who will perform critical voice (instrument) parts, musical interpretation, and perhaps even create appropriate arrangements.

Younger Students

Several students who are demonstrating good progress in singing and playing in class evaluate whether their music is ready for performance. They collaborate in the selection of a few short pieces that they perform well, perform

(*continued*)

Box 2.2 (contiued)

for the principal and staff and for teachers and students in other classrooms. This select group and other small groups from the same class sing frequently for each other. Groups evaluate their own performances using criteria given by the teacher and with contributions from the students.

Among several choices given by the teacher, small groups of students (chosen by the teacher) select which song or instrumental accompaniment they will sing or play. Groups sing or play for their classmates.

The process of transition planning can be applied to any long-term adult goal, although to illustrate the next two steps (which focus on analysis of contexts and related school experiences), I've chosen two adult goals that are valued by many music teachers: attending concerts of classical music and performing music with and for others in a small ensemble. As you read these next few steps, think about how the two goals are interrelated and can be taught (practiced) in the same context. Boxes 2.2 and 2.3 show how the three steps for a transition music program apply to these particular goals.

Step 2. Analyze the adult music experience as it would occur in a realistic context; identify related activities in contexts (people, places, materials, etc.) and functional prerequisites

Attending a concert of classical music is not a single activity; it is multidimensional, in that it consists of many related activities. Some of the activities fall within the scope and sequence of traditional music curricula, such as listening to and describing music and even demonstrating appropriate concert etiquette. Transition planning, however, goes beyond goals and objectives and includes a thorough analysis of the adult experience, including the identification of related tasks and contexts. For example, attending a concert most often involves watching the performers while listening to live performances, reading concert programs and notes, relating descriptions of music to the performance, and describing and evaluating the music and the performance when talking to companions during intermission and after the concert. In order to talk intelligently about a music performance, an individual may need to identify groups of instruments by sight and sound, read descriptions of music and identify events when they occur, and use conventional terminology to describe and analyze music and discuss preferences with companions.

Box 2.3

SCHOOL MUSIC EXPERIENCES BASED ON A PRINCIPLE OF TRANSITION: ATTENDING CONCERTS

ADULT EXPERIENCE: ATTEND CONCERTS OF CLASSICAL MUSIC

Related activities in contexts and functional prerequisites (examples):

Watch performers while listening to live performances.
Read concert program and notes and relate descriptions of music to the performance.
Describe and evaluate music and performance when talking to companions during intermission and after the concert.

Functional prerequisites (examples):

Identify groups of instruments by sight and sound.
Read descriptions of music and identify events when they occur.
Talk about music using conventional terminology.

Similar, age-appropriate experiences for older and younger students (examples):

Include live concerts in communities, schools, and classrooms by professionals, students, teachers, or other individuals along with concerts on high-quality videos.

Older Students

Listen in small groups with peers, discuss preferences, and verbally identify and talk about the stylistic features of the musical selection. Describe any compositional devices used to evoke feelings or emotions.

Younger Students

After listening to two short performances, use conventional terminology to relate preferences and talk about any aspect of the music with a partner or in a small group. As needed, music terminology is prompted or chosen from lists.

Before each performance, listen to melodic or rhythmic patterns played by a student or teacher. The teacher and/or students quietly and discreetly nonverbally show when the patterns are heard.

The music experience of performing with and for others in a small ensemble also consists of many related activities, some of which are familiar in the traditional music curricula (singing or performing on an instrument a varied repertoire of music, demonstrating ensemble skills, reading instrumental or vocal scores). Again, transition planning requires attention to tasks in contexts: various learning settings such as homes, classrooms, or concert stages and the people in those settings.

Performing in large ensembles under the leadership of a conductor who chooses the music is a different experience from performing as a member of a small ensemble. Small ensembles often do not have conductors, and members are the ones who select the music, schedule rehearsals, and decide where they will perform. Again, related activities and prerequisite knowledge and skills for the related activities should involve tasks that traditionally would be associated with the activity, such as singing and playing with technical accuracy and with a good tone in small ensembles, sight-reading ensemble music with several other peers, demonstrating good practice skills when working on ensemble music, and maintaining a steady tempo while performing with others. Only prerequisites that apply directly to the activity should be identified.

Step 3. Develop a hierarchy of realistic, age-appropriate experiences for students at each grade level that are as similar as possible to the adult experience, that can occur frequently throughout the school year, and that can be practiced frequently using contextual variety

In order to keep the school experiences as close to the adult experience as possible, it is useful to develop experiences for the "exit" grade level first. Ideally, twelfth grade should be the exit grade for music, although the exit grade may be the last grade level taught by the same teacher (e.g., fifth for elementary) or the last time music will be a required subject for students. Activities for each grade level, with age-appropriate modifications in task complexity and contexts, can then be developed from the exit grade level to the lowest grade level in a top-down process.

Although school experiences will vary somewhat from the adult experience of attending concerts of classical music, it is important to keep the related activities, contexts, and tasks as similar as possible to those that occur in the adult experience and to choose those that provide frequent opportunities for practice. Occasional field trips to concerts in the community may have some benefits for students, since they involve real concert venues; however, these experiences are infrequent and provide limited opportunities for students to learn and practice the range of skills and knowledge that are important parts of the experience.

Compared with field trips, opportunities for practice and transfer of knowledge and skills increase when teachers structure frequent concert experiences, short performances that are given in the classroom or rehearsals. Live "concerts" can be given by the teacher, classmates, parents, or other members of the community. Professional videos of performances of great artists and ensembles also provide excellent opportunities for students to practice related activities that are associated with concert contexts. Although the venue is certainly different, in this situation, teachers have flexibility to structure a range of experiences and opportunities for students to practice skills and apply knowledge (e.g., choice of music, length of music, type of ensemble, performers, topics and music terminology for discussion). For example, consider the related experience of adults talking intelligently about music with companions during intermission or after the concert. For a primary-level experience, after students listen to the teacher perform several short musical excerpts or watch and listen to a short performance on video, they select at least two words from a list of familiar music terminology and use those words to describe the music to a partner (the teacher monitors and expands discussions). Upper-elementary students may use appropriate music terminology in small-group discussions to explain their personal preferences after listening to different short videos or live musical excerpts, and older students may verbally identify and explain the stylistic features of the music selection and some of the compositional devices that were used to evoke feelings or emotions.

The complexity of the tasks and contexts for school experiences involving small-group performances will also vary for students at different grade levels. Again, the experiences that are developed for transition should provide frequent opportunities for practice and be as similar as possible to those that occur in the adult experience. Year-end concerts, holiday concerts, and performances of small ensembles at contests may have benefits for students, but, as with field trips to concerts, these experiences usually occur infrequently and may not offer opportunities for students to learn and practice valued skills and knowledge (e.g., understanding the technical requirements of music and making appropriate selections for performance; working cooperatively with other musicians making independent decisions regarding the music, interpretations, programming for particular audiences, rehearsal schedules, and rehearsal strategies; evaluating individual and group performances).

Teachers can structure numerous age-appropriate experiences and provide frequent opportunities for all students to learn and practice performing in small ensembles in various informal contexts with friendly audiences. Some students will also perform in more formal concert venues. For a primary-level experience, teachers can, on a regular basis, choose several students to sing (and/or play) familiar songs with or without accompaniment in class. Throughout the month, perhaps several students who are demonstrating good progress in singing and playing in class can be selected to evaluate music as being ready for performance or select a few short pieces for an informal performance at the principal's office or for peers and teachers in other classrooms. Similar experiences can be structured for students in upper-elementary, middle, and high school by simply varying the music, audiences, and complexity of tasks that involve independent and small-group decisions regarding selecting music. Teachers who rehearse large ensembles can structure experiences for older students where students select group members for a small ensemble (with some supervision from the teacher) and perform current repertoire for students in lower grade levels. This type of experience provides students with additional opportunities for decision-making in the selection of members who will perform critical voice (or instrument) parts and perhaps in creating appropriate arrangements.

Creative teachers will find many ways to extend the experiences of attending a concert of classical music and playing with and for others to other meaningful music activities performed by adults. It is important, however, that principles of transfer (e.g., learning something well, frequent opportunities for practice, learning principles) are applied to any learning experience.

Music and music making are valued by a large majority of individuals in our society, many of whom have experienced only a few years of formal music education. Music and music making were integral to the lives of individuals long before music education was a part of our school curricula. How will the quality of life of future generations change for the better as a result of children's attending required or elective music classes with competent music educators today? How will music education change so that all people will continue to be involved in meaningful music participation? What good can music education do?

The idea of deciding what is important and meaningful for others is difficult. Many people may want educators to "expose" children to different music experiences, all valued and good, and let children decide for themselves. Competent music educators understand the importance of time for practice and study, key ideas supported by transfer research in all disciplines, and they subsequently make intelligent decisions that significantly affect their students' musical lives. Yet it appears that many children and adults do not choose to continue many of these music experiences outside of school. Perhaps we need to plan more directly for the future musical lives of students. Curricular and instructional decisions must be based on the reality that students leave school and that the frequency of their successes in school will greatly influence their opportunities for choice outside of school.

Transition planning begins with thinking about the future and the music experiences of generations of future adults, and decisions focus on how to bring adult music experiences that are most valued into school music programs, beginning at the earliest possible age. Well-established principles of instruction will result in students who become more skilled, knowledgeable, independent, and confident within enjoyable learning contexts that are age-appropriate and similar to those valued for adulthood.

As children and adults, we experience many transitions in life. Whether transitions are seen as planned, capricious, or just an inevitable part of time and growing older, many transitions bring different responsibilities, decisions, and choices requiring different skills and knowledge. In order to make these transitions smoother, many forward-thinking adults engage in transition planning for retirement, medical and health care for their families, college for their children, vacations, and "rainy" days. We should do no less when planning for the musical lives of future generations.

CHAPTER 3
Where Do I Start?

OVERVIEW

Teaching is complex and really hard to do. It is hard to do because teaching is only successful if students learn, when they learn what we intended to teach. What is it music teachers intend to teach?

If the focus is on the end goal, that of preparing students to participate happily and successfully in meaningful music experiences throughout their lives, then you would think everything else would fall into place. That is where the complex part comes in. Knowing the end goal is extremely important, but there is the business of providing an appropriate curriculum and educational opportunities for all children in inclusive settings to reach this goal. What should those educational opportunities be, and how do you make them happen?

To the degree possible, competent teachers use well-established principles of teaching and learning to reach goals important for their students. Principles are a theme throughout this book; some have emerged from research and others from the ideas and wisdom of individuals who are highly recognized in their respective disciplines. The value of relying on principles for inclusive classrooms is that they are not differentiated among age and ability levels but are universal in the sense that they are applicable in ways that engage diverse groups of students in common experiences. For example, you've read about designing a curriculum based on a principle of transition and principles of transfer. You've also read about principles related to equity and attitudes toward various groups in our society. As with other principles in this book, the principles in this chapter and the principles in the final chapter on accomplishing music goals will apply to your teaching situation, regardless of grade level or area.

The principles described in this chapter have evolved through many forms throughout my career. Although I could have created more, or possibly fewer, I've arrived at a list of four that I describe as governing principles, because they serve to guide all decisions regarding children's music experiences in school. The four governing principles will help you think about ways to create a culture of inclusion and meaningful experiences for children where they will participate happily and successfully with their classmates in a wide variety of music activities; where they will develop cognitively and socially through interactions with peers; where they will develop emotionally through feelings of well-being, self-efficacy, and autonomy; and where they will benefit from your collaborations with a group of knowledgeable and caring adults. Can't we just teach music rather than dealing with other things that will take up our time? From years of experience preparing music teachers for classrooms, I understand the eagerness just to get to the music, but ignoring these governing principles will greatly impede the musical development and well-being of students.

The principles are not independent of one another, although they are presented separately for purposes of focus and clarity. The first is short, but it provides a broad foundation for all other actions of teachers, students, and members of society. Principles 2 and 3 focus on ways to positively affect attitudes and music learning by facilitating children's social and emotional development. The all-important issue of coordination and collaboration is presented in the final principle.

In brief, the four governing principles state that the musical lives of children can be improved when

Culturally normative music experiences and participation in socially valued roles and socially valued activities with a diverse population of children are part of the routine of daily life.

Interactions with same-age peers in inclusive music environments are frequent, positive, and reciprocal.

Self-determination is fostered in music environments where children feel safe and secure and where they experience autonomy, demonstrate competence, and make choices and decisions about music, music making, and other music activities in their lives.

The design, implementation, and evaluation of an individualized music education program involves collaboration and coordinated efforts among parents or guardians, professionals, other significant individuals in the child's life, and the child, when appropriate.

PRINCIPLE 1. CULTURALLY NORMATIVE MUSIC EXPERIENCES AND SOCIALLY VALUED ROLES

Culturally normative music experiences for children are those that are available for most children of the same age, and socially valued roles and music activities are those that are valued by and for most children of the same age. When culturally normative music experiences and participation in socially valued roles and socially valued activities with a diverse population of children are part of the routine of daily life, the musical lives of children can be improved. This principle is based on the premise that quality music experiences have cognitive, emotional, and social benefits for all children and that positive, shared music experiences among seemingly diverse groups of students will increase positive attitudes and behaviors among those students.

Theory and Research: Quality of Life

People strive for quality of life for themselves, for their loved ones, and for others deemed in need. The core dimensions associated with quality of life (e.g., education, employment, living environments) are at the forefront of laws to ameliorate inequities and discrimination.[1] Four questions are helpful in assessing the quality of life of a person: (1) Where is the person (home, community, and school settings)? (2) With whom does the person interact (classmates, acquaintances, friends, paid professionals, diverse populations)? (3) What does the person do (music and other curricular activities and programs, daily living activities, employment)? (4) How does the person feel (what a person says or does that tells us something about the person's emotional well-being and sense of autonomy)? These questions, particularly those having to do with living environments, led to the development of a principle of normalization, the basis for this first governing principle for inclusive music classrooms.

A principle of normalization was first introduced in the 1970s as it concerned the quality of life of individuals with disabilities. The principle was often misconstrued as an attempt to make individuals with disabilities more "normal." That was not the intended purpose. Normalization focuses on ways to improve the quality of life for people with disabilities by providing them with the same types of experiences that are available to most people without disabilities. Because of its broad application concerning the quality of life of diverse populations, the principle of normalization remains an influential concept in policies and practices worldwide.

The most influential names associated with the principle are Bank-Mikkelsen, Nirje, and Wolfensberger.[2] The normalization movement began in Scandinavia in 1959, when Niels Bank-Mikkelsen, then head of the Danish Mental Retardation Service, had a principle written into Danish law to create an existence for the mentally retarded as close to normal living conditions as possible. Actions in Denmark influenced the Swedish disability advocate Bengt Nirje, then secretary general of the Parents Association for Persons with Mental Retardation, to coin the term *normalization* and to clarify its application to the normalization of life's conditions and not the normalization of a person. A strong advocate for normalization practices in Europe and the United States, he influenced educator and scholar Wolf Wolfensberger, a widely recognized advocate for the normalization principle in the United States beginning in the early 1970s.

Among the earliest and most striking victories in the United States for people with disabilities were changes in federal and state laws associated with the deinstitutionalization movement during the late 1970s and 1980s. Public awareness of discriminatory practices was dramatically increased through the work of two individuals, Burton Blatt and Fred Kaplan. Blatt, an advocate for deinstitutionalization and a leader in special education, and his colleague Kaplan, a talented photographer, were among the first to chronicle the blatant inequities of physical and social segregation, which fostered negative stereotypes and discriminatory behaviors toward individuals with intellectual and developmental disabilities. Their startling 1966 photographic essay on life in institutions, *Christmas in Purgatory*, had a dramatic impact on its readers.[3] The contrast between the beginning of the book, with its stark black-and-white photographs of children and adults with intellectual disabilities in institutions, and the book's second half, presented in color and depicting children and adults in their homes and communities, was shocking to many who were unaware of living conditions in institutional settings. Efforts to address these inequities continue to the present day. (Read more about the history of the deinstitutionalization movement, civil rights, and pioneer music teachers in appendix B.)

Although its initial outcomes were less than ideal, deinstitutionalization was an important step toward improving the living conditions and daily routines for children with disabilities, many of whom now reside in their homes with their families and attend neighborhood schools. Deinstitutionalization precipitated education reform for the hundreds of thousands of children who were moving into their family homes and into their communities.

Education reforms have had far-reaching consequences affecting culturally normative music experiences for children, one of the most significant being the Individuals with Disabilities Education Act (IDEA), first signed into US law in 1975 as the Education for All Handicapped Children Act (P.L. 94-142).[4] As you have read, this law requires states and local agencies to place children in the least restrictive environments (LREs) and to develop procedures to ensure that "to the maximum extent appropriate, children with disabilities, including children in public or private schools or other care facilities, are educated with children who are not disabled, and special classes, separate schooling, or other removal of children with disabilities from the regular education environment occurs only when the nature or severity of the disability of a child is such that education in regular classes with the use of supplementary aids and services cannot be achieved satisfactorily."[5] This single statement, this law, dramatically changed the lives of children with disabilities, many of whom would have been relegated in the past to live and be educated in institutional settings. This law also requires that to the extent appropriate, children have access to the regular curriculum, including extracurricular activities available to their typically developing peers. The requirements of IDEA for the same educational opportunities for children with disabilities as those provided to their same-age typically developing peers reflect a principle of cultural normalization.

Requiring the same educational opportunities, however, does not ensure that all children with disabilities are receiving those opportunities. Research reports from the Office of Special Education Programs (OSEP) show that children with multiple disabilities spend a majority of their six-hour school day in separate, not regular, classrooms. During the 1970s and 1980s, Brown and other reformers in special education advocated for least restrictive environments for students with severe disabilities and for regular classrooms and a school day that was typical in length and organization. Among other actions, these leaders proposed a distribution of students in a typical classroom comparable to the distribution that might be found in "desegregated, heterogeneous, postschool communities."[6] They proposed the term *natural proportion* to define the proportion of students with disabilities that should ideally be in any classroom.

The concept of natural proportion, consistent with the principle of normalization, is useful today to approximate the number of children with disabilities who should be a part of any group of children in school. Nationally, schoolchildren and youths ages six through twenty-one who receive services through IDEA represent 9 percent of students in that age group, and about 1 percent to 2 percent of those who receive services have severe disabilities. Think of students in any classroom as a population distributed on a normal curve. Following this idea, in a classroom of twenty-five students, no more than three would have a disability, and among these, one may have a severe disability. Of course, exact classroom examples of proportions proposed by this concept rarely exist, but actions *guided* by natural proportion can prevent unnecessary segregation of services and resources or the placement of too few or too many children with disabilities—or too few or too many with the same type of disability—in any classroom.

Living in a community and participating in a music classroom with a diverse population of peers are important steps toward cultural normalization; however, normalization practices do not ensure social inclusion and positive social interactions. In 1983, Wolfensberger broadened the principle of normalization to include what he called social valorization, valuing people with disabilities as a result of their social roles.[7] He proposed that when an individual with a disability performs roles that are valued, the individual's social image or value is enhanced.

As children participate with a diverse classroom of peers in roles and activities that most of them value, the music-learning environment is enriched as a result of influential social interactions. The influence of social roles and participation in socially valued activities has since been substantiated in the research literature with respect to individuals of different races and ethnicities and provides strong support for all four principles in this chapter. For example, positive attitudes among diverse populations of students can be fostered in schools as a result of extended, direct, positive interactions among groups. Also, when children who may be perceived as incapable actually do more than is expected by most of their peers or adults, whether keeping a beat, improvising a melody at the keyboard, or identifying a music composition, negative stereotyping may begin to diminish. (See numerous research citations throughout the discussion of principles related to peer interactions and fostering self-determination elsewhere in this chapter.)

Applications and Strategies: Quality of Life in Music Classrooms

For many years, rich music experiences were not available to large numbers of children with disabilities. They were not in regular music classrooms (*where*), and they had few opportunities to interact and make music with their typical peers (*with whom*) or to learn and increase their ability to make music and use music knowledge (*what*). This limited their opportunities to experience autonomy, demonstrate competence, and make a variety of choices and decisions about music, music making, and music activities in their lives (*feelings*).

Federal laws, regulations, and policies have begun to ameliorate blatant discriminatory practices, although some children are still isolated from the types of culturally normative and meaningful music experiences most other children enjoy. When cultural normalization is a governing principle in music classrooms, teachers are more likely to provide all students with the same types of quality music experiences, to the extent possible, and structure positive interactions among seemingly diverse groups of children so they may learn from one another. This principle, among all others, provides the broadest foundation for all decisions and actions of music teachers who intend to improve the quality of life of their students.

Because this principle is overarching and affects all decisions and actions, it can be applied in many different situations. Let's take for example the larger issue of where children receive their school music instruction. The application of a principle of cultural normalization recognizes the diversity of abilities and disabilities of children and yet guards against what has been the common practice of segregating children of seemingly similar characteristics in separate classrooms. Separate classrooms exemplify the most blatant violation of cultural normalization; therefore, no music classes within any school should consist of only students with disabilities. A principle of normalization is also violated when large numbers of children with disabilities are included in any single music classroom or music ensemble.

Although some schools follow a principle of cultural normalization, whether they use this terminology to describe their practices or not, some schools do not. Some children may need separate instruction throughout the regular school day through tutoring or classes to meet their particular learning needs, but do they also need a separate music class? And if students with disabilities are included in regular classes, how many students with disabilities can a music teacher realistically accommodate? What can you do if your administration wants you to teach separate music classes for students with disabilities only or if your administration places too many students with disabilities in one of your regular music classes? It is not uncommon for classroom teachers known to be "good with" students with disabilities or students who are struggling in school to find increasing numbers of these students placed in their classrooms. When a principle of natural proportion is violated, the quality of instruction is greatly diminished, resulting in negative outcomes for all members of the class, including the teacher.

In these situations, as you are continuing to provide music instruction under less-than-optimal conditions, you will need to collaborate tenaciously with your principal, your regular and special education colleagues, *and* parents as a way to move toward a reasonable solution regarding student placements. I've given you strategies for these collaborations in governing principle 4. The arguments for appropriate placements are those that concern the quality of your students' experiences and the opportunities they will have to participate successfully in the regular music program, arguments that are supported by requirements in IDEA for regular placements and access to the regular curriculum. It is not easy to change traditional practices, but I have seen the positive results from convincing teachers who have moved students with disabilities, one by one, from separate to regular music classrooms where they and their typically developing classmates participate successfully and learn by being together.

After diverse learners are included in regular classrooms, in numbers that approach those proposed by the principle of natural proportion, there are many ways you can apply the governing principle of cultural normalization and social value to decisions about your music program, curricula, and instruction. Begin by using music activities that you value in your music program as a standard by which to evaluate the quality of participation of diverse populations of children. To the maximum extent possible, all children should attend regular music classes taught by music specialists; participate in regular school music concerts and field trips; participate in a variety of activities as part of the regular music curriculum (singing, playing instruments, listening, creating, talking about music, etc.); make choices and communicate music preferences, ideas, and feelings about music; and demonstrate accomplishments.

Using standards for your regular music program, you can informally assess a student's musical life by means of quality-of-life questions posed earlier (where, with whom, what, feelings). Although your questions may vary from those I list below, you will find that these types of questions will quickly reveal the similarities among and differences between activities of one student and most of his or her same-age peers. Consider asking some of the following questions:

1. *Where is the student before, during, and after the lesson activities?* Where is the student during special music events (e.g., school concerts, symphony field trips)? Where is the student when class begins and ends? Where does the student sit?

2. *What is the student doing throughout the lesson?* Does the child participate as fully and independently as possible or with prompts and/or assistance? Does the level of participation or success vary across different types of activities (listening, singing, instruments, talking, etc.)? What

kinds of meaningful activities can the student perform as independently as possible in the classroom, and are these activities that can transfer to music activities in the student's home or community?

3. *With whom is the student interacting most frequently, and are interactions with diverse populations positive and reciprocal?* Does the student interact most frequently with adults, other students with disabilities or typically developing children, or only with classmates of the same race or ethnicity? Do casual or positive interactions occur naturally during unstructured time before and after class? Is the student included in conversations, even if an alternative communication system or language other than English is used by the student?

4. *What feelings can you infer from your observations of the student's participation?* Have you observed the student making choices and communicating preferences, ideas, and feelings to classmates? Does the student have opportunities to demonstrate accomplishments that are valued by the student, classmates, and others?

Asking these questions about students who have disabilities or who are struggling academically and/or socially in your classroom will help you make curricular and instructional decisions that are consistent with the principle of cultural normalization, decisions that will foster the students' musical, social, and emotional development. As an example of an instructional strategy that reflects this principle, when designing activities for small groups and peer interactions (principle 2), teachers will assign only one child with a disability to a small group of four or five typically developing classmates. In another example focusing on the development of independence (principle 3), teachers will provide opportunities for students to set goals, make plans to reach those goals, and self-evaluate, behaviors that are valued by society. And when determining curricular goals, teachers will consider students' preferences and use universal strategies with minimal adaptations only when necessary (chapter 4). The principle of culturally normative music experiences and social valued roles has wide application for teachers' decision-making and applies to almost all of the strategies and ideas throughout this book.

PRINCIPLE 2. FREQUENT, POSITIVE, AND RECIPROCAL PEER INTERACTIONS

Talking about music, exchanging glances and smiles with classmates at the end of a music performance, being chosen as a partner for a dance, performing with a small ensemble of peers, helping a classmate learn to sing or play a musical phrase—these and many other seemingly unexceptional interactions among children can all contribute to their overall development, including their musical development. Music scholars have examined in depth the interplay between individual and social characteristics of children within cultural conventions and the impact of these factors on music practices, music learning, and the musical development of children.[8] Extensive research on the influences of social and cultural contexts on learning and development suggests that the musical lives of children can be improved when interactions with same-age peers in inclusive music environments are frequent, positive, and reciprocal.

Theory and Research: Social Ecology Influences Learning

The effects of positive social relationships on a child's well-being and success in school are well known. In brief, we know that relationships among children, unlike children's relationships with adults, are more open, more spontaneous, and in many ways more creative, because children develop their own rules, solve their own problems, and construct how and why things work the way they do. Children develop cognitively and socially when they can learn from one another and engage in intimate, constructive conversations.

When children first begin to experience friendship, usually around the age of two, they engage in positive reciprocal interactions and begin to experience social and emotional support. The need for companionship and support becomes more important to their emotional well-being as they grow older. For some adolescents, feelings of loneliness and inferiority along with poor school performance can be traced to their lack of personal, trusting, supportive, and reciprocal relationships with friends and the lack of a circle of supportive classmates. Although other variables can influence success in school, the significance of positive peer relationships is unarguably one of the most powerful.

Positive social interactions influence more than social development. Several noted theorists have identified social ecology as a powerful influence on learning outcomes—cognitive, emotional, and social—and research that is grounded in these theories has led to effective educational practices for children with a wide range of abilities. Albert Bandura proposed that learning is closely tied to the environment created by others in the group.[9] Research and practices in education related to observational learning and modeling are directly tied to his theories. One of the more striking examples of modeling can be observed by comparing one student's behavior with different classmates or groups of classmates. We know, as teachers and parents, the strong influences of peers, how some peers will bring out the best in a child and others will not. Also striking are observations of groups of children in separate special education classrooms and classrooms that are inclusive. Children will imitate peers' behaviors in any type of setting. You need only talk to music teachers who work in both separate and inclusive music classes to understand the dramatic differences in the types of behaviors being modeled and imitated. Who is Jessica going to learn from when all of her classmates exhibit many of the same types of communication, behavioral, learning, or emotional challenges that she does?

With few exceptions, positive models for academic and social behaviors are abundant in regular classrooms, and this fact alone provides a strong case for inclusive experiences. Yet many children may not learn appropriate social skills from watching their peers, or they may watch or interact with peers who model inappropriate behaviors. Although music teachers cannot structure social interactions for children outside of school, in school, we can arrange meaningful interactions with appropriate models and also, when necessary, give students explicit, direct experiences to practice appropriate social skills.

Developmental theorist Lev Vygotsky believed that social interactions are necessary for overall cognitive development.[10] He emphasized cooperation among peers as a way to build new skills and acquire new knowledge valued by a culture. Vygotsky's ideas led to a practice that is widely recognized among professionals in psychology and education: cooperative learning. A large body of research evidence in educational psychology supports the use of cooperative learning strategies. Based on the early work of Maller and Slavin, Johnson and Johnson developed explicit protocols and strategies for teachers.[11] Children teaching children, whether through structured small groups or peer tutoring, is an idea that has gained wide acceptance among parents and professionals.

Tomasello viewed the inclination of individuals to teach others, even among the very young, as a distinctly human characteristic.[12] The inclination for children to teach and learn from one another is thought to enable the socialization of children into their culture, and it can be observed worldwide in the informal music games of children on playgrounds and in families where music practices reflect cultural preferences.[13] There are any number of examples in society where we can see these inclinations to teach—children teaching one another, older children teaching younger children, and children helping and teaching children who appear to be in need.

During many years after the passage of IDEA in 1975, music classes, along with lunch and recess, were the first choices of IEP teams to meet the mandate of the "least restrictive environment." They were in music classes not for music learning but for "socialization." With a directive to provide inclusive experiences for students with disabilities to the extent possible and with social development as the curricular priority, music classes appeared with regularity on IEPs well into the 1990s. In extreme examples at secondary levels, students without any prior experience playing instruments were placed in instrumental ensembles for socialization. Students with disabilities sat in rehearsals, watched ensembles and listened (or not), but rarely interacted with classmates and did not participate in meaningful ways. Neither socialization nor music objectives were met. Unfortunately, some of these practices continue today.

The ongoing practice of placements in music for socialization often reflects many adults' misperceptions about goals and instructional practices in music education. The belief that everyone loves music is just fine, but what if adults also believe that the primary goal for music classes should be only for enjoyment and social activities and that learning music skills and knowledge is only for those students who are labeled as "talented"? It's certainly a good thing that music classes are viewed as happy places for children to spend time and interact with their classmates, but when music class is viewed only as a place for socializing and enjoyment, many opportunities are missed. What about the child's musical development? And will simply being in a music class result in positive social experiences with peers?

Not all classroom activities (singing, listening quietly to music, and playing instruments) require social interactions. In fact, the last thing most teachers want during their instructional time is socializing. "Stop socializing," the teacher pleads, "and let's get back to work." Socialization during instruction, when unplanned by the teacher, is synonymous with off-task behavior. And who wants that? True, there are many occasions when students can interact informally and appropriately with their classmates in music (and even before and after class, during bus rides on field trips, and so on). Social relationships can develop through peer interactions in classrooms, but these types of interactions can also occur in social studies, math, language arts, and physical education classes. So why would it be so closely tied to music?

Perhaps associating music with socialization has its historical roots in the early custom of making music at social gatherings with friends and family, a custom that in many ways is diminishing in contemporary society in the United States. Whether that is the case or not, I leave this issue to others who have expertise in the sociological and historical foundations of music. Getting back to the issue at hand, first, as music teachers, we most likely agree that opportunities for social interactions are not the primary reason for school music programs. But if social interactions are identified as important goals, then instruction must be designed specifically to reach those goals. Also, why are parents, professionals, and teachers so concerned with children's social development? What are the benefits of positive peer relationships and interactions for children, and are there ways for teachers to structure opportunities for social interactions in music classrooms and rehearsals and also to maximize positive outcomes for music learning? Can we, should we, do both?

Research documenting the positive influences of social interactions on learning and the inclination of children to teach has led to effective classroom strategies for peer-assisted learning. Peer-assisted learning, or PAL, as this concept appears in the research literature, usually refers to dyads or small groups that are structured with students across an extended period of time and designed to accomplish particular tasks assigned by the teacher. However, in a less formal manner, dyads and small groups can be set up spontaneously and last for brief periods of time. For example, I've observed elementary teachers who give students a question or task to discuss briefly in dyads with classmates who are seated next to them ("pair share"), and this idea, of course, can apply to all levels and even with small-group structures.

In dyads, interactions usually involve same-age or cross-age tutoring, when one student is assigned the role of teacher and the other is the learner, or tutoring that is reciprocal, when each student has a turn in the role of teacher or learner. Small groups, whether defined specifically as cooperative learning groups (with an established set of procedures) or not, are most often made up of same-age students (usually three to five in a group), and each group is as heterogeneous as possible (mixed abilities, mixed genders, students with and without disabilities, and any other mix that is possible given students' characteristics). There can be other variations for dyads and groups, given the age of the students, the goals, and so on. Some strategies follow models with explicit procedures (e.g., cooperative learning groups, some specific tutoring models), and others have few established rules other than those set by the teacher.

For purposes of this chapter, unless specified otherwise in a research study, I will use the concept of PAL broadly, to mean any dyad or small-group structure that is specifically designed by the teacher to achieve music learning and/or social learning goals. These dyads and small groups can be for an extended period of class time or can happen frequently for shorter periods of time throughout the year.

In a meta-analysis of hundreds of studies observing elementary school children teaching one another, positive academic outcomes (primarily for reading, math, and social studies) were found for PAL strategies (defined as peer tutoring, small learning groups, and small cooperative group strategies).[14] Although students of various ages and abilities can benefit academically from the strategies, they were found to be particularly effective for students defined as vulnerable—students in the lower elementary grades, minority students, students at-risk, and students with disabilities. A smaller number of studies examined both academic and social outcomes, and findings were positive for both measures. In some, self-concept was also measured, again with positive outcomes.[15]

Academic achievement outcomes are related to peer interaction variables, but dramatic outcomes also occur in attitudes, attitude formation, and attitude change. Theories on the nature of prejudice[16] led to hundreds of studies examining the question of whether intergroup contact with face-to-face interactions between members of clearly defined groups based on race, ethnicity, disability, and other factors reduces prejudice. In a meta-analysis to test intergroup contact theory, intergroup contact not only reduced prejudice between members of the different groups but also generalized to individuals outside the group.[17]

These meta-analyses suggest positive outcomes for both social and academic goals when students teach one another; however, in music research, data have been collected for one or the other, either social or academic goals. In music education research, social variables are most often examined as they affect music learning. In music therapy research, we see the reverse; music variables are examined most often as they affect social behaviors. Several studies in music education and music therapy present interesting examples of the ways structured social interactions benefit students.

When students' social behaviors are topics in music education pedagogical and research literature, the behaviors are often those that concern classroom management and not peer interactions related to music learning.[18] The only music study found to date has examined small-group peer interactions to improve music learning (i.e., self-evaluations of undergraduate music students of their music performances) and did so through two experiments; the second examined modified group procedures used in the first study.[19] As a result of multiple peer-group sessions where students sang and played for one another and discussed one another's performances, self-evaluations of performances (tone, intonation, technique, and interpretation or musical effect) became closer to the evaluations of peers across time, but the evaluations did not become more accurate as compared with those of the instructor.

The strong influence of peers is well documented in the literature, and the influence can be positive or negative. As you just read, the students' self-evaluations in the small-group music study were influenced by their peers (self-evaluations became more like those of peers in their group), but self-evaluations and peer evaluations were not accurate. What would it take for self-evaluations to have become more accurate using small-group strategies? The researcher suggests that sessions should last a longer period of time and that the teacher should play a larger role in oversight of the groups, particularly in the early stages.

When complex teaching strategies such as peer-assisted learning are examined in the research, it can take many studies to develop a model that is deemed most effective. Much of the research outside of music that has shown the effectiveness of small-group procedures (specifically, cooperative groups) examine procedures that are implemented across time and that include a significant role for the teacher in monitoring the progress of the groups. Small-group strategies, even if they are implemented with adult students, require the presence and attentiveness of a music teacher, at least initially.

Even without music studies of peer-assisted learning, music teachers can feel confident about implementing these strategies, given the strong support from a substantive research base outside of music and with the understanding that the strategies may need to be revised and refined. You may already be using PAL strategies. Many elementary music teachers regularly have students work in dyads or small groups, and many secondary music teachers rely on their students to assist one another with particular fingerings, hand position, notation, or other technical issues. Several choral teachers I know have students work in pairs, tape-recording each other, evaluating each other's performances, and working to make improvements. Although some peer tutoring and small-group procedures can be difficult to establish at first, particularly when they involve complex tasks, the benefits for students are well worth the effort on the part of teachers. (Ideas for setting up groups will be discussed in the applications section below.)

As you have read, the implementation of peer-assisted strategies benefits all students, although they are most effective for students described in the research as the most vulnerable, students who are at-risk and those with disabilities. In many cases, students described as "at-risk" attend schools in cities with high-poverty concentrations—typically urban schools—as do many children who have poor health or disabilities as a result of living in poverty. Deservedly, the complex issue of urban music education is gaining greater attention among music teachers, scholars, and researchers.[20] Numerous studies outside of music and several in music education have identified a lack of resources, adequately prepared teachers, and any number of factors that negatively affect the quality of music education for teachers and students in such school districts.[21] As we learn more about the demographics of music programs in urban schools, scholars and researchers are approaching ways to better prepare teachers, to assist teachers in the schools, to engage parents and community resources, and to develop meaningful programs and effective strategies. The end goal, of course, is to prepare and motivate students so that they will participate more fully and successfully in their school music programs, particularly at the secondary level, when they are most vulnerable to positive and negative peer influences.

There are any number of social benefits of music programs and music making for adolescents. Positive musical engagement can occur in diverse contexts (schools, communities) and can be highly influential in young people's perceptions of themselves, thus influencing their musical development.[22] Several model music community programs with at-risk students report numerous emotional and social benefits.[23] The value of participation in a small music ensemble was empirically demonstrated with sixth-grade at-risk students who participated in a creative percussion ensemble with a teacher-mentor.[24] Students' perceptions of their musical competence increased significantly, as did their rankings of the importance of music in their lives.

Meaningful and positive social interactions, when structured in music classes, can provide students with any number of social and music benefits—but the students have to be there! The issue for secondary music classes is to get students there and then to use effective strategies, thus allowing for greater opportunities not only in school but also for their adult lives. In a study of high school seniors, it was found that 21 percent participated in performing ensembles (choir, band, orchestra), and most scored high on academic tests and were female, white, native English speakers, and children of parents with advanced degrees and high socioeconomic status.[25] Does this seem to be the profile for most students in urban schools? Not really, but interestingly, it looks very much like the profile of students in urban schools who are in *performing ensembles*.

The issue of recruitment and retention of students in secondary ensembles is complex, and it has been addressed frequently at conferences and in the pedagogical literature; a number of articles have examined the relationship between nonmusic factors (e.g., family income and structure, ethnicity, academic achievement) and students' decisions.[26] In a recent large study of two urban middle schools, higher academically achieving students and those from two-parent or two-guardian homes were found to be more likely to begin band; students with these same demographics who were female and from higher SES were also more likely to persist in band.[27] These predictors were consistent regardless of ethnicity. Any further discussion on this topic is well beyond my purpose for this chapter. The few facts I've presented are powerful enough to make the point that many secondary students who could benefit most from meaningful interactions with their peers in music classes are not there—they are not in secondary music classes to the extent that we would hope. For those who are, their music learning experiences are enriched when teachers implement effective peer-assisted learning strategies.

Music ensembles have been described as "close-knit" circles that reach the level of specific cultures where students teach and learn from one another—a "home away from home," as some students have said.[28] In this study examining interviews of students in band, choir, and orchestra ensembles, we learn that the social climate of the music classroom was a pervasive element in students' responses, that they often mentioned social benefits such as friendships and learning to work collaboratively, and that the music classroom was thought of as a place to develop friendships.[29] It should be noted that these students attended a school in an upper-middle-class suburban area, most were white, and most all had plans to attend college. I suspect it is unlikely that ethnicity or race would make a difference in ensemble students' perceptions of social benefits.

From the comments of students in this interview study, however, the degree of importance of social aspects of ensemble membership varied (although still positive), and some members described a few members using the terms "outcast" or talked about members who "just don't fit in." And many of the social interactions were described as occurring outside the classroom, interactions that did not involve music making or activities related to music learning. If music teachers are to take advantage of the social aspects of the music classroom and the potential benefits for music learning, specially designed peer interactions will need to be structured as a part of the regular class session.

Given the research on prejudice toward individuals who may be perceived by peers as not fitting in, or as "different," intergroup contact through positive interactions will most likely decrease negative attitudes and increase positive attitudes toward different groups of students (based on race, ethnicity, gender, disability, and other factors). With extended positive intergroup contact with classmates in school, it is likely that positive attitudes will generalize to other individuals of a group with similar characteristics. In a review of music research on the topic of attitudes toward individuals with disabilities, direct contact, through either small groups or peer tutoring, increased positive interactions between students with disabilities and typically developing students and increased positive attitudes of typical students toward their disabled peers.[30]

In reviews of music research related to students with disabilities, a large majority of studies were found to focus on the effects of music interventions on social outcomes such as increasing attention and/or decreasing problem behaviors.[31] Overall, these reviews report the interventions as effective; however, few studies were conducted in inclusive settings, and few studies examined interactions between children with disabilities and their typical peers.

Direct experiences positively change attitudes and behaviors toward children with disabilities, and context influences perceptions and expectations about individuals with disabilities. Attitudes developed through experiences with classmates with disabilities also may have a lasting effect. In one study, secondary-level music students were asked about their past experiences with classmates with disabilities. When asked about future interactions with students with disabilities, they responded more positively than did students who had not interacted with peers with disabilities.[32]

Two studies involving preschool children illustrate that music activities alone will not result in positive interactions among children; interactions must be structured. In one study, typical preschool children increased their choices of peers with intellectual disabilities as partners after several weeks of musical partner games with specifically created songs about partners.[33] In another study of a regular school playground, a music "hut" was designed with instruments and musical adaptations to facilitate interactions among typical peers and a child with autism.[34] The availability of music materials did not increase interactions with the child; interactions increased only when the typical peers learned how to play and interact with the child with autism using the music equipment and materials provided.

As you have read, structured interactions through small groups and peer tutoring influence the quality of the interactions among children and also influence children's attitudes. This was the case in a study of four classrooms of elementary children who participated in small-group activities with their classmates with severe disabilities for several weeks.[35] Positive interactions were observed during their small-group activities, and small groups increased positive interactions between typical children and children with severe disabilities during free time in class. Interactions during free time were slightly more frequent when groups also received a music listening reward for "cooperating" in their groups, although effects were most noticeable for children in classrooms that began the small group intervention early in the study. Results suggest that small-group music activities should be structured for diverse groups of students as soon as possible in the school year, in order to increase the probability of positive attitudes, positive social interactions, and generalization.

Positive social outcomes were also observed in a study involving cross-age peer tutoring; upper-elementary-age children who were described by their teachers as having behavior disorders tutored kindergartners with low social and academic skills.[36] Music cassettes were among the rewards earned by the tutors. Kindergartners with tutors made significant academic gains compared to a control group without tutors, and both tutors and tutees reported positive attitudes toward the learning experience. College students who viewed videos of the tutoring sessions and who were unaware of the teachers' labels for the tutors described the tutors as "gifted, on-task, positive, socially appropriate, above grade level, and behaviorally normal." Outcomes from this study show that children with disabilities, put in the right situation and with the right support systems, can exceed the low expectations that are often associated with their disabilities.

Developing teaching strategies directly from the music research is challenging, particularly considering the scarcity of studies on interventions to achieve social and musical goals. However, given the positive findings from the few studies that exist and given the wealth of research from special education and psychology, there is more than enough evidence to support the application of findings to music classrooms and rehearsals.

Applications and Strategies: Music and Social Development in a Climate of Inclusion

Pick up any book on teaching, whether intended for future teachers, experienced teachers, or faculty in teacher preparation programs, and you are sure to see the first important task for a teacher: "Establish a positive socio-emotional classroom environment." What is a positive socio-emotional environment? It is a place for learning where each child feels a sense of belonging; where each child feels comfortable, safe, and secure; and where each child has numerous opportunities to make choices and experience autonomy. It is a place for learning where children respect one another and the teacher, where they show kindness toward one another, where they collaborate and cooperate with one another, and where children laugh together and joyfully celebrate one another's successes. Wouldn't you want to be a student or teacher in such a classroom?

Although much emphasis in schools is placed on students' academic progress, a child's successful academic development is in many ways dependent on the social-emotional fabric of the classroom. So what is one of the first tasks for the teacher? Establishing a positive socio-emotional classroom environment, one that includes many opportunities for students to interact positively with one another.

There is no shortage of advice for new teachers about how to create a positive classroom environment: be patient, cheerful, kind, respectful, accepting of the individual, fair, and on and on. Anyone would be hard pressed to find a teacher, or a future teacher, who would disagree. (Note that some of the attributes I mentioned are also desirable for politicians, sales clerks, doctors, receptionists, flight attendants, administrators, and so on.)

To build a positive climate of inclusion in your classroom, it is important to answer hard questions, beginning with an honest evaluation of your own attitudes and those of your students—attitudes that may reflect learned negative stereotyping regarding different groups of people. It is important to keep at the front of your reflections the word *learned*; negative stereotyping is learned, and it can be unlearned. Part of what we do as music teachers is build a sense of community among students in our classrooms and schools, and this can be done to some degree by developing a climate of inclusion. Good intentions of teachers and students need to be accompanied by actions if classrooms are to become happy places where children will feel safe, will be welcomed, and will be successful. I've listed several ideas to get you started:

- Guard against low expectations and dangerous assumptions. (Such attitudes on the part of the teacher and typical students are not uncommon. Praise yourself for working against unproductive learned attitudes, and focus on what students can do and have learned.)
- Collaborate with positive, knowledgeable, supportive individuals outside of the classroom. (The teachers' break room can be fertile ground for reinforcing negative stereotypes. Avoid negative individuals and the doughnuts. Find colleagues and others who will contribute positively and realistically to your concerns and who have a good sense of humor.)
- Learn, and have your students learn, how to communicate with students who use alternative forms of communication, assistive listening

devices, or other types of assistive technology. (Special educators, parents, and the student can be your best teachers.)

- Defuse tension and stress through humor and enjoyable music activities. (Engage everyone in upbeat music or an activity that both you and your students will enjoy.)
- Set yourself up for success with expectations that are realistic, and give yourself positive feedback for your accomplishments.
- Integrate topics of civil rights into teaching; give examples as they relate to music contexts (e.g., access to performance halls, interpreters at concerts, person-first language in written and spoken communication).
- Develop a sense of community and giving through music projects, performances, and tutoring. (Engage all of your students in planning, developing, and implementing ideas—everyone contributes, cooperates, and celebrates collaborative efforts.)
- Prepare students for "all kinds of children" by giving them specific responses (and, for younger children, simulated practice) for those occasions when a classmate may be uncooperative, rude, insensitive, distracting, and so on. (Consult with counselors and special education teachers about specific behavior plans for your more aggressive and vulnerable students.)
- Teach routines and rules and social skills that show "with-it-ness" (e.g., respecting others' space, ignoring distractions, requesting assistance and permission, working cooperatively in a group and with a partner).
- For some students, particularly children with disabilities, peer interactions may occur only in school and when structured by teachers. Nurture friendships that you see developing in the classroom. (For younger children, if you suspect parents will feel positive toward the friendship, tell them about the positive interactions you have observed. Some parents, when they are aware of this developing friendship, will find ways for children to have play dates and enjoy each other's company outside of school).
- Structure informal opportunities for students to find commonalities in experiences, preferences, and activities. (Discussions between students can be integrated into any lesson or rehearsal or structured for a few minutes before or after the lesson. Assign partners to ensure positive, reciprocal interactions and productive outcomes.)
- Redirect interactions when well-intended typical students are hovering or helping too much. (Teach students when and how to help.)
- Structure occasions, no matter how brief, when students with disabilities and students who may lack self-confidence demonstrate their capabilities and teach and help their typical classmates. (Structure

occasions when the students are sure to be successfully and outcomes positive.)

- Structure frequent opportunities for positive social interactions and cooperation in small groups with interesting music activities and materials early in the school year. Plan a short, simple, highly structured but interesting activity for the first day of class. Keep it enjoyable, and include upbeat music in some way. For example, write topics for preferences on the board (food, pets, music), begin with one that will be sure to get them talking, then move to music preferences. Play background music (socially more comfortable than silence for talking). Partners (or groups of three) face one another, introduce themselves, say something about music or other preferences, whatever gets them talking. They might decide among the topics. Also, you might then call their attention to the music that is playing. They listen, say something about the music to their partner and continue talking about other music preferences and music experiences. The younger the students, the more structure needed. Keep it short, and use a cue if necessary to control how long each student talks. If students are new to you, do this activity at the end of class, after you have observed them carefully and can make some decisions about partners and groups.

Music instruction in inclusive classrooms provides a multitude of opportunities for positive social interactions (e.g., short face-to-face interactions with a stand partner, discussion groups to plan performances or tours, small groups to create improvisations, peer tutoring on individual parts). Young children with multiple disabilities who cannot play instruments with melodic or rhythmic precision can participate with classmates in the creation of soundscapes or sound effects. In this activity, students in small groups choose their instruments, create plans (who plays what, when, and for how long), and perform. The overall objective for each small group is to develop a piece in which everyone contributes in a meaningful way, and the outcome is musically satisfying to everyone in the group. Consider another example in a rehearsal setting. Natural peer supports exist in choral and instrumental ensembles among students who sit in the same section. Short face-to-face interactions can be structured easily throughout the rehearsal. Also, teachers can set up interactions to discuss issues such as music programming and upcoming performances.

In the cooperative model and in other variations based on small-group protocols, students can achieve academically and socially by accomplishing assigned tasks with their peers. Groups should be heterogeneous (mixed ability levels in a single small group), each group member should contribute to a common goal (e.g., compose melodic lines or rhythms for a poem), and tasks toward the common goal should be individualized based on each student's strengths (write the notation, say the words of the poem, play or sing the melodic line, tap the rhythm of the created melody while others sing or play, and so on). There are expectations for small groups: everyone participates, everyone cooperates, only one person speaks at a time, and everyone listens to the person speaking.

As we know, there are children who will naturally and positively interact with their classmates, regardless of their classmates' culture, ethnicity, gender, or ability levels. Many teachers have inspiring stories about their students' interactions, kindnesses, and sensitivities.[37] There are also children who will need to learn how to interact with other children who seem different from themselves, and they can learn best through interactions that are structured by their teachers. When positive interactions are structured early in the school year, the mutual respect and understanding that are nurtured through these interactions will generalize to informal interactions among students. More and more children will begin to help their classmates in meaningful ways. They will begin to view their classroom as a place where every one of them belongs. They will begin to teach one another and collaborate on ways everyone can participate more fully. Children learn best in a positive classroom environment, and children, learning together, vividly remind us of this fact.

PRINCIPLE 3. FOSTERING SELF-DETERMINATION

We talk about people as being in control of their lives. We observe individuals who make sound decisions, solve problems, set attainable goals for themselves, and regulate their behavior (e.g., exercise, study hard, practice) or not. In most cultures, to be a self-determined individual is viewed positively. Research documents positive outcomes for children who have learned skills related to self-determination, positive outcomes for their social development, academic development, and well-being. Positive outcomes can also extend to children's musical development. The musical lives of children can be improved when self-determination is fostered in music environments where children feel safe and secure and where they experience autonomy, demonstrate competence, and make choices and decisions about music, music making, and other music activities in their lives.

Consider the many choices you have in life and the variety of decisions you make in any given day. You set goals, solve problems, make decisions, communicate preferences to others, monitor your actions, and even praise yourself for your accomplishments. You chose to be a teacher. You chose to read this book. You are a self-determined individual. You have any number of skills, many of which are components of self-determination.

Self-determination can be fostered or repressed. Consider individuals who live in countries with oppressive governments, who have limited educational opportunities, and who are unable to escape their unfortunate situation for any number of reasons. Institutional living and poor educational services diminish opportunities for individuals to be independent and take control of their lives—where they are, with whom they interact, what they do, and subsequently, how they feel about themselves, their capabilities, and their future. Advocacy and self-advocacy groups have struggled for decades to change the structure of services for people who are often marginalized by society. Their goal is services to enable individuals to have more independence, more choice, freedom, autonomy, and responsibility. This struggle continues, particularly for people with significant disabilities.[38]

Throughout children's lives in school, teachers work to provide them with the knowledge and skills that will lead them to happy, successful adult lives. And throughout school, teachers try to teach their students to be more independent and to show elements of self-determined behavior (problem solving, decision-making, self-evaluation). Children who learn these skills are generally happier and more successful in school and life than children who do not.

Many children learn to become more independent and acquire the knowledge and skills associated with self-determination implicitly, although other children require more guidance and instruction. We observe children on a daily basis who, when compared with most same-age peers, have problems making decisions, require too much adult assistance, lack confidence and discipline, and cannot accurately evaluate themselves or their skills. We worry about them and their ability to be happy and successful in life.

Although children's needs and individual characteristics influence how quickly and successfully skills are learned, children's home and school environments will have much to do with fostering skills required for a meaningful adult life. This fact was made vividly clear by observing adults with disabilities who grew up in restrictive living environments (e.g., institutions) and who lacked skills for employment, domestic living, and independence. These restrictions began to change with IDEA, particularly with requirements for IEPs and individual transition plans.

The idea of transition appears in almost every aspect of education. In chapter 2, you read about the importance of designing and implementing a music curriculum built on a principle of transition. You have also read about requirements in IDEA for transition plans beginning at age fourteen and, beginning at age sixteen (or younger), a statement of transition services focusing on employment and other postschool adult living objectives.

Consider the possibilities for any child when adults in the child's life give attention to the child's transition throughout school years and into adult life—transition to meaningful postschool adult activities, including those associated with music. If students are to be successful as adults in postschool activities, they will need the skills and knowledge to engage in activities as independently as possible—skills and knowledge that are a part of the general education curriculum and skills and knowledge associated with self-determination. Providing for self-determination is essential for successful transition. But can it be taught?

Whether self-determination per se can be taught as a curricular goal is questionable; however, there is a general consensus among professionals that skills *associated* with self-determination (e.g., choice making, self-regulation, problem solving) can be taught and that acquisition of these skills results in positive outcomes for life. The importance of transition and the necessity of self-determination behaviors have led to the development of specialized published curricula on these topics.

Skills needed for employment, domestic living, and independence are often included in students' IEPs, since they are also considered important for success in general education classes. The role of music teachers is to work collaboratively with special educators, parents, music therapists, and other professionals to incorporate IEP goals and strategies into a student's music activities, not as a substitute for music learning but as an integral part of music learning. Behaviors associated with self-determination can be integrated easily into a variety of music activities for all students.

Theory and Research: The Concept of Self-Determination

The scientific community generally agrees that behaviors defined as "determined" (not to be confused with "self-determined") are those caused by prior factors and events, from the genetic makeup of individuals to events in nature such as rain, temperature, or hurricanes. As we are well aware, environmental factors in children's homes and schools, including the actions of parents and teachers, can determine children's behavior. Almost all adults can identify many factors that act as causal agents in their lives.

Self-determined behaviors, on the other hand, are volitional acts. It is the individual who acts as the primary causal agent in order to maintain or improve his or her quality of life. For centuries, philosophers have debated the existence of free will and have raised questions regarding the reconciliation of determinism and free will. I will not contribute to this debate in this book, but I will give an introduction to several prominent theorists and researchers who have contributed instructional interventions that foster self-determination.

In the work of Albert Bandura, behavior is explained by extrinsic motivation (external causal agents) *and* intrinsic motivation (self as causal agent). Bandura depicts people as self-organizing, proactive, self-reflective, and self-regulative in their actions, rather than merely reactive to social environmental causes. You read briefly about his contributions to social learning and modeling in the 1980s. In the 1990s, he began a research agenda to understand more deeply the constructs of self-efficacy (self-perceptions of one's own capabilities) and self-regulation (self-control of one's actions and thoughts). In his definitive book on the topic, Bandura proposes that beliefs about one's capabilities regulate all aspects of human functioning.[39] Self-efficacy beliefs affect individuals in either a positive, self-enhancing way or in a negative, self-debilitating way. He attributes these beliefs to how well individuals motivate themselves and persevere in the face of difficulties, the quality of their emotional well-being, their vulnerability to stress and depression, and the choices they make at important decisional points—all elements of self-determination.

Ryan and Deci are most closely associated with self-determination theory.[40] Their theory is derived from a review of research that identifies optimal social-contextual conditions that facilitate healthy psychological development and self-motivation. From their examination of the research, Ryan and Deci propose that self-determination encompasses three innate psychological needs: competence (feeling a sense of achievement), autonomy (feeling in control), and relatedness (feeling safe and secure with other people). They postulate that these needs, when satisfied, can lead to self-motivation and physical and emotional well-being and, if *not* satisfied, can lead to physical and even mental illness.

The concept of self-determination in the psychological literature and subsequent research has led to the development of definitions and strategies in education. Wehmeyer is cited frequently for his work promoting self-determined behavior in children with intellectual and developmental disabilities, and he has put forward several broad definitions. You will see commonalities among them. In one, he and his colleagues define self-determination as "a combination of skills, knowledge, and beliefs that enable a person to engage in goal-directed, self-regulated, autonomous behavior."[41] In another, self-determination is defined as "*solving a sequence of problems* in order to construct a means-end chain—a causal sequence—that moves us from where we are—an actual state of not having our needs and interests satisfied—to where we want to be—a goal state of having those needs and interests satisfied."[42] You can see how both definitions reflect the idea of "needs" proposed in Ryan and Deci's self-determination theory. Wehmeyer's work to develop curricula, however, required him to delineated component elements of self-determined behavior.[43] Among the components are:

- Choice-making skills
- Decision-making skills
- Problem-solving skills
- Goal-setting and goal-attainment skills
- Independence, risk-taking, and safety skills
- Self-observation, evaluation, and reinforcement skills
- Self-instruction skills
- Self-advocacy and leadership skills
- Positive attribution of efficacy and outcome expectancy
- Self-awareness
- Self-knowledge

Considering the critical impact of self-determination on many aspects of an individual's development and well-being, you might think that the construct of self-determination is a well-researched topic. This is not the case. Although hundreds of articles have addressed the topic (and similar concepts such as independence and autonomy), self-determination has received sparse attention in the research literature, primarily because of the difficulty of defining the term and measuring the presence or absence of self-determination per se. Each definition of the term presents yet more concepts requiring definition.

Several researchers have studied specifically defined behavioral outcomes that encompass many behaviors associated with self-determination. Two research reviews examined self-determination research with individuals with disabilities and found that a large majority of the studies were shown to focus on choice making; a few examined more complex actions such as setting goals, problem solving, self-regulation, or other behaviors associated with self-determination.[44] Researchers, theorists, and educators agree that making choices is not, in itself, self-determination, although choice making is an important skill that can be taught, even to very young children.

Guided by self-determination theory, the research of Deci and Ryan and others has examined more complex behaviors and shows that students in learning environments that foster autonomy will take more risks, will be more curious and self-motivated, and will think creatively.[45] More recent research with students with disabilities also shows positive effects on academic outcomes when they learn complex actions that involve cognitive strategies (learning to learn), self-monitoring, self-evaluation, and problem solving.[46]

When writing about ways music teachers help and hinder the develop of a learner's independence, Duke interprets a body of research in psychology and in music learning to explain why providing more assistance to students than is actually required inadvertently limits the learners' development over the long term.[47] Music research is consistent with research in psychology and shows benefits for learners who acquire and use skills associated with independence and self-determination. Positive outcomes in motivation, practicing, music achievement, and music performance have been found for music students who learn how to set goals and work toward them incrementally, learn how to solve problems, and learn how to self-evaluate—and they outperform students who lack these skills.[48]

Findings from research studying behaviors associated with self-determination have direct implications for many of life's domains, including those related to music learning and performance. In the next section, you will read how these findings can be applied to facilitate all aspects of development, including musical development.

Applications and Strategies: Experiencing Autonomy, Competence, and Good Feelings

Transition, social interactions, the climate of the classroom, collaboration, and access to the curriculum involve behaviors associated with self-determination. Throughout childhood, throughout school, parents and teachers make many of the decisions that will affect a child's learning. With adulthood come the independence and responsibility to make decisions—about employment, place of residence, social network, recreation and leisure, and music. A successful and happy adult life has a great deal to do with the ability to make responsible choices and decisions (and having some good luck).

Almost all children become more concerned with their transitions to different schools, classes, careers, and adult life as they advance in grade levels. And almost all of them want to be involved in making decisions about their futures. By law, students with disabilities are entitled to participate (as appropriate) in making decisions about their IEPs and transition plans.

What decisions will any of your students make regarding their music participation? Will they have real choices, and will they have the skills and knowledge necessary to choose from a wide variety of options? Will they have the skills to perform in their elementary Orff ensemble, play in a band or orchestra, or sing in a choir if they choose? Will they have the skills that will allow them to set music performance goals for themselves, and further, will they know how to take independent action to improve their skills? Will they have the skills and knowledge to make reasonable choices about the music they will listen to, perform alone, or perform for others?

Decisions about music, music making, and other music activities in life require other kinds of decisions about contexts—places where activities will occur and people who will be involved. With the guidance of music teachers and parents, students can learn to consider realistic options and make good decisions about their music education and music experiences. Students can learn music skills that will increase their competence and confidence and thus give them greater opportunities to enjoy participating and making decisions about music in their lives.

Social relationships, friendships, family relationships, and relationships with teachers all influence a child's development and behavior. These influences motivate (entice, pressure, teach) a child to engage in behaviors and develop attitudes that can have highly positive or negative consequences for the child and may continue throughout the child's life. What would we do without a social network of friends who generously provide us with support, kindness, love, and help? Recall here that Ryan and Deci propose "relatedness" (feeling safe and secure with other people) as one of the psychological needs for self-determination. They also propose two other psychological needs: competence (feeling a sense of achievement) and autonomy (feeling in control). There come times in everyone's life when choices, decisions, preferences, solutions to problems, goals, evaluation, advocacy, and accomplishments need to be (and to feel) personal. In his book of poetry for children (and adults), Shel Silverstein makes this point beautifully in the last few lines of his poem entitled "Helping":

> And some kind of help is the kind of help
> That helping's all about,
> And some kind of help is the kind of help
> We all could do without.[49]

Adults and peers who are unaware of the importance of autonomy and choice may inadvertently diminish important music learning opportunities for children. I recall a particular situation in an inclusive elementary music classroom when a child with a disability was learning to play a mallet instrument. Instruments were being used to accompany the class singing; the teacher and a paraprofessional were at either side of the child as he knelt behind the instrument, mallets in his hands. As the children began to sing and play, the paraprofessional immediately held both of his arms with the intention of helping him keep a steady beat. In frustration, the child said emphatically, "Go away." And with a second "Go away," he firmly pushed the aide with his elbow while still maintaining his grip on the mallets and not missing a beat. He continued to play through the entire song—confidently, independently, and with rhythmic precision. What a happy child.

It's not uncommon to see situations where a student with a disability, who is completely capable of completing a task, is drawn off-task by a well-intended aide or classmate who pats the student's arm, rubs his back, hovers, or helps too much. You've read about the problems of excessive and inappropriate helping. In a study of typical peers seated next to their classmates with disabilities, I observed typical peers unnecessarily assisting, prompting, and interacting.[50] There were individual differences among the typical children—a few were able to refrain from unnecessary helping and remain attentive to the music instruction even when seated close to their classmate with a disability—others were distracted and inattentive in this same situation. Unnecessary helping can be counterproductive to any student's learning and to his or her sense of autonomy and achievement.

There is an abundance of research showing positive benefits for children who are taught in classrooms where they feel safe and secure to make choices, express preferences, make decisions, and otherwise experience a level of control that substantially affects their motivation to participate and learn. Consider the issue of choice again. Many teachers know that students will be more on-task to music instruction and more motivated to participate when they have options and when they think of activities as meaningful, interesting, and within their capabilities. All of these factors interact. For example, asking a fifth-grader to chose a song to sing from a class list won't increase his motivation to sing if he doesn't find the songs interesting, doesn't like to sing, or doesn't think of himself as a good singer. When a middle school band student is asked whether he would rather put new music in folders or just sit and listen to the rehearsal of a piece determined to be too difficult for him, that's not much of a choice when he just wants to play music with his group. If the student is disruptive or does a poor job at the task of his "choice," wherein lies the problem? And what will he feel about his own capabilities?

Because students may be compliant and even enjoy the task that has really been chosen for them by the teacher, a teacher may mistakenly believe that the student has had an opportunity to experience autonomy and a sense of achievement. Not at all. Teachers must consider more deeply what choices are being presented (level of complexity, type of choice, preferences), when they are presented, and why particular choices are important for the student.

Introducing choices to students, teaching them how to self-regulate (set goals and reach them), giving them increased autonomy, honoring their preferences, giving them problems to solve within their capacity and strategies to solve them, and providing opportunities for them to experience individual achievement require teachers to be aware of the short- and long-term consequences of students' actions and also to make students aware of these consequences. Many of us have experienced a situation in which we have gone along with a student's choice or given in to a request, or sometimes a demand, only later to regret our actions. These errors are common among undergraduate students in teacher preparation programs during their first teaching experiences.

There is much to be said about knowing students' needs, characteristics, and capabilities as teachers prepare them for greater independence and much to be said about teachers who hold high expectations for their students and who are consistent in their use of effective strategies to help students reach achievable goals. When teachers give in and give up, so will students.

The notion of self-determination in the field of special education has led to the development of specialized curricula, teaching strategies, and training programs for teachers.[51] Special education departments at several universities are advancing efforts to foster self-determination through specifically designed curricula. Although many of these ideas were developed specifically for children with disabilities, they can be broadly applied to different situations including all students and their music learning.

One specialized curriculum cited frequently in the literature is the Self-Determined Model of Instruction developed by Wehmeyer and his colleagues.[52] The model is presented in great detail and includes information for planning and implementation. What catches my attention is the organization of this curriculum. It focuses on three broad instructional areas, with questions for students to ask and answer:

- Set the goal (What is my goal?)
- Take action (What is my plan?)
- Adjust goal or plan (What have I learned?)

I think you can see how these questions could apply to all students and to music teaching and learning and how they could be helpful in teaching students to become more competent and independent in their music making and decisions about music. For goal setting, a student can ask and answer the following questions: "What music do I want to learn?" "What can I play or sing now?" "What must change for me to learn how to play or sing this music?" "What can I do to make this happen?" The student could develop a plan and evaluate the outcome. An action plan could include a student's answers to such questions as "What can I do to improve my singing?" and "What is keeping me from improving my singing, and can I change or fix that?" and "When should I take action?" Of course students also need to learn how to evaluate their actions by asking frequently, "What have I learned?"

You, as the teacher, would, of course, offer support as necessary to help individual students ask and answer these questions, and the level of your assistance would vary with the age and particular needs of the students. As you consider questions for your students, you'll find some that are appropriate to ask individuals and others that are appropriate for everyone in your class. Asking questions can become a part of the routine of every session (e.g., "What have I learned?"), and students can give their answers to classmates seated close by. Students of all ages and with varying capabilities can experience a degree of autonomy by learning how to ask and respond to these questions. When students learn what questions to ask themselves and what actions to take to accomplish their goals (social or music), they are well on their way to becoming more independent and competent individuals.

You'll recall that the focus of this guideline is on ways to foster self-determination. You, as the teacher, are fostering, nurturing, guiding, in other words, teaching skills, knowledge, and values that will help your students to be happy and successful throughout life. Our responsibility is to help all of our students become independent learners, independent musicians, and nice people. To this end and to this section, I've summarized some of these ideas and listed a few more strategies that may helpful.

- Provide frequent opportunities for students to express their interests and goals for continuing music throughout their school years and into their future lives as adults.

- Teach music skills and knowledge that will enable students to develop competence, experience personal achievement, and have opportunities for real choices regarding music, music making, and other music activities.
- Provide opportunities for students to assess their music abilities, interests, and preferences related to school and outside of school activities.
- Provide students with nurturing mentors, older students or peers, who have similar interests (e.g., singing, playing, listening); discuss with them, and parents, of course, how they can attend school and community music programs and events together.
- Consider students' various interests, skills, and accomplishments, and find more ways for them to share these with others and feel good about what they know and what they can do.
- Look for opportunities in daily routines and music activities where students can be more involved in making decisions and solving problems.
- Following the principle of normalization, provide opportunities for choice making and problem solving that are as similar as possible to opportunities available to same-age typical peers.
- Give students increasingly difficult problems to solve and increasing responsibility and autonomy in music settings.
- Encourage self-initiation when the student's actions will most likely result in positive consequences.
- Anticipate undesirable behaviors that may arise under conditions when students feel a lack of control, when they feel they are "managed" or helped too much by other students or paraprofessionals. Teach peers and paraprofessionals when and how to help.

Although we teachers spend most of our lives in school, the reality is that students leave school; they leave us. The degree to which they will become independent, competent musicians, choose to participate in music activities in their lives, make good decisions, solve problems, and feel good about themselves in the process will in part be influenced by school and by us. The goal for music teachers is clear: to teach children to be as independent, competent, and self-confident as possible and to help them enjoy and take pleasure in life's many experiences.

PRINCIPLE 4. COLLABORATION AND COORDINATED EFFORTS

Collaboration is more than communication; it is a conscious effort on the part of individuals with different areas of expertise to come together for the common purpose of improving the educational experiences of children. The musical lives of children will be improved when the design, implementation, and evaluation of each child's individualized music education program involves collaboration and coordinated efforts among parents or guardians, professionals, other significant individuals in the child's life, and the child, when appropriate.

Theory and Research: The Process of Collaboration

Performances of two or more musicians provide some of the most vivid examples of collaboration and coordinated efforts toward a mutual goal, that of creating beautiful music. Even when musicians differ in their expertise specific to singing or playing different instruments, beautiful music will happen, particularly in small ensembles and duos, if musicians of comparable levels of skill have a common vision of the final musical product, if they share responsibility in decision making, and if they value their colleagues' opinions and expertise. When any of these components is absent, or when any member exhibits excessive frustration or anxiety, rehearsals and performances suffer (as does the listener).

Collaboration is often defined in the literature as an interactive, dynamic process that allows people with diverse capabilities to develop solutions to mutually defined problems. The keywords mentioned most often in research literature on cooperation are *sharing* (shared values, ideas, information, responsibilities), *partnership* (mutual trust and respect, open and honest communications, pursuit of common goals or outcomes), *interdependency,* and *power* (empowerment of each participant based on knowledge and experience rather than titles of individual members).[53] Collaboration can occur between two individuals, among members in small and large groups, and between and among organizations, schools, states, and nations. At its best, collaboration is a process that can begin to resolve complex mutual problems to the benefit of everyone.

You've read about cognitive and social benefits for children when they engage in learning activities that have a common goal, when they have opportunities to share ideas, and when they learn from one another. Through these activities, they also learn what it means to cooperate, how to share, to listen to one another's ideas, and to reach a consensus on goals and actions for the group. Adults who have learned these lessons are welcomed members of collaborative teams.

Collaborations can occur formally or informally and can take on many different forms. Many responsible teachers regularly work with parents. There is a wealth of research on home-school relationships, much which shows academic and social benefits when communication is reciprocal, when parents and school personnel work together to exchange information and implement interventions to help children succeed in school.[54]

Whether interactions are informal or occur through more formal means, music teachers have much to offer to the process. They often have information about students that might otherwise be unavailable. We hear from teachers and know from research that children are more on-task in music classes compared with other types of classes, that music can elicit other desirable behaviors, and that music activities can be structured to teach special education objectives, motivate students, and reinforce behavioral responses. The music therapy profession is grounded in historical, clinical, and empirical evidence substantiating the positive effects of music on behavior.[55]

Because of the numerous benefits of collaboration for teachers and students and its importance in successful inclusion practices, the goal is to increase opportunities for collaboration without adding excessive amounts of time and paperwork to music teachers' busy schedules. In the following sections, you will find many ideas that will help you initiate interactions and build and maintain positive, professional, and productive relationships with parents, administrators, special educators, and other professionals, specifically paraprofessionals and music therapists.

Applications and Strategies: Getting Involved and Building Relationships

Music teachers need to determine the extent of their commitment to the process of collaboration. Adding one more responsibility to an already busy schedule may seem overwhelming, but sometimes the idea of doing something is more overwhelming than actually doing it. Teachers who have made decisions to get more involved seem happy about their decisions, mostly because they see positive outcomes for their students. They also enjoy the experience of sharing their students' achievements with others. Over time, collaborating with parents, teachers, and paraprofessionals; contributing ideas to students' IEP or RTI plans; and even attending some IEP and team meetings will become a natural and important part of what you do as a teacher.

In this section, you will find specific ideas about collaborating with parents, paraprofessionals, and music therapists, but first, read through these broad ideas about how to start and stay involved.

1. *Request to be notified of students receiving special education services who are entering your classroom for the first time, and request that all students' IEPs and intervention plans be made available to you at the beginning of every year.* IDEA requires public agencies (schools) to make IEPs available to each regular education teacher, to inform them of responsibilities for implementing the students' IEPs, and the specific accommodations, modifications, and supports that must be provided. You may, however, need to initiate a plan to make this happen as a matter of routine. You'll want these records to help you ensure the health and safety of students in your classroom and to make appropriate curricular and instructional decisions. Parents can help with access to this information, although your first approach should be through your administrator and special educator. Some information will be protected in the interest of privacy. Ask to be informed about important changes in students' individual programs (special education, RTI plans) and other changes that may affect students' behaviors in class.

2. *Prioritize problems and students' needs, and seek help for some students before others.* Many music teachers see hundreds of students, many with disabilities or at-risk. It is unrealistic to think that you can gather in-depth information about each student at the beginning of the school year, but through day to day observations of students and other information gathered from parents and colleagues during the first month of school, you will eventually know more about all of them.

3. *Attend meetings for as many students as possible, but especially for a student whose needs are a priority.* Be prepared to describe briefly your goals for all of your students and, to the extent possible, this particular student. Because you would have reviewed the student's files, would have talked with parents and other professionals, and most likely would have seen the student in classes before this meeting, you will have some, but not all, of the information you need. Before meeting, refer to the categories discussed in chapter 4 ("Gathering Information"), and prepare your notes and questions. Don't hesitate to ask questions, but as the expert in music education, be sure to describe briefly your goals for all of your students and, to the extent possible, this particular student. This is a good opportunity for administrators, other teachers, and parents to hear about your exciting program and the benefits for all of your students.

4. *Build rapport with parents and special educators early in the school year, and gather as much information as possible.* A quick phone call to parents will begin to build the rapport you want to establish. "Hello. I am your son's music teacher, and I just wanted to let you know that I look forward to having him in class and working with you throughout the year." Parents tend to remember constructive contact with individual teachers. Also,

during those busy teacher days at the beginning of the year, try to find time for short discussions with your special educator and other specialists who work with your students; gather as much information as possible.

5. *Collaborate on assessing students' progress. As part of your regular teaching, take notice of small (but notable) behaviors and behavior changes that will be important for your planning and that you may want to relate to parents and colleagues.* Record the specific behaviors and the context (situations, activities, materials, other students involved). It's useful to specify first the behavior(s), then context and possible interpretations of why these behaviors occurred. Develop a convenient way to record and file this information. Welcome colleagues into your room to suggest observation strategies and to observe and assess students' progress on IEP and RTI goals.

6. *Identify and request the type of support you want and need.* Prioritize your requests for instructional support (large and small needs, which may include materials, assistive devices, information, instructional strategies, training, classroom observations, paraprofessional assistance). Also, ask for moral support when you need it. You may want to hear "You're doing just fine" and "Keep up the great work." Find colleagues who will provide both kinds of support, instructional and moral.

7. *Set a positive tone for conversations.* Conversations, informally and in meetings, can take on a "tone" depending on the attitudes of individuals. Begin your conversations with a brief description of the positives you have seen and real possibilities for the student's music learning and participation. Most likely, many of your colleagues and students' parents will not have seen your music class or know about different students' levels of participation and behaviors in your class. From there, go to your questions, and begin to get the information you need. Some of your questions may go unanswered simply because of a lack of time. Team meetings will be useful, but it is only one part of the collaboration process, which must continue informally throughout the year.

8. *Persevere in building relationship with parents and colleagues.* Building rapport takes time. Relationships with parents and colleagues are nurtured when there is a sustained interest in sharing information and in learning from one another and when everyone has a genuine concern for students' well-being and success in school. For music teachers who will see the same student (parents, colleagues) across several years, the effort is well worth it.

You have just read several points about collaborating with a number of individuals—parents, special educators, administrators, and other professionals from schoolwide teams. More ideas for collaborations are presented in the next several sections, with a focus on parents (of course), paraprofessionals who may be in your classroom frequently, and music therapists who may provide services for the same students you teach.

Parents

Parents are their children's first teachers. The term "parent" is used throughout IDEA to mean any natural, adoptive, or foster parent; guardian; or other adult legally responsible for the child. Adults who are parents of children with disabilities and children who are struggling academically and/or socially need support and cooperation from schools and teachers. As a music teacher, one of your most important responsibilities will be to communicate frequently with parents.

You may detect different degrees of comfort from parents regarding involvement in their children's school activities. Not all parents want to be involved or to be involved in the same way, but the benefits of positive parent-teacher collaborations for students are well worth your efforts.

Culture and language may account for the extent of parents' willingness to engage in parent-teacher collaborations; some may prefer interpersonal, informal communications, and others may prefer written notes. In some cases, you may need to rely on an interpreter or make written information available in the parents' language. It will also be helpful for you to learn a few words and forms of greeting in the parents' language. Although you should not assume values based on the parents' cultural roots, if they live in a community with a common non-English language and for the most part share the cultural values of the community, your rapport with the parents and the community will be be enhanced if your music program includes music of the culture.

It will help your interactions if you try to put yourself in their shoes. What would you want from schools and teachers if this child was your child? Parents want their children to be successful, and they rely on schools, for the most part, to prepare their children to have successfully lives. When parents are asked about their dreams for their children, whether their children have disabilities or not, almost all will talk about their children having happy lives—enjoying good health, rewarding employment, a residence with some material comforts, and a social life that includes pleasurable activities and friends. Many of the skills that will lead to these outcomes are learned in school, and it is no surprise, then, that parents whose children are at-risk for not having a happy, rewarding life desire frequent contact with schools to make inquiries, suggestions, requests, and even demands. This is completely understandable, although obviously there can be points of contention.

Parents want their children to develop to their fullest potential, and many may have strong ideas about what their children should learn in school. Music teachers should not be surprised that many parents of children with disabilities view social relationships and friendships as important goals for their children, often more important than music goals. Social development themes are prominent in the literature, and even with the growing demand for access to the general education curriculum, social goals remain a priority for many parents and teachers.

Although music classes and performing ensembles, when structured for positive interactions, provide opportunities for students' social development, students' musical development should not be ignored. Music teachers will do well to inform parents of their children's music goals and achievements, along with opportunities for continued study and enjoyable music recreation activities throughout life. And since good news may not come frequently to some parents of students with disabilities or to parents of students who are struggling in school, make a point to let them hear about their children's progress and achievements. This news can reinforce the idea that music education is a valuable subject in their children's education and in the school curriculum. Music teachers, particularly at the secondary level, rely heavily on support from parents for their programs. Several characteristics of instrumental programs in specific (instrument rental, method books, repairs, and supplies) and secondary programs in general (on- and off-campus performances) contribute to more frequent contact with parents than is typically experienced by elementary teachers. If elementary teachers participate infrequently or not at all in the development of the IEP or other intervention plans and if they have few contacts with parents (except when there are problems), parents may have little information about their children's participation and musical development.

When parents and teachers focus on the musical development of children when they first enter school, greater numbers will learn to sing, play instruments, choose music ensembles as a part of their secondary programs, and ultimately enjoy rich musical lives in their schools. Given the many issues and concerns that accompany parenting a young child with a disability, parents may not be looking ahead to ways their child can participate more fully in music activities at the elementary level and perhaps even learn to play an instrument and continue to participate in middle school and high school ensembles. The elementary teacher, in collaboration with the middle school teacher, can inform parents of realistic music possibilities for their child—opportunities for the child's music participation not only in school but also for recreation and leisure outside of school and throughout life.

Paraprofessionals

Paraprofessionals, also called instructional aides in some school districts, can provide invaluable support to teachers. However, don't assume that all paraprofessionals have received preparation for your classroom, that their help is always necessary, or that their actions will always function positively for the student. There were few paraprofessionals in classrooms before the 1950s. Paraprofessionals were part of an answer to the teacher shortage that occurred as a result of World War II, and increasing numbers were added to classrooms as a result of several programs during the 1960s (e.g., the Elementary and Secondary Education Act, Head Start). With the passage of P.L. 94-142 and the dramatic increase of students with disabilities in public schools came a corresponding dramatic increase in the employment of paraprofessionals. Although historically, there has been no specific training required of paraprofessionals beyond a high school diploma, with the No Child Left Behind Act of 2001 (NCLB), paraprofessionals working in schools are now required to have at least two years of college, although there are no requirements for specific coursework or tests.[56] Some states have additional requirements beyond those mandated by NCLB, and given increasing pressure from teachers, parents, and advocates, it is possible that we will see more stringent requirements in the future.

In any discussion of paraprofessionals, the first question to ask is whether a paraprofessional is necessary at all. When support from a paraprofessional is needed, often in cases of students with severe disabilities, their use should be considered temporary and evaluated on a regular basis. Too often, the paraprofessional remains with the child throughout the day, even when the child has progressed and needs less or perhaps different types of support.[57]

Paraprofessionals can provide effective support, but if their roles are not defined, they can be detrimental to a student's learning. A paraprofessional can impede the student's overall development by assuming the role of music teacher, determining when and how the student will participate, thus limiting the child's opportunities for choice, autonomy, and interactions with the music teacher and classmates. I've observed paraprofessionals happily participating in classroom music activities to the point where they ignore their responsibilities to the student.

Music teachers can encourage paraprofessionals to work more creatively and productively when everyone understands his or her roles and responsibilities. Music teachers can have a good start at understanding and defining the role of paraprofessionals in music classes by collaborating with the special educator who supervises the paraprofessional. Although collaboration with special educators, parents, and others may be required at times, it is ultimately the music teacher who makes curricular and instructional decisions for all students in their classrooms.

When you have a clear understanding of roles and responsibilities, you are prepared to talk, collaborate, and develop effective, efficient, and meaningful ways for paraprofessionals to support your students with disabilities. Some additional points may be helpful, as follows.

1. *Learn about existing policies and guidelines.* Ask your administrator about policies and guidelines regarding paraprofessionals, and talk with the special educator about ways they have been implemented in special education and regular classrooms. Most likely, you will revise existing guidelines to meet your needs and those of your student. Check out some of your ideas with the special educator and other classroom teachers who may see the same student and paraprofessional.

2. *Orient the paraprofessional to your program and classroom and the student's goals at a meeting early in the school year.* These meetings should be pleasurable and productive and should happen with paraprofessionals you have worked with before and those who are new to you. Your most important goals for the meeting are to build positive rapport, to share your enthusiastic concern for the musical development of all of the students in your classroom, including your students with disabilities, and to define roles and responsibilities. A written list of general expectations for classroom routines and for specific types of activities (movement, recorder, sectionals, small-group activities) will be useful. Below is a list of music and social goals that are applicable to many students with disabilities, students who may have behavioral intervention plans, and students who may be struggling academically in school. Personalize it for your own situation and student. You will see that the goals are consistent with other governing principles presented in this chapter. Depending on the individual student, examples of goals might include the following:

- Enters and exits the classroom in much the same manner as other classmates (on time, picks up materials, finds place, etc.).
- Engages in lesson or rehearsal routines and performances in the same manner as classmates.
- Travels to music events in the same manner as classmates.
- Partially participates, with minimal adaptations, in activities that cannot be performed as they are by classmates.

- Performs music in a variety of settings, home, school, and community.
- Receives feedback from the music teacher (when appropriate for music or social behavior) and also feedback from the paraprofessional that is consistent with that given by the teacher.
- Makes choices and decisions similar to those made by classmates.
- Communicates about music and socializes with classmates when appropriate (e.g., small-group activities).
- Uses the same or similar types of materials, music books, and instruments as classmates.
- Actively participates in different types of activities that are associated with leadership and control (e.g., roles centering on daily routines such as distribution of materials, group leader, errands to the office).
- Receives assistance only as necessary, and assistance is faded as soon as possible.
- Receives assistance from classmates, when appropriate, and not only from adults.
- Shows individual achievement and is a part of music ensembles with classmates.

3. *Ask the paraprofessional to give you important information before class about any major changes in the student's medications, behavior, or other incidents that you should know about.*

4. *Ask for information about assistive devices or alternative communication systems used by the student, if the student cannot provide this information.*

5. *Give feedback frequently.* By discussing goals early in the school year, you can refer to them easily when giving feedback to the paraprofessional. For example, "Thanks for making sure that Jack is always here on time with the rest of the class." Or "I see that Jack played most of that passage on his own before you helped him. Great. Next time, let's see if he can go even longer before you help him, and when you do, don't forget to fade your help from time to time when he looks like he has it." Feedback should be specific and not always positive. Negative feedback can be given in a way that is respectful.

6. *Resolve major problems in consultation with others.* If problems arise, talk with someone who you believe will give you candid advice about working with your paraprofessional. Your administrator will need to know about any major or persistent problems.

7. *Develop effective ways to communicate during class.* Together, you can find ways to convey ideas during a lesson or rehearsal. In one case, a teacher simply held up two crossed fingers as a signal to ask the

paraprofessional to provide more support for the student, to stop assisting the student, and even to move away from the student to allow for more independence.

8. *Ask for feedback and help when needed.* Working together to solve a problem can be very reinforcing; however, think carefully about your requests. If you reject most of the paraprofessional's ideas and feedback you have requested, you will quickly diminish the positive rapport you are trying to build.

Music Therapists

If a student is identified as having a disability and is eligible for special education services, the student may also receive related services and supplementary aids and services. Related services are defined as those that can help children benefit from their special education by providing extra support.[58] For example, students may benefit from music education or special education if they receive assistive technology devices and services that will allow them to communicate or move more easily. Counseling services may be required to lower a student's level of anxiety so he or she may focus on school instruction and assignments. There are any number of services that are identified as related services and that can be funded through special education funds. The types of related services available for students is dependent on school district and school policies. Some school districts include music therapy as a related service.

If a school district and respective schools decide to make music therapy available as a related service, several actions need to be taken for any given student to receive those services. First, a qualified professional music therapist will need to conduct an assessment to determine if the student is eligible for music therapy services—*eligible* meaning that music therapy services will help the student with a disability benefit from special education.[59] Second, on the basis of the assessments and recommendations of the music therapist, the IEP team determines whether music therapy will be included as a service in the student's IEP.

The music therapist, who most likely is a member of the IEP teams, provides specific goals for each student served, most often for students who have significant disabilities. Since music therapy goals are similar to those in special education (language, mobility, academic, social, and so on), students should also be in inclusive music classrooms where they can accomplish music goals. Music therapists can provide valuable learning experiences for children with disabilities, but music therapy is not a substitute for music education.

As a result of a music therapy assessment, some of your students may receive music therapy services, and others may not. Although you may see students who could benefit from music therapy, the caseload for the music therapist and the eligibility requirement will limit the numbers of students who receive direct music therapy services. Some music therapists only provide direct service to students and have a large caseload; others provide direct services and consultation to teachers and other professionals as part of their responsibilities.

Whether music therapy services are defined as related services or school districts provide services through local or district funding, all music therapists should be qualified according to standards established by the American Music Therapy Association (AMTA). Qualified music therapists are those who have completed degree programs and clinical training approved by AMTA and who have received board certification (MT-BC) or the designation of Registered, Certified, or Advanced Certified Music Therapist (RMT, CMT, or ACMT). Members of AMTA adhere to a strict code of ethics and standards of practice that govern the clinical practice of music therapy.

Although standards require music therapy students to have clinical experiences with at least three different populations, they typically develop an area of specialization during their culminating clinical internship, which is typically six months in a single setting. If you are seeking a music therapist for your school, in addition to ensuring that the therapist has the appropriate credentials, choose someone whose specific interests, experiences, knowledge, and skills are related to school-age children. A careful screening of candidates will be important to the success of a music therapy program in your school district.

As you may suspect, there is a wealth of information about the music therapy profession—its history, the preparation of music therapists, employment, applications with different populations, and research. I encourage you to learn more about AMTA and the effectiveness of music therapy practices through AMTA's highly informative website, from resources in this book, and especially from music therapists in your community and state.[60]

Many of the general points related to collaboration discussed earlier in this section apply to your interactions with music therapists. Below are some additional points that will facilitate your interactions with a professional with whom you have much in common.

1. *Make inclusive music education a goal for all students with disabilities, to the extent possible.* With rare exceptions, every student with a disability should have inclusive music education experiences, and music teachers

and music therapists can work together to make those experiences successful. Music therapy services will be discontinued when ongoing assessments show that they are no longer needed by the student; music education, it's hoped, will continue throughout the student's school years. Some school districts meet fine arts state requirements for students with disabilities by structuring "adaptive" (separate) music classes. If you teach one of these separate music classes, it is likely that some of your students also have sessions with music therapists. In other cases, the music therapist may be responsible for the separate class, and you may not see these students at all. A reasonable goal for music therapists and music teachers working together is the elimination of special music classes in favor of inclusive music classes with resources and support that would allow students, even those with severe disabilities, to participate successfully.

2. *Share information about goals, strategies, and adaptations.* Music therapists are well informed about students' specific strengths and characteristics, their educational programs, and strategies for reaching IEP goals. And the music therapist would have completed a music therapy assessment of the student and may have interesting information about the student's music responses. Also, you have important information about the student in a large-group setting with typical peers, whether IEP goals are transferring to your class, and additional information about the student's social interactions and music behaviors. Collaborate on ways to incorporate IEP goals into music activities and still keep a focus on important and appropriate music goals. Consider in your discussions short- and long-term objectives for school music experiences and music experiences outside of school.

3. *Develop transfer activities for music education and music therapy goals.* History and research show that students who remain only in small special education classrooms for most of the day have difficulty transferring skills and knowledge to different contexts. Skills learned in special education, music therapy, and music education should be practiced in a variety of contexts. Develop activities specific to music and IEP goals that could occur frequently in a variety of school settings, in addition to home and community settings.

4. *Collect observational data, and assess student progress.* Assessment of students' progress is an important part of what you do, and collaborations with the music therapist can be helpful in planning observation strategies, observing the student, and collecting data. All music therapists take research classes and should be prepared to develop appropriate observation tools, whether the tools are simple checklists or systematic observation procedures. From the data, you will be able to assess the effectiveness of strategies and adaptations and make informed decisions about music

goals and strategies. Share the data informally and at meetings with parents and teachers throughout the year.

5. *Enjoy and share your successes and those of your student with each other.* Collaboration regarding problems and solutions is essential for the educational growth of the students, but the powerful effects of success, humor, and camaraderie on the emotional well-being of teachers and therapists should not be underestimated.

Many of us have have witnessed school spirit portrayed by the banners, colors, mascots, and a school song that we hear being rehearsed in a room at the far end of the building. This collective, communal spirit is also seen, although not nearly as vividly, among competent, responsible teachers and administrators who, on a daily basis, interact with each other, trying to provide their students with the best education possible.

Among the most uplifting and powerful actions that any group of adults can undertake are those that will influence a child's future, a future that is dependent most often on success in school. An important premise of IDEA is the stipulation of an IEP team, which requires people to come together to prepare an appropriate educational program. Underlying this requirement is the powerful assumption that teachers, parents, administrators, and other professionals will *want* to work cooperatively for the benefit of children, and that they will be successful in their efforts to improve children's lives.

Individuals who drew up the regulations for IDEA had a great deal of confidence in the collective expertise and goodwill of people. The lawmakers were correct in their belief in that responsible teachers, parents, and schools have always collaborated throughout the school year, and without a federal mandate to do so. For these caring adults, collaboration is a personal core value and process that will benefit their students and define the character of their schools.

CHAPTER 4

Now What?

OVERVIEW

Much of what we understand about learning and teaching applies to children across spectra of abilities. And the principal features of learning experiences that effectively prepare children for meaningful musical lives beyond school are not differentiated among age and ability levels but are universal in the sense that they are applicable in ways that engage diverse groups of children in common experiences. All children can develop musically when a meaningful music program is designed to be accessible, equitable, and flexible; instructional practices are effective; individual adaptations are used only as needed; and students' progress is assessed frequently—in other words, when a universal approach is used in music teaching (see box 4.1).

The perspective of a universal approach moves away from the view of students in separate groups and toward a view of students on a continuum of all learners. Universal strategies are designed based not on group membership (disability, learning needs, or other characteristics such as gender, race, ethnicity, culture, or language spoken) but on students' individual strengths and needs and the requirements of activities and tasks. In a positive learning environment with a universal approach, students learn to value diversity among their classmates and celebrate one another's successes.

An important characteristic of a universal approach is flexibility. Flexible strategies allow all students to be successful and accomplish meaningful music goals. Highly effective teachers use a variety of ways to present information, engage and motivate students, and structure ways for students to participate in the same activities but in different ways. Of course, some students will need individual adaptations to enable them to participate successfully—to move, to communicate, to learn.

Box 4.1

PRINCIPLES OF A UNIVERSAL APPROACH FOR INCLUSIVE MUSIC CLASSROOMS

- Learning differences are viewed on a continuum, and expectations are high for all students.
- The regular music program is designed to be accessible, equitable, and flexible.
- A universal approach is a proactive process, not an afterthought, and requires:
  - Knowledge of students' needs and characteristics.
  - Knowledge of activity and task requirements.
  - Universal strategies first (flexible and multiple strategies) to meet students' diverse needs and, only as necessary, individual adaptations.
  - Strategies built into regular instruction.
- Universal strategies are designed to allow all students to be successful and progress in the same music curriculum and with the same performance standards, to the extent appropriate.
  - Students participate in the same classroom activities, tasks, and routines to the extent appropriate.
  - Flexible and multiple strategies meet students' diverse learning needs and may reduce or eliminate the need for individual adaptations.
  - The quality of the music learning experience is not compromised for any student.

Individual adaptations (e.g., braille, modified tasks, assistive devices, personal support) are adjustments to any aspect of the curriculum, instruction, or teaching environment that are necessary for students to participate in the music program to the fullest extent appropriate. Individual adaptations are designed for and apply to one student only. Sam sings more accurately when words and notes are in large print, Heidi feels calmer and will talk about the music when her partner is soft-spoken, and the orchestra will benefit from Estelle's beautiful playing when she has less complex cello parts.

Students with disabilities and who are struggling in school can inspire teachers to employ well-established teaching principles in creative, flexible ways that can benefit other students or, at the least, not compromise program goals. Effective teachers often develop group activities while keeping particular students in mind. Here are several examples where teachers might have used only individual adaptations and separated students from their classmates but instead implemented universal strategies:

- A teacher who gives a student with asthma several breaks during marching drill practice is implementing an individual adaptation. When the teacher, knowing about the individual student's needs, gives everyone several shorter breaks rather than one longer break and this action does not compromise the quality of the practice, the teacher is using a single universal strategy. Everyone has more frequent breaks at the same time.
- If one student who uses a wheelchair plays a percussion instrument as other classmates dance in a particular movement activity, the teacher has implemented an individual adaptation for that student. In contrast, the teacher who implements multiple strategies with this particular dance has all students learn instrumental accompaniments for the dance and also gives students opportunities to create upper-body movements for particular sections. There are now three different actions in one activity (dance, upper-body movements, and accompaniments), different ways for students to respond musically and show what they have learned. At different times in this activity, typically developing students can participate fully by doing any of the three actions, and the student using the wheelchair partially participates by doing two of the three: accompanying and upper-body movements. With multiple strategies, the student with a disability has more opportunities to participate successfully with classmates.
- Early in the school year, a high school teacher frequently talks to her students about the schedule and expectations regarding routines and daily rehearsals. She thought of giving a printed sheet with this information to one of her students who has difficulty remembering spoken information. Then she thought of several other students who seemed to be forgetful. She tells the class about expectations, distributes printed copies of important information for their binders, and calls attention to a special area in the classroom where expectations, messages, and other information pertinent to rehearsals and concerts are posted. On occasion, students are asked to look at their sheets or the posted information, and she also gives verbal reminders. Checking printed information becomes a habit for students, with benefits for everyone.

In the examples above, there are two different questions a teacher could ask: "When my students are doing this activity, what changes can I make for Miguel so that he can participate more fully?" and "When my students are doing this activity, without compromising my goals, what changes can I make for all my students so that Miguel can participate more fully and in ways similar to his classmates?" These are two different ways of thinking. Thinking about individual adaptations is often the default, but think universal first.

Why think about universal strategies first? There are several reasons. First, a universal approach involves each and every student in regular classroom activities; strengths and weaknesses of students are considered in the development of multiple strategies so that every student will accomplish important music goals. Also, a universal approach guards against overuse and overspecialization of individual adaptations. Students who are marginalized, who are struggling academically and/or socially, or who have disabilities are often subject to negative stereotyping and isolation. The default action of some teachers is to develop individual adaptations or to exclude students from the activity. Even though some individual adaptations maybe necessary, the overuse and overspecialization of adaptations can result in negative outcomes.

The unnecessary separation of students from activities and their classmates will contribute to negative stereotyping and lower expectations, thus limiting opportunities for music achievement, positive peer interactions, and the development of self-determination. When all students participate successfully in the same activity, experience personal success, and contribute to the success of their classmates, a culture of inclusion is fostered. Students feel competent, experience a sense of belonging, and feel good about themselves and their classmates.

This chapter focuses on ways you can approach curricular and instructional decisions that will allow all students to participate happily and successfully in your regular music program. Throughout, you will find many examples of universal strategies and individual adaptations; more examples are found in the online resources.[1] I organize this material around a model that will take you through the steps necessary to design and implement a program that is accessible, equitable, and flexible. Before discussing this model, I describe briefly the development of a universal approach in education and also some interesting changes that have led us to employing more effective curricular and instructional practices. I recommend that you also read the summaries of changes to educational practices that I've outline in appendix D.

UNIVERSAL APPROACH: ARCHITECTURE TO EDUCATION

A universal approach in education is grounded in principles of universal design in architecture, in the design of buildings, public spaces, and products. The fundamental idea of universal design is applied in products and environments, including teaching environments, and is studied at several centers in the United States.[2] In IDEA, universal design relates to requirements for state- and district-wide tests for children with disabilities. IDEA uses a lengthy definition. I like the shorter, more useful one by Ron Mace, a highly respected architect who coined the term *universal design*. He used the term to describe the concept of designing all products and built environments to be aesthetic and usable to the greatest extent possible by everyone, regardless of age, ability, or status in life.[3]

Using the description put forward by Mace for universal design, a universal approach in music education can be described as designing an equitable, flexible music curriculum that is accessible for all students to the greatest extent possible. Universal design incorporates many of the ideas and advances from laws and policies that specifically apply to individuals with disabilities, although it has come to benefit all people, not just those with disabilities.

Universal design had its beginnings with the barrier-free movement of the 1950s, which was driven by World War II veterans with disabilities, other individuals with disabilities in communities, and their advocates. Although the focus of this movement is associated with access to buildings, it is important to think beyond buildings to services and participation in activities in those buildings. Through rehabilitative engineering, devices were developed that would assist WWII veterans to see, hear, manipulate objects, navigate environments, read, and communicate. Assistive technology (AT) devices and equipment were leading to greater opportunities for individuals with disabilities in employment, housing, education, and overall quality of life.

The civil rights movement of the 1960s and the disability rights movement, which began in the 1970s, drove changes in public policies and laws related not only to architecture but to all activities of daily living. Section 504 of the Rehabilitation Act of 1973 is a civil rights act that protects individuals with disabilities from discrimination in public sectors that receive federal funds (e.g., schools), and more recently, the Americans with Disabilities Act of 1990 and 2008 (ADA) ensures access for children and adults to all programs and services that are public *and* private, including music programs and services.[4]

The most obvious architectural changes brought about by early laws were retrofittings to buildings that were financially expensive and aesthetically ugly in the eyes of architects and others. Imagine a wooden ramp next to the stairs leading to a beautiful historic building. A ramp built next to stairs is not an example of universal design. Other early changes were curb cuts to allow individuals using wheelchairs to cross streets more easily. Now a requirement for the design of new sidewalks in public places, curb cuts benefit many people: individuals using wheelchairs, bicyclists, adults pushing strollers, and others. In one beautiful art museum, a graceful, seamless ramp transports individuals up or down several floors as they view paintings and sculptures. This spiral architecture of the Guggenheim Museum in New York City was designed by Frank Lloyd Wright in 1959, long before the term *universal design* was coined. Nonetheless, the outcome is clear; the design is effective, and everyone has easy access to the art.

New laws and financial incentives to address issues of access attracted the attention of professionals in other fields, not only architects. Common examples of designs that were originally intended for people with disabilities proved beneficial to everyone: curb cuts, smooth ground surfaces at entryways, ramp access to buildings and swimming pools, lever-type handles for doors and sink faucets, and light switches with large flat panels. The idea that new designs could be usable by everyone became marketable and popular. It's easier to enter hotel rooms with luggage when entryways are wider, to use kitchen tools with thicker grips, and to know when to walk (and how much time you have remaining) when icons and audio signals are at crosswalks. Icons and audio prompts are now used on any number of household items (e.g., ovens and washing machines) and electronics (e.g., computers, phones, televisions).

As battles in the disabilities movement were being won through new laws and policies, special educators and other professionals developed strategies, structures, and devices to provide more services and programs for students with disabilities. With architectural changes and technology, students began to experience greater access to and more independence in the physical environments of their schools. With the passage of IDEA, requiring access to the general curriculum, materials, and testing, universal design became an increasingly prominent approach in education.

You can see how ideas of equity, access, barrier-free design, and technological advancements, combined with new policies and laws, have led to the idea of universal design in education. Meeting individual needs of children in a single classroom is certainly not new. What is new, however, is the focus of this approach relative to meeting the learning needs of diverse populations. A universal approach moves in a direction that, to the extent possible, increases opportunities for students with disabilities and those who are struggling academically and/or socially to participate successfully in the same types of activities as those experienced and enjoyed by their classmates.

SIGNIFICANT CHANGES IN CURRICULAR AND INSTRUCTIONAL PRACTICES

Many significant changes in practices came about because of laws, but significant changes also resulted from the efforts of smart, strong-willed people who assessed thinking and practices and found them sorely lacking.[5] Regardless of new laws, research, and advocacy that have resulted in dramatic changes for the lives of individuals with disabilities, outdated practices are still used in some schools and music classrooms, practices that reflect the thinking of the 1960s and 1970s. Having been a part of that early history, I believe that we all did the best we knew, at the time, but dated ways of thinking and ineffective practices must be replaced with thinking that includes evidence-based practices.

Until the mid-1970s, the concept of mental age and the developmental model dominated decisions in special education, meaning that the curriculum was sequential and based on what children of a particular age and/or grade level should know and do before advancing to any of the goals designated for the next age or grade level. The intent was to help individuals with disabilities "catch up" to their typically developing peers.

Programs for individuals with intellectual disabilities included a multitude of prerequisite academic skills from curricula for typically developing preschool children. For example, identifying colors, shapes, and alphabet letters was considered necessary before introducing words to read. Hours were spent teaching individuals with disabilities to point to everything—point to the letter A, point to the dog, and so on. Music activities consisted primarily of preschool songs designed to teach the alphabet, colors, numbers, names of fruits and vegetables, eating utensils, and other objects.

In the minds of many who opposed this approach, prerequisites were barriers to improving quality of life, and parents were among the first to oppose this ineffective developmental model for their children. To make this point, at a conference I attended for people with significant disabilities, attendees wore buttons that read, "Pre- Means Never."

You see the problem. If time is spent on prerequisites, is it possible for children to learn the functional skills necessary to live as independently as possible in their communities, engage in recreational activities, and get jobs? History shows that many children never caught up and never learned important skills for adult life. Rarely, if ever, can children move through the number of prerequisites and learning sequences at a rate that would enable them to participate in the activities enjoyed by their same-age peers.

On the basis of decades of observing adults with disabilities, the developmental model was deemed ineffective and, for the most part, eliminated from special education practices. We no longer talk about the mental age of children and adults with disabilities or plan educational programs around this outdated idea.

Pressed to optimize instructional time, teachers began to prioritize meaningful learning outcomes and remove unnecessary prerequisite skills. Advances for individuals with significant disabilities were applied in educational practices for all children with disabilities and for those who struggled academically and/or socially in school, prioritizing and teaching skills and knowledge for adult life.

Curricular and instructional practices of the 1980s were transformed; they became chronologically age-appropriate, community-referenced, and focused on functional outcomes. For the first time, individuals with disabilities learned how to live and work in their communities, as independently as possible. The use of chronological age as a criterion for including children with disabilities in a wide array of settings required higher expectations for students.

The principle of partial participation, an important new concept introduced in the 1980s, allowed for even greater numbers of students to participate in regular classrooms.[6] This principle has applications for any child who is unable to learn or do the myriad age-appropriate skills that are required of their typical same-age peers for tasks and activities. Earlier practices had followed the thinking of "all or nothing," that if a person could not do *all* of the activity, then that person could not do *any* of the activity. If a student could not hold a guitar or make changes quickly among several chords while accompanying class singing, the student was excluded from guitar activities. With partial participation, the student could play a guitar tuned to a single chord as some classmates play all of the chords in a three-chord piece, and as appropriate and meaningful for students, some switch between playing one, two, or three chords (consistent with a universal approach). The concept of partial participation led to highly effective practices in inclusive classrooms and is discussed again in the section on curricular modifications.

The past several decades have seen many changes in educational practices. Self-advocates, families, and professionals are selflessly dedicated to maintaining these advancements and meeting new challenges. For now, we have laws that support what many know to be true, that individuals' quality of life is greatly affected by their school experiences. Students need access to a meaningful general education that includes academic goals (for some children, also functional goals) and extracurricular and nonacademic activities. I would argue that music should be among the academic goals—music goals that are meaningful, appropriate for students' needs, and accomplished by implementing effective instructional strategies.

A MODEL FOR EFFECTIVE INCLUSIVE MUSIC PROGRAMS

As you might imagine, there are many things for teachers to think about and do to develop and implement accessible, effective music programs. I've organized what follows around four broad ideas: (1) creating a quality music program and a culture of inclusion; (2) gathering information; (3) planning and implementing strategies; and (4) thinking ahead (see box 4.2). (See examples using this model on the companion website.)

Creating a Quality Music Program and a Culture of Inclusion

You have read about the importance of developing a meaningful music curriculum based on a principle of transition and the importance of using evidence-based instruction to meet the needs of all students.[7] A meaningful, accessible program, however, considers students' overall social and emotional development. Since ideas in this section have been discussed at length in previous chapters, only brief summary statements are presented here for review.

Design a meaningful music program based on a principle of transition, one that is accessible, equitable, and flexible. The long-term goal for all students is to experience meaningful music participation throughout life, alone and with others in their schools, homes, and communities.

Provide culturally normative music experiences with frequent opportunities for positive peer interactions and experiences to foster self-determination. Positive outcomes in students' musical and overall development occur when students participate in experiences that are typically available for most students of the same age, experiences that are valued by most students of the same age, experiences that provide frequent opportunities for positive peer interactions, and experiences in environments where they feel safe and secure, experience autonomy, demonstrate competence, and make decisions about music, music making, and other music activities in their lives.

Establish positive learning environments. Positive, inclusive learning environments exist when teachers create motivating learning experiences, teach tolerance and generosity, teach cooperation and a sense of

Box 4.2

A MODEL FOR EFFECTIVE INCLUSIVE MUSIC PROGRAMS

1. CREATING A QUALITY MUSIC PROGRAM AND A CULTURE OF INCLUSION

- Design a meaningful music program based on a principle of transition, one that is accessible, equitable, and flexible.
- Provide culturally normative music experiences with frequent opportunities for positive peer interactions and experiences to foster self-determination.
- Establish positive learning environments.
- Build positive relationships and collaborate frequently with parents or guardians, knowledgeable professionals, and students.

2. GATHERING INFORMATION

- Learn about students through observations and interactions with them, through collaborations with knowledgeable individuals, and by reviewing individual plans (IEPs, 504 plans, others).
- Establish curricular priorities and performance standards consistent with meaningful long-term goals.
- Conduct broad and in-depth assessments of environments and activities.

3. PLANNING AND IMPLEMENTING STRATEGIES

- Meet students' diverse needs using a universal approach that considers:
  - Frequency of opportunities to practice and significance of activities.
  - Universal strategies first, then individual adaptations as necessary.
  - Effective strategies and adaptations for elements of the learning environment.

4. THINKING AHEAD

- Use authentic assessments to determine students' progress and the effectiveness of strategies and adaptations, and make changes as necessary.
- Share and discuss outcomes with parents or guardians, schoolwide teams, and students as appropriate.
- Continue collaboration, and develop, implement, and assess new strategies and adaptations as needed.
- Focus on the degree to which students develop musically and experience meaningful musical lives in and beyond school.

community, and teach students to celebrate their own successes and those of their classmates.

Build positive relationships and collaborate frequently with parents or guardians, knowledgeable professionals, and students. Frequent collaborations and coordinated efforts are essential to students' musical, social, and emotional development. Through formal meetings and informal interactions, music teachers gather information about their students, seek assistance to solve problems, and talk about students' goals and achievements.

Gathering Information

What's important for students to learn, and what's necessary for students to be successful? The purpose of gathering information is not only to determine important curricular priorities that are consistent with long-term goals but also to determine when universal strategies and individual adaptations will be needed and how they should be implemented.

Student Information

You've read at length about the important governing principle of collaboration. Gathering information is an ongoing process and will require conversations with parents and other professionals in formal meetings or informal interactions. You will also need additional information from students' plans (IEP, RTI, 504, or other plans developed by teams and behavior specialists) and from observing and talking with students. Schedule specific times to talk to parents, teachers, and students as early as possible in the school year.

Use the list in box 4.3 to organize your thinking and to develop student profiles. This can function as a checklist for information that you already have and information you need to get. Take it with you when you meet with schoolwide teams and parents. As you look through the list, you can see that the process of gathering information requires time but not necessarily large chunks of time, and it doesn't need to be done all at once. Make medical and health concerns a priority, and get this information as soon as possible. (Examples of student profiles can be found at the companion website.)

As with most music teachers, it is likely that you will teach the same students for several years, so it's particularly helpful to organize this information. Develop a way to document and retrieve information easily. Get

Box 4.3

GATHERING INFORMATION FROM OTHERS: STUDENT PROFILE

Talk with parents, teachers, other professionals, and the student, as appropriate, and read the student's individual plans to gather information for the following:

- *Medical/health (physical needs):* overall health, precautions, and interventions; medications and expected behavioral outcomes; other.
- *Strengths and past accomplishments (what the student can do and has accomplished):* music, other academic/arts subjects, physical activities/sports, social interactions, other strengths.
- *Characteristics and needs (which may require adjustments to the learning environment, activities, and/or classroom management routines when students work alone and/or with others):* cognitive, sensory, physical, behavioral, emotional, social, other.
- *Ongoing preferences and interests (likes and dislikes):* music and other academic subjects, school and out-of school activities, people (including students and adults), things (materials, instruments, equipment), other.
- *Special education services, related services, other services (when and how often):* music therapy, speech, tutoring, physical therapy, occupational therapy, social skills classes, paraprofessional support, other.
- *Goals (what's important to learn, short- and long-term goals):* music, academic, social, other (short- and long-term goals for success in school and in postschool activities).
- *Strategies and individual adaptations (what works best for presenting information and content to the student, for the student to show what he or she knows and can do, to motivate the student, for classroom management, other):* modes of communication; instructional methods; assessment of progress; physical environment; materials, instruments, equipment; technology (assistive technology and devices); support from peers and others.

as much information as possible, particularly when students are new to your class. A student's interest in astronomy may initially seem to be of little importance for music learning, but a teacher may use this information to create opportunities for the student to tell his classmates what he knows. This topic could also be used to motivate composition activities, other scholarly inquiries, and music listening activities, perhaps around Gustav Holst's *The Planets*.

Sometimes the first information you hear about students may be the most important, but dig deeper, and ask about specific strategies and adaptations to help students be more successful. As you go through questions on your list with parents and other knowledgeable colleagues, keep your conversations focused and specific. As appropriate, ask students the same questions. Many students are experts about their assistive devices, alternative communication systems, medications, and physical needs, although confirmation of their information may be necessary. And all students can verbally or nonverbally communicate their music preferences, important information for their profiles.

You can learn much from your students through informal assessments of music preferences, interests, and skills conducted at the beginning of the year. Gather this information in different ways (written/spoken, gestures, using alternative communication systems or computers), and vary formats (individual audio recordings, games with large or small groups, students' interviews of each other in pairs). Also, watch students during regular routines and activities; observe choices of instruments, how long they listen attentively to a piece of recorded music, and so on. A student may be off-task for several minutes and then be alert when a particular piece of music is played. For some students, indicators of preferences, interests, and skills will be subtle and nonverbal.

Important information about goals will come from written individual plans. Academic and social goals are often decided by teams, and although you are the best person to develop written music goals for your students, ideas for goals can come from parents and other individuals. Here is an example of a music goal being developed for all students, although it was inspired by the IEP goal for one student; goals were accomplished through the use of multiple strategies in a universal approach:

> A child's grandparents were having an anniversary party. The parents wondered about their daughter performing a few pieces at the party; the daughter was in beginning band. Early in the year, her music teacher offered the IEP goal "perform alone three short pieces for classmates and family." In consultation with all of the beginning band students, the teacher chose appropriate music, all class members learned the melody lines for the pieces, and everyone had frequent opportunities to practice and perform in class, alone and in small groups. They also played for the principal and staff. The culminating experience for all students was to play the pieces for their own families in their homes. It was an enjoyable experience for everyone—students, families, teacher.

Curricular Priorities and Performance Standards

Curricular goals and assessments are inextricably related. Develop tentative goals and assessment standards, but don't hesitate to change them after observing your students and talking to more people. To the degree possible, select and prioritize goals for students that are already an important part of your music program, based on a principle of transition for meaningful participation throughout life.

Selecting curricular priorities for students can be challenging, particularly for those students who you know will not be able to accomplish the wide variety of goals offered in your regular music program. To help in the process, I provide an important list of questions to ask yourself when determining priorities (see box 4.4).

As you develop goals, read the students' IEPs and consider how your goals for students also meet requirements for IEPs or other intervention plans. As you read in the previous chapters, schools are required to

Box 4.4

DETERMINING CURRICULAR PRIORITIES AND PERFORMANCE STANDARDS

Among the wide variety of possible goals in your music program, and considering information you know about the student and the importance of music participation in school and throughout adult life, determine curricular priorities for the student. Ask yourself the following questions:

- What are the most important music skills and knowledge that will allow this student to participate in meaningful music experiences now and in the future, alone and with others?
- What other skills and knowledge will allow this student to function more efficiently throughout life?
- Is the student capable of learning these skills given the amount of instructional time available?
- Will the student learn these skills by observing appropriate models? If not, what other strategies are needed?
- Are there frequent opportunities in school and outside of school for the student to practice learned music skills?
- What are the student's interests and those of parents or guardians? Will parents or guardians be sources of support?
- What level and quality of performance should be expected, and how will progress be assessed in and outside of school?

make IEPs accessible to regular education teachers, as well as information about specific accommodations, modifications, and supports that must be provided students.

IEPs must include both academic and functional goals along with coordinated activities and transition services that focus on improving the students' achievement and movement from school to postschool activities. They must also include statements identifying adaptations and supports toward goals, the students' progress in the general education curriculum, participation in extracurricular and other nonacademic activities, and participation with other children.

Consider how students' individual plans can assist in making curricular decisions for students and the ways instruction can be designed to improve students' music achievement and movement from music activities in school to postschool music activities. What would those goals be and in what contexts would they occur? Postschool music activities could include singing or playing instruments in community groups, attending concerts, composing and arranging music using appropriate technology, playing keyboards, and so on. Recall suggestions for ways to design a curriculum based on a principle of transition that were discussed in chapter 2. Once priority postschool activities are determined, relevant skills and knowledge become a focus for instruction.

Children with disabilities, particularly those with physical or intellectual disabilities, are often relegated to activities that involve only music listening or playing uninteresting percussion instruments. I once wrote an article entitled "Life Beyond the Jingle Stick" to make the point that children with disabilities deserve meaningful music making experiences, the kinds of experiences enjoyed by their typical peers and the kinds they see in the media, in the real world.[8] I used the ubiquitous jingle stick to represent the poor sounding classroom instruments that are unfortunately pushed upon young children with disabilities.

Singing and playing instruments are valued activities in most all societies. These activities provide rich opportunities for group and individual enjoyment in many contexts throughout life. For example, playing chords for familiar school and holiday songs on a keyboard or guitar is not only a culturally normative and socially valued skill, but also a skill that can lead to a sense of personal achievement and heightened self-esteem.

Singing and playing instruments beautifully in classrooms, talking with classmates about music they have heard, examining the way music works—all are important for students' musical development. The development of skills, however, needs to be considered not only for traditional, authentic school contexts, but also for participation in extracurricular music activities and for transition to postschool music activities. Are there possibilities for students to continue singing and playing instruments in their homes and communities throughout the year? What are the possibilities for participation in traditional and nontraditional ensembles such as mariachi or percussion?

One wise teacher I know found an ideal opportunity for a high school student with a disability who could not, for several reasons, participate in traditional band ensembles. When introduced to steel pans and the school's famous steel pan band, this student was delighted. The steel pan band provided an alternative ensemble experience for this young man. His classmates were positive music models and were kind and accepting, his parts were carefully written, and he went on to perform with his band at school and community concerts, at conferences, and at state contests. After graduating from high school, he continued to participate in the community steel band and even worked as an assistant for his former teacher, giving lessons to beginning students.

In summary, meaningful music curricula include both long- and short-term goals that focus on the quality of students' lives now and in the future. Parents or guardians and teachers who know individual children's strengths and needs can help identify appropriate music goals by considering the following: (1) the student's interest, (2) the authenticity of the context for instruction, (3) the number of skills and kinds of knowledge to be learned in the time allotted, (4) whether frequent opportunities are available to observe positive models demonstrating the skills and knowledge, (5) whether frequent opportunities are available to practice the skills and knowledge, and (6) whether the student will use the skills and knowledge to participate as independently as possible, alone and with others, in authentic music experiences in school, at home, and in the community.

Although the primary focus of activities in music classrooms is music learning, all activities have a natural overlap with other types of goals that may be identified in students' individual plans. Goals in special education are often categorized as follows:

- *Traditional academic curriculum:* Basic skills (reading, writing, math), other content areas (social studies, sciences), the arts, and physical education.
- *Supplementary goals:* Social, behavioral, communication, motor, self-management, self-determination, and other skills and knowledge that are embedded in most all subjects.

- *Functional goals:* Skills and knowledge needed to perform daily routines required for activities in various environments (home, school, work, community).

Goals in music programs may be thought of using two categories:[9]

- *Music goals:* Skills and knowledge needed for accurate and expressive music performance and successful participation in a variety of music activities (keep a steady pulse in body movement and music performance, change dynamic levels and tempo following verbal and nonverbal cues, perform independent parts coordinating pulse and dynamic level with the ensemble, assume appropriate posture for singing and playing instruments, read and notate music, identify melodic/rhythmic motifs in written and performed music).
- *Social goals:* Skills and knowledge needed for successful interactions and participation with others in music classrooms (follow rules and routines, work cooperatively with others, practice self-control, express preferences and interests, compliment performers, evaluate one's own performance and feelings).

Of course, various goals can be integrated. For example, consider an activity in which students listen to music and in pairs, talk to a classmate about the music, explaining their preferences for interpretation and identifying several compositional techniques. The primary goal is a music goal, but clear communication of ideas and appropriate social behavior, goals that may appear on a student's individual plan, are essential to a positive and productive interaction.

People can underestimate the capabilities of students with disabilities or those who are at-risk. One purpose of teachers gathering as much information as possible about their students is to guard against possible low expectations, on their part or on the part of others. I have seen examples of low expectations in classrooms when students with disabilities are engaged in activities that simply keep them busy with performance criteria that reflect the thinking "good enough" or "fine for someone with a disability."

Once curricular priorities are established, performance standards should be set beyond the student's initial level and quality of performance. Progress for any student requires the refinement of skills, which requires appropriate goals and performance criteria skillfully sequenced in levels of difficulty and complexity. The bar must be raised—for all students.

Broad and In-depth Assessments of Environments and Activities

As you are gathering information about students, ask yourself a lot of questions about how students can participate in classroom routines and activities to the fullest extent possible. To answer those questions, more information is needed about your classroom and your students' day-to-day activities.

Consider the many behaviors involved in routines such as entering and leaving the classroom or setting up for a rehearsal or participating in music activities such as playing instruments, singing, dancing, talking about music, and so on. Even experienced teachers can overlook the many behaviors that are required in a single routine or activity. Every behavior, no matter how seemingly small, is an opportunity for participation and learning. When teachers analyze activities, they are often surprised to find behaviors they had not thought of before. By creating a simple list

Box 4.5

GATHERING INFORMATION: A BROAD ASSESSMENT OF ENVIRONMENTS AND ACTIVITIES

Consider the student's profile and goals, and conduct a broad assessment to determine if changes are necessary for these areas:

- *Climate of inclusion:* classmates' attitudes and behaviors toward the student, student's participation in roles valued by classmates, other responsibilities.
- *Physical environment:* seating or positioning used frequently, location of materials, instruments, equipment used frequently, light and sound, other.
- *Classroom management:* expectations and consequences for appropriate and inappropriate behavior.
- *Routines:* before, during, and after class, routines for frequently occurring activities.
- *Music curriculum and assessment criteria:* music goals, assessment, and grading procedures.
- *Instruction:* frequently occurring teaching strategies, including formats (whole class, small groups, etc.), use of visuals, routine teaching sequences, other.
- *Materials, instruments, equipment:* used in frequently occurring routines and learning activities.

Box 4.6

GATHERING INFORMATION: IN-DEPTH ASSESSMENT OF ACTIVITIES

Consider the student's profile and goals, and conduct an in-depth assessment of frequently occurring music activities (tasks and/or routines) by following these steps:

- List, in sequence, students' behaviors in small steps as typically performed (what students will do) and how information and content will be presented to students.
  - Number steps beginning with an action verb, and include any materials, instruments, or other equipment.
  - Analyze steps further, and add smaller steps as necessary for particular tasks (task analyses).
  - Determine how information and content are typically presented (visually, aurally, other modes of communication).
- Review behaviors in steps, the sequence of behaviors (including materials, etc.), and how information and content are presented. For each step, determine if, when, and what universal strategies are needed to allow the student to participate in the same way as typical peers, to the extent possible. Identify individual adaptations as necessary.
- Identify other appropriate goals for the student that are or can be embedded into the activity (e.g., fundamental music skills and knowledge, social skills, goals related to self-determination). Determine if applications are also appropriate for other students.
- Implement, assess effectiveness, and make changes as necessary.

of behaviors for any activity, routine, or small task, you can arrange for your students to participate to the fullest extent possible, independently and with adaptations and assistance as necessary. You can also identify ways to integrate goals from their individual plans, assess their skills, and identify future music goals.

One of the best ways to get a lot of information is to think about your students' needs and characteristics and do a quick assessment of your classrooms, activities, and routines (see box 4.5). In-depth assessments require more deliberation (see box 4.6). (Examples of broad assessments and in-depth assessments can be found at the companion website.)

Broad assessments are best made on the spot, in your classroom, and by watching your students, wherever they are. However, given the hectic pace of school days, imagery can help. Try to imagine how your classroom looks and the sequence of activities that will occur. Imagine your classroom without students—just the floor space, lighting, placement of chairs, stands, equipment, and so on (physical environment). Imagine the students entering the classroom, perhaps talking with one another, or not, and moving into routines, following your classroom rules throughout the class period (classroom routines and social behavior). You engage students in music activities and have expectations for their performance, whether singing, playing instruments, listening to music, reading music, or other music activities (music curriculum and assessment). Activities may require books, orchestra or band instruments, music, computers, and other stuff (materials, instruments, equipment). Throughout the activity, you are relating information, giving directions, using visuals, asking questions, giving feedback, and so on (instruction).

Now, imagine a particular student in your classroom. Scan box 4.5, quickly determine whether adjustments are needed, and jot down any ideas. The following is an example of a stream of thoughts in a quick assessment for a student named Jake. I'll begin with the first category, "climate of inclusion" and move on quickly to other categories from there.

> As you think about this idea, you feel confident that your classroom is a positive learning environment for students, but you decide to set up more opportunities for positive social and cooperative experiences among students and opportunities for Jake to show personal achievement. From your knowledge of Jake's characteristics and your consultations thus far, you know that some adjustments are needed, even though you are not sure about details yet. From what you've seen, many students seem to shy away from him. You recall from talking with a colleague and the behavior specialist that Jake works best alone or with a nurturing partner, but you frequently ask groups to work together (instruction; format). You want to give some future thought to his participation in larger, interactive groups. Perhaps you are thinking vaguely about a way to restructure an activity or the distribution of materials (routines) using partners—Jane would be the ideal partner for Jake (social). Your thinking cues in changes for seating (physical environment) when students enter the classroom. Is there a way that you can offer more choices to all students (social) and particularly to Jake? You think it's important, but you're not yet sure how you will do this. He needs some graphic organizers; you read this on his RTI plan and think you can do this for some printed materials (instruction visuals, materials). Perhaps there is a way to involve the class in developing maps and organizers showing routines and music content. Now you wonder if you can give Jake some leadership responsibilities, perhaps for those times when students are transitioning between activities and to rehearsals on stage. You're not sure how yet but will think about this later.

Throughout this exercise, you are making brief notes to yourself. Keep in mind that you are assessing routines and activities that occur frequently in your classroom and rehearsal spaces and where students spend most of their time, physically, whether seated in a circle, in chairs, or on risers. It may be that you have concerns for your upcoming field trip or contest, but focus first on activities and routines that occur frequently, since they provide students with many opportunities to practice skills. What are students asked to do frequently (tasks, activities, routines), and what equipment and materials are used most frequently (contexts)? When activities and routines are assessed, it is easier to see how the same strategies can be used in many similar situations.

In-depth analyses give teachers a closer look at specific activities and tasks. In special education jargon, an in-depth analysis can be called an ecological assessment (coming from the sciences, meaning a study of all aspects of the environment) or a task analysis (a sequence of all specific relevant steps required to complete a task such as buzzing lips to play brass instruments or performing a particular dance step). In-depth assessments are step-by-step listings of the typical behaviors students exhibit in the activity or task within the context (other individuals present, the physical environment, materials, and so on).

By conducting in-depth analyses, teachers can identify if and when adjustments are required for behaviors, for steps in the sequence, for materials and equipment, and so on. These analyses provide information for the development of appropriate strategies and adaptations as needed and information to determine whether to add or revise steps, adjust materials, and so on. Also, adjustments may provide more opportunities for peer interactions or opportunities to foster self-determination. Knowing what does not have to be changed is as important as knowing what does. Without in-depth analyses, opportunities for partial participation may easily be overlooked. In-depth assessments guard against the outdated "all or nothing" way of thinking.

Planning and Implementing Strategies

Strategies will be designed based on students' strengths and needs, although some strategies can be developed in the absence of specific student information. For example, you are already aware that many students benefit when information is presented visually in addition to vocally and that students will be less distracted when seats are turned away from the windows or the entry door. Before the first day of class, you can create multiple strategies that will most likely apply to everyone in the class. Other strategies are best developed after you have assessed your teaching environments, considering students' specific strengths, characteristics, and needs.

Frequent Opportunities to Practice and Significance of Activities

As you design strategies, consider first strategies for behaviors that occur frequently in activities and routines and those for behaviors that are significant in the students' musical lives. Frequently occurring behaviors provide many opportunities for students to practice skills and apply knowledge. Strategies may be needed for daily routines and activities, such as locating materials and instruments and preparation for the classroom or rehearsal performance; entering and exiting the room; instrument care; classroom management rules; singing and/or playing instruments. However, there are also times when the significance of the behavior requires attention, regardless of its frequency. For example, participating in performances onstage with classmates may be an infrequent event, but it is an important one for many students and their families.

Elements of the Learning Environment and Strategies

You are thinking about your activities and routines, your students, and ways to plan and implement lessons so that everyone will participate as independently and successfully as possible. You think about ways to sequence activities, present information, arrange the room, and make materials available to everyone. You also think about how you can provide more opportunities for students to make choices, express preferences, and

Box 4.7

ELEMENTS OF THE LEARNING ENVIRONMENT

Think about the following when designing strategies to meet students' needs:

- Modes of communication.
- Curricular goals and performance standards.
- Instructional methods.
- Assessment procedures.
- Physical environment.
- Materials, instruments, equipment.
- Technology.
- Support from peers and others, as needed.

interact with one another. All of this information will be helpful to you as you go about designing and implementing strategies.

Strategies can involve any of the elements of the learning environment (see box 4.7) and can range from simple ideas, such as adjusting lighting in the room or changing students' seating, to ideas that may be less familiar, such as making computers accessible or using alternative communication devices. In the remaining sections here, I describe elements of the learning environment in detail and provide many examples of ways to maintain flexibility in designing strategies for your students, illustrating many possibilities for diverse groups of students to participate successfully in common music learning experiences. You'll find several examples of individual adaptions among the many possible strategies for a universal approach to music teaching.

As you read through the many details in these sections, keep the bigger picture in mind. Think about the elements as numerous opportunities to develop flexible, effective strategies to present information to students, to engage and motivate them, and to allow all of them to participate successfully in the same activities. Let's begin.

Modes of Communication

In education, modes of communication are typically thought of as the various ways students perceive and respond to information in their environment, most often using hearing, sight, touch, and movement. Since modes of communication overlap all other elements of the learning environment and are included in examples in sections to follow (e.g., instructional methods, materials, technology), I will present only a few of the more obvious examples here.

You are aware of braille (touch) as an alternative for printed visual information and American Sign Language (visual/movement) as an alternative for auditory information. These are adaptations for individual students, but many students will more easily comprehend information when multiple strategies are used to communicate. For example, students may hear a teacher talking but may grasp what is said more quickly when the teacher refers to visuals, and students may read printed music but make fewer errors playing a difficult repeating rhythm when they circle the rhythm throughout the music, play it out of context several times, then play it in context. When music is presented visually and aurally, compositional techniques are more understandable to many students, and they more easily understand how their individual parts contribute to the overall sound.

Options are also needed for students to express their ideas, to show what they know and can do. For example, some students can improvise music but have difficulty reading music, some read music fluently but have difficulty talking about it, some can use their bodies or draw to show expressiveness in music but cannot read and follow dynamic markings in printed music, and some can compose using computers but have difficulty using writing tools.

Curricular Goals and Performance Standards

Curricular issues have been discussed at length in this book. Students will have a meaningful musical life when music programs are based on a principle of transition and when important music goals are curricular priorities for all students. Music teachers may work on fundamental music skills and knowledge and necessary social skills, but they do not lose sight of important music goals that will allow students to participate successfully in school and postschool music activities.

Although most students will progress toward the same music goals, other students will require curricular modifications. Before making modifications, review the questions that were presented in box 4.4 to determine first if the skill or knowledge that would be modified is important for the student to learn and then whether it will still be important after it is modified. Some modifications can render a goal or task meaningless.

When considering modifications, think about broad activity goals such as learning to perform a particular Orff arrangement and smaller tasks or behaviors such as playing an open fifth on the bass xylophone. In-depth analyses of the sequences of activities (box 4.6) will reveal behaviors (tasks) that require modifications and others that will not, thus revealing opportunities for partial participation. For students who are unable to learn the myriad skills that are required by an activity, who do not have the physical stamina to participate throughout the entire sequence, or who, for any number of reasons, cannot participate fully, partial participation allows them to join their classmates in the same activity, do as much as is possible, and participate as independently as possible.

Be aware of common errors that can occur when the strategy of partial participation is narrow and limits the students' range of activities and learning.[10] Errors occur when partial participation (1) is limited to one activity or one small part of an activity, such as only playing simple percussion instruments or only starting the CD player and then watching classmates participate in activities; (2) does not include extracurricular music activities, such as performing with other ensemble members

Box 4.8

MODIFYING CURRICULAR GOALS AND PERFORMANCE STANDARDS

Ways to think about modifying goals and performance standards to meet students' needs:

- Modify music goals/tasks and performance standards.
  - Level of complexity.
  - Amount of content.
  - Partial participation (number of activities/tasks performed).
- Identify alternative music goals/tasks and performance standards.
  - Music-related goals that match activity themes.
  - Fundamental music skills and knowledge.
- Identify supplementary goals/tasks and performance standards.
  - Social skills and knowledge.
  - Others (e.g., IEP, 504, RTI goals; peer interactions; elements of self-determined behaviors).

in holiday community concerts or attending field trips to concerts; (3) requires a high degree of assistance from other adults or students; (4) occurs only in the presence of the teacher and has no application to other music contexts; (5) involves an activity that is not valued, respected, or preferred by peers; and (6) requires changes in the activity in such a way that the activity loses its musical or educational value for other students in the class.

Partial participation in music activities can be considered one of several kinds of curricular modifications (see box 4.8). Curricular modifications can involve adjustments to the level of complexity and/or amount of content students are asked to learn or, in some situations, the selection of an alternative music goal that relates closely to the focus of the activity or to fundamental music skills and knowledge. There are also any number of supplementary goals that can be integrated into the regular music activity, including goals from students' individual plans (e.g., communication, motor, social, and self-determination behaviors). Whether modified, alternative, or supplementary, goals should be those that are meaningful for students and not simply alternative activities to keep them busy.

A few examples of different types of curricular modifications are given below, with performance standards to define students' success. The first example is not a curricular modification but an accommodation that is presented only as a point of comparison with other examples. With accommodations, goals and performance standards are unchanged, although adjustments are made to other elements (e.g., instruction, physical environment, materials).

No adjustments to music goal/task and performance standard: A student who is blind is held to the same performance standards in an audition for a select choir. She sings beautifully, and the teacher provides multiple means for her to learn the music through frequent repetitions in rehearsals, audio tapes, and assistance from classmates.

Modified music goal/task and appropriate performance standard: An orchestra teacher rewrites several parts for a student, making the parts less complex. The student is assessed on fewer pieces than his classmates and only on his modified parts but is still expected to play accurately and musically.

Alternative music goal/task and appropriate performance standard: The goal for a student who is too frail to participate in movement lessons is to play accompaniments with a few classmates as other classmates dance. She is still expected to play her accompaniment part accurately and musically and refine fundamental skills in her playing (e.g., rhythmic precision, appropriate dynamics).

Supplementary goal/task and appropriate performance standard: A band teacher wants her students to communicate meaningful evaluations about their own and their group's performances. In frequent class discussions of repertoire, students talk with stand partners, discuss preferences for pieces, express opinions regarding the group's performance, and use conventional music terminology in their explanations. Several goals for one band student relate to the broad areas of communication and self-determination. This student, who is reluctant to talk in a large-group setting, is expected to look at the person he is talking to and state at least one idea (opinion, preference) to his partner, to members in his small group, and eventually to the entire class. Although expectations for the frequency and quality of his verbal responses and communication differ from those of his typical classmates, he otherwise is held to the same standards for his music performance and classroom behavior.

Assessment

Did they learn what we intended to teach? Curricular and assessment decisions are inextricably related. Assessments should be determined *before* instruction, at the same time as curricular decisions are being made. When assessments are developed before instruction, teachers have a clear idea of what the student will "look like" after instruction, and this picture will drive instruction toward this outcome. Duke writes about this idea eloquently: "The process of effective instruction begins with designing meaningful assessments, and at the core of meaningful assessment is a vision of students as accomplished learners."[11]

Music assessments, unlike state and district tests, happen frequently, they vary in format, and results are known almost immediately. Every note played or sung, every response to a teacher's direction, every behavior performed in a specific activity provides an opportunity for assessment of students' progress.

Almost all music assessments can and should be authentic. In talking about the importance of authentic assessments and instruction for students with significant disabilities, Brown writes, "However [students are] labeled, it is the responsibility of instructional personnel to arrange and empirically verify that each skill being taught is performed in meaningful contexts in school and nonschool environments and activities."[12] Applied to music assessments, the audience behavior of your students at a performance of a visiting ensemble or at a concert hall is an authentic assessment compared with their reponses in class to questions about good audience behavior. And clearly, assessing music performance is just that, not naming notes and key signatures or clapping rhythms but assessing students' playing and singing beautifully alone and with others in a variety of performing contexts. (You will read more about assessing students' progress in the section "Thinking Ahead.")

For decades, students with disabilities were excluded from class assessments and from state- and district-wide tests. That has changed as a result of amendments in IDEA 2004. IEPs must include a description of how students' progress will be measured and when periodic reports will be provided to parents. You may be asked to document the progress of students who have IEPs and also those with 504 or RTI plans. Further, IEPs are to specify accommodations necessary to measure students' performances on state- and district-wide assessments and include statements about why students cannot participate or why alternate assessments will substitute for regular tests. Universal design principles are to be used in assessments to the extent feasible.[13] Multiple design strategies can involve

Box 4.9

DESIGNING STRATEGIES FOR INSTRUCTION

Think about the following when designing instructional strategies to meet students' needs:

- Format (individual, partners, small groups, entire class).
- Presentation of information and content (includes instructions, questions).
  - Modes of communication (written, spoken, gestures, alternative systems).
  - Level of complexity, amount of content.
  - Repetition.
  - Pacing and response time.
  - Modeling and prompts.
  - Proximity to student.
  - Visuals to clarify, organize.
- Sequencing of learning activities.
  - Order of instructional sequence.
  - Small approximations, task analysis steps.
  - Positive practice of steps throughout sequence.
- Feedback (frequency and magnitude).
- Transfer.

any of the elements of the learning environment, beginning with students' mode of communication and including other elements found in instruction (see box 4.9). Teachers may read the directions aloud and then show the directions in print, give many opportunities for questions, use double spacing between questions, capitalize or underline key words, use short sentences, require different response times, vary the sequence in which musical examples or questions are presented, use repetition frequently, give frequent words of encouragement, and assess content across several weeks rather than in one longer session.

Assessment data should be shared and may be added to reports for parents. Although positive words about students' progress are welcomed by most all parents, your words take on particular importance for parents of students who are struggling academically and/or socially in school. Music teachers in large part can determine the success of students as a result of curricular and instructional decisions but also based on the frequency of assessments, content, and the assessment procedures.

Instruction

Instruction is the presentation of information by teachers and other individuals or through the use of materials, equipment, and technology (books, CD players, computers, etc.). Instruction involves all modes of communication and behaviors, such as asking questions, giving directives, and presenting information and content. As you have read, IDEA 2004 has several explicit statements requiring schools to use scientific, research-based instructional practices. These include well-established elements of instruction, many of which are listed in box 4.9.

There are many ways to consider instructional elements within a universal approach. Here are a few examples of multiple strategies used in a listening lesson with elementary students:

> A teacher considers the attention span of several students and chooses short excerpts so he gets to the interactive part of the lesson sooner. Knowing that a few students will have difficulty expressing their ideas in a class discussion of the music, he plans to use partners and small-group formats and selects partners and group membership based on students' characteristics and needs. Some students will need to have more time to express their ideas; working with a partner will allow more time. He designs and projects a simple visual of printed instructions and plans to ask a few students either to read or repeat the instructions. As always, he plans to move among the partners and groups and knows that he will walk by some frequently to keep them on-task. He knows who will be a good partner for his student with significant disabilities and plans to ask the aide to assist with the student's communication board only when necessary. There is also one student who has been working to control anxiety attacks. As part of this student's plan, the student may leave any activity and sit in a screened break area in the classroom, where he does breathing exercises and calms himself. His regular seat is at the end of the row close to the break area, and that is where he will work with his soft-spoken, supportive partner. As he shows fewer signs of anxiety throughout the semester, the teacher plans to move his seat gradually to the center of the row.

Any change in a lesson can be inspired by one or several students. The challenge is for teachers to plan and implement multiple means to present information and multiple ways for students to respond successfully and as independently as possible. Giving more (or less) feedback, modeling, giving students strategies for organizing information as it is presented, allowing breaks during a lesson or during the rehearsal of a difficult piece, changing the order of the activities—all are factors that have been shown to influence students' success and motivation and are applicable to many learning activities.

Physical Environment

We've all been in situations when we can't hear a soft-spoken individual, a room has faulty lighting or is too cluttered, chairs are uncomfortable or too close together, and books and materials are hard to reach. We've also experienced times when we cannot concentrate on a task because of distracting sounds from others in the same room, from a malfunctioning heating or cooling system, or from musicians practicing in the adjacent room. We make adjustments when we experience problems and inconveniences related to the many environments in our lives; however, some children must rely on adults to adjust physical environments that are barriers to their learning and well-being.

With knowledge of students' strengths and needs, teachers know what changes are necessary for mobility; access to materials, instruments, and equipment; and access to instruction. Changes can involve lighting, furniture, carpeting, seating, shelving, ventilation, floor space, sound and acoustics, and the location of students' seats, risers, and storage lockers or cabinets, to name a few. I've observed situations where teachers have designed simple universal strategies to solve problems. When a very "live" classroom was carpeted, everyone, not just the student who was sensitive to sound, benefited from the improved acoustics. The behaviors of one student in this classroom made the sound problem all the more obvious, and carpeting became a priority. A teacher of young beginning string students found that they handled their instruments more carefully when her list of rules for instrument care were posted not only at the front of the class but also on each student's cubby where their instruments were stored. In another situation, a teacher formed another aisle for students to have easier access to books and instruments at the rear of the room, also making it easier for the student who used a walker. When it was apparent that the overhead lighting was too bright and distracting for one student in particular, the teacher had a dimmer light installed and used it when full lighting was not necessary. All students, including the teacher, welcomed lower lights, particularly when listening to music.

Some elements of the classroom can be changed easily by the teacher; others may require construction (e.g., addition of ramps, wider door frames) to be in compliance with 504 and ADA requirements. You will want to be included in discussions regarding ADA standards and specifications for your classrooms, practice rooms, and performance spaces. Laws require access to programs and buildings for all individuals, and that means not only your students but also members of the general public who want to attend school events. Be sure to include in your announcements information regarding access. Your school will have ADA statements that can serve as models for these announcements.

Materials, Instruments, and Equipment

There is a great deal of stuff in our music classrooms—instructional music materials, a variety of instruments, and other equipment such as sound and video reproduction systems. Universal design strategies can make almost all of your materials, instruments, and equipment accessible.

IDEA requires accessible materials and technological devices and services for the implementation of educational programs and assessment of students' progress. The focus of federal and state agencies has been on the development of accessible instructional materials for core subjects such as reading and math. I am unaware of developments for accessible music materials, but many universal strategies and technologies are transferable to music materials, instruments, and equipment.

Print and audiovisual materials On any given day, music teachers and students engage in reading music and different types of print materials (newspapers, textbooks, books for leisure reading, professional journals, popular magazines, advertisement flyers, etc.). Apart from the content of the material, reading can be a pleasant or unpleasant experience. When you analyze some of your more unpleasant experiences with printed material, you quickly identify solutions that would relieve some of your physical discomforts, eyestrain, or a neck ache, and make the information more perceptible and the reading more pleasant.

Other examples are found in poor video and sound reproduction systems. How can we expect students to be thrilled by a performance of the Chicago Symphony Orchestra when they are asked to watch a video played on a small monitor with poor speakers? All of us, including students, are justifiably agitated when speakers crackle or the volume is too loud or too soft. High-quality sound reproduction systems for CD players, video players, and computers are necessary if audible materials are to be instructional, although the quality of systems in many music classrooms remains poor. In addition to simply having good equipment, there are any number of strategies and adaptations for audio materials, and many involve the use of assistive technology. Because listening to music is much of what we, and our students do, multiple strategies are described at length in the section on technology.

Excessive or insufficient information, in addition to the organization and style of any presentation, affects our experience with instructional material. I'm sure you've seen presentations and lectures with too many words on a PowerPoint slide, and then there are icons, borders, and even animations that are intended to clarify information but only weaken the presentation. Similar examples are found in children's music books, where the printed music seems secondary to the artwork. Rather than looking at cluttered pages in their books, trying to find the rhythm the teacher is asking them to find, students will benefit from a projected visual of the music notation only, with minimal highlighting of rhythms, phrases, or intervals as necessary.

Printed text and music materials can be designed and adjusted to meet the needs of students by considering the following:

- Print format: font and size of letters or notes, ink color (light or dark; color), alignment and spacing, bullets and numbering, borders and shading, margins, background material, length of paragraphs.
- Pictures and symbols.
- Highlighted text or music notes or phrases.
- Print page: type of paper (dimensions, weight, texture, color).
- Covers and binding: hard or soft covers, spiral or solid, information on covers.
- Book or music adapted for page turning.
- Assistive technology: magnification aids, high-intensity lighting, tactile aids such as braille text or braille music, speech scanners, variable speech control tape recorders for prerecorded text or music, adapted books and music stands, computer music programs.

Instruments Ensembles provide an ideal example of a universal approach to music teaching. All of the students are participating but in different ways as determined by their particular parts and the instruments they are playing. Also, parts and instruments have been carefully selected by the music teacher based on students' capabilities and characteristics.

Consider the important decision of selecting appropriate instruments for students. Most deliberations in schools involve choices among traditional band and orchestra instruments, but instruments may include acoustic guitar, harp, piano, recorder, folk instruments, electronic keyboards and guitars, steel pan, drum set, and others. When a poor match is made, students most likely will not be successful, they will drop out of their ensembles, and many may feel they lack music abilities. We have all met some of these students when they are adults, who describe themselves as not good at music or untalented. Interest and physical characteristics are typically considered in the selection of instruments. Factors that can influence students' success and continued participation include:

- Student's interest.
- Personal characteristics (ability to stay on-task for increasingly longer periods of time and follow instructions).

- Compatibility of physical characteristics (physical stamina, strength, coordination, length of arms, height, position of teeth) and instrument characteristics (size, weight, ease of handling, ease of making a characteristic sound, mouthpiece and embouchure).
- Opportunities to play in school ensembles and social settings.
- Opportunities to play at home, alone or with family and friends.
- Availability of lessons, individual and/or group.
- Music availability, variety, and levels of difficulty.
- Instrument availability and cost, school instruments and individual purchase.
- Support from parents (interest, time, financial).
- Opportunities for continued instrumental experiences as an adult in community music organizations.

Physical characteristics and learning needs are important considerations when selecting instruments and ensembles for students, but teachers must guard against automatically denying students instrument experiences based on these factors alone. Can students with sensory impairments, hearing or visual, play instruments? And what about students who have limited use of their arms or who learn at slower rates than their classmates? Will students who have poor eye contact, lack appropriate social skills, read poorly, tantrum occasionally, or have conditions affecting their health be successful in a school instrumental program? The probability of answering yes to these questions is high if decisions about instruments are made carefully, if students show interest, if teachers use effective teaching practices with appropriate adaptations, and if families, other adults, and classmates support the students' music study and praise achievements. With the exception of the addition of necessary adaptations as needed, this kind of support would predict success for almost all students.

When it comes time for "instrument day," and elementary children are asked to consider studying an instrument and joining band or orchestra, those with disabilities are often left out of this activity. Sure, they've enjoyed playing classroom instruments in the elementary grades, but what are their opportunities to play real instruments? We know from interviews with children with disabilities that when they say they play an instrument, it is rarely keyboard, guitar, wind, string, or brass instruments.[14] They name classroom instruments, most often percussion. My advice to teachers is to refrain from their instinct to think about percussion as the first instrumental experience for students with disabilities.

If percussion is considered an area for serious music study for students and not just a default activity, then students' skills should be refined. In an example to make this point, you read about the high school student whose disability made playing traditional band instruments difficult but who was guided by his wise teacher to the steel pan. Steel pan became a passion for this student. His teacher set appropriate performance standards for him, and he advanced to a level where he could play modified parts in the high school steel pan band. This student also composed and played his own music for classmates, and after graduation from high school, he assisted his former teacher and played in a community steel pan band.

When you are considering the appropriateness of an instrument, also consider the possibilities of adapting instruments, which can increase the number of options for students. When an instrument is altered in a reasonable manner, what may initially seem impossible becomes possible. For example, a tenor trombone was not initially considered for a student who loved the instrument but had limited range of motion in her right arm. With the use of an extension, playing the tenor trombone became a reality; she also played bass trombone. In yet another example, a highly motivated young teen who was interested in playing clarinet in her school band progressed to such a level that she auditioned for and won first chair in a major city's youth symphony. That's not an unusual story, except that she had severe arthritis in her hands. How did she advance to such a high level of playing? An occupational therapist built key extensions from a synthetic material. Several adjustments were made to the synthetic keys throughout the year, and with the help of her tenacious music teacher, a patron funded the purchase of a new clarinet, complete with adapted *silver* keys.

You will also want to consult with professionals about ways to use assistive technology (AT) devices such as foam, Velcro straps, stands, grips, and other materials to alter an instrument, instrument stand, or picks or to assist with playing positions. (See also the section on technology below and note 18). Many handy parents, neighbors, and custodians have enjoyed designing and building devices for students. Don't hesitate to recruit them. Again, adaptations should only be as specialized as necessary; players should look professional, as should the instruments, materials, and equipment.[15]

To continue with the idea of using real instruments and materials, almost all students, including those with significant disabilities, can be successful with keyboards, playing harmonies, arpeggios, or drum effects. Young beginning Suzuki violin students have tape markings on their fingerboards to remind them where to place their fingers, a technique that could provide support for students who need additional reminders about finger placements; markings should be as small as possible. Students who are playing a guitar, although it's tuned to one chord, are still playing a guitar.

Equipment Some equipment is standard in classrooms, such as risers, stands, and sound reproduction systems. Other equipment might include computers, iPads, appropriate software, printers, MIDI equipment, CD-ROM-compatible computers and music-related CD-ROMs, video cameras, monitors, VCRs, and other multimedia equipment. I'll discuss several adaptations for equipment from computers to audio recordings in the next section on technology. For now, consider the various ways students can be involved in designing and operating the equipment.

In a universal approach, all students can have opportunities and responsibilities to use and operate equipment as they accomplish music goals. As one example, using multiple strategies in a universal approach, in groups, with a partner, or alone, students can use electronic keyboards, computers, and MIDI equipment to compose and/or arrange music for a class performance. Assignments in the lessons would vary, with some students creating melodic lines over a single chord, others playing chord progressions, others in charge of loading audio files, and others imitating melodic material. Students would, however, have experiences with all assignments, to the extent possible.

In a different example not directly related to music learning, consider the many roles that are possible in the operation of equipment for performances—lighting, sound, curtains, and so on. I watched a K–3 music performance where a fifth-grade class served as the tech-support team. Roles varied among students. Some worked together, but everyone added to the success of their younger schoolmates' performances. The "Tech Team" completed the necessary tasks, including operation of the sound equipment, providing support for children performing accompaniments, and arranging access and adequate spaces for students who used wheelchairs, walkers, guide dogs, or other mobility devices. When the team members were recognized and took their bows, you could see how proud they were, wearing black T-shirts with "Tech" in white letters.

Technology

Some students cannot sit in an upright position to see the teacher and classmates without an adapted chair or stander; cannot read without a magnification device or braille; cannot hear without a personal amplification system or hearing aid; cannot turn on the CD player without a large switch; cannot communicate without a simple voice output device; or cannot access information on a computer or iPad without software that provides text to speech. Students who might otherwise have difficulty notating a composition, understanding music instruction, or listening independently to music can be successful using computers, iPads, iPhones, and other types of music technology. Technology is prominent in education and daily life. Assistive technology (AT), simply put, is anything that helps individuals with disabilities accomplish tasks that otherwise would be difficult or impossible to perform and that enhances their functional independence.[16]

Early laws stimulated technological advancements that continue to have significant implications for the lives of all individuals with disabilities (e.g., Section 504 of the Rehabilitation Act; Technology-Related Assistance Act, or Tech Act; Assistive Technology Act; Section 508 of the Rehabilitation Act of 1998).[17] Most of the technological advances in education were driven by requirements in IDEA 1997 for an accessible curriculum, and IDEA 2004 which requires instructional materials in accessible formats (e.g., braille, audio, large print, e-text).

Most music teachers are aware of advances in music technology, particularly those used for theory instruction and composition. Information about music technology is readily available. All lessons using music technology can be designed using a universal approach. In the preface to her instructive book on music technology and composition, Freedman writes: "Technology allows a musical experience for all skill levels—an opportunity, never before available, to compose, manipulate, save, instantly listen to music electronically, and even print standard Western music notation for others to play without having to know much about traditional music theory or notation."[18] To make this point, lessons in her text provide ideas for students capable of engaging in more complex tasks and those who may need modifications. Although music teachers may be familiar with types of music technology, even experienced music educators may lack knowledge about assistive devices, equipment, and their uses in music.[19]

Several types of applications of technology are found in schools, and they range from low-tech items such as foam cushions to assist with playing position or laminated pictures showing icons for routines to high-tech items such as speech recognition devices and alternative communication devices. Technology products and devices are used for mobility, positioning and seating, speech communication (augmentative and alternative communication systems), access to information (computer access, telecommunication, listening and print access), academics (music, reading, writing, math, studying), adult independent living (control of environment, daily living activities), and recreation (music activities, toys, sports, games).

Some technologies are specialized for individuals, such as alternative communication systems or mobility devices, and are referred to as assistive technology (AT). Others are universally designed products that can be used by all students. A computer, iPad, or iPhone is an AT device when it is a necessary means of communication by an individual who cannot speak, when it is used as a tool to improve motor skills, or when it is used as a therapeutic strategy to relieve stress and lower anxiety. A simple lever handle on a sink and a touch-sensitive table lamp are AT devices when they are the only ways an individual with a physical disability can turn water or a light on and off. Many low-tech devices can be developed by music teachers, although music teachers may need to be trained in the use, handling, care, and storage of more specialized devices. AT training can come from any number of individuals, such as music therapists, physical and occupational therapists, teachers, parents, or commercial vendors. By law, AT services must be available for the student, family members, and any individual who works with the student. Ask for training so you can learn how to listen to and understand students' communications using augmentative communication devices, learn the ways in which students use computers and voice recognition software or learn how to adjust bolsters or adapt chairs for students to be positioned and seated properly, and so on.

To help increase your knowledge about how to design universal strategies using technology and AT devices, I describe below several technologies for students to (1) access information and communication (print and audio), (2) access computers and on-screen information, (3) operate equipment using switches and other similar devices, and (4) participate more fully and comfortably from an appropriate position and seat.

Access to print or audio information and communication Various types of AT devices have been developed for students to access print and audio information, and several have applications for music classrooms. Examples include magnifying glasses and magnifiers on stands for reading music, a reading stand adapted with an extended arm, enlarged print for text printed on paper or downloaded to computers or iPads, changes to print contrast such as a black background with white letters or notes, high-intensity lamps for reading print material, and optical character recognition (OCR) systems, which can scan and translate print into a format that can be read or spoken by a computer or translated into braille. Some online sites advertise software programs that will scan music and produce output files and programs to translate printed music to braille or versions for individuals with low vision.

Accessible instructional print materials are made available free of charge through several agencies. When IDEA 2004 was reauthorized and amended, among the amendments were requirements for accessible instructional materials and the creation of the National Instructional Materials Access Center (NIMAC) to facilitate their production and distribution. NIMAC is a federally funded, national electronic file repository that makes National Instructional Materials Accessibility Standard (NIMAS) files available for the production of core print instructional materials to specialized formats (braille, audio, large print, or digital text formats). NIMAS is a technical standard that is used to prepare electronic files that can be used to convert printed instructional materials into specialized formats. States are required to adopt the standard and provide accessible print instructional materials to students identified as having disabilities.[20]

The National Library Service (NLS) for the Blind and Physically Handicapped will provide transcription services and, for print music, will provide a free library program of braille and recorded materials. NLS also has a special music section with copies of braille and large-print music scores, texts, and instructional recordings about music and musicians.[21] Some students enjoy the independence and variety of music-making experiences that can come from learning how to write and read braille music. Other students may prefer to use literary braille and write out their parts or chord progressions using the braille alphabet.[22]

Recordings can be used by students who are blind or have low vision, but they are also useful for almost all students. Recordings of class songs, individual parts, or entire rehearsals are useful for learning individual parts and increasing auditory discrimination and memory skills. Teachers have designed recording projects with any number of roles for students. Recording activities provide multiple ways for students to participate, and when equipment is universally designed or adapted, all students can participate and benefit. Consider the following points when making recordings for teaching purposes and designing learning activities to meet diverse needs:

- Record using high-quality equipment, and for listening, use equipment that has variable speed and pitch controls operated by easily manipulated dials or slides.
- Provide brief reminders of performance fundamentals (e.g., tempo, style, key) at the beginning of the recording, even though students will hear this information in class.
- If available, play a CD of the piece, and show the score to provide a context for individual parts.

- Record entire sections as they are to be rehearsed, and give section numbers, phrase numbers, or choral text as start and stop cues.
- Use the best musical model for recording parts, preferably classmates in the same section.
- In class, provide students with goals, what is to be prepared for each rehearsal, and information about the organization and content of the recordings. Some students may be recorded giving this information.
- Give recordings to individuals or pairs of students who will work well together and, as part of the learning process, perform for each other, provide good feedback, and answer questions.
- Use recordings as teaching tools for students, who, alone or with classmates, listen to several of their own recordings, evaluate them, and provide improved versions (e.g., improvements in technical accuracy, expressiveness, other criteria or goals specific to students).
- Provide checklists in different formats (typed, braille, large print) with criteria for students to evaluate recorded performances.

For sight-reading printed music, there are a few options for students who are blind or who have low vision. Students can learn exercises from recordings in advance of class sessions (although not really sight-reading), read from braille transcriptions or large-print versions of the music, or engage in an alternative task such as using literary braille to notate what is being sung, a type of dictation exercise using note letters only. On some occasions, there may be benefits for students to learn exercises in advance; if they choose, they may be able to serve as evaluators for their ensemble peers who are reading exercises for the first time.

Many teachers have students who use hearing aids. These devices are worn in the ear canal and amplify frequencies matched to individual hearing losses. With a hearing aid, however, it is not always easy to determine which person you are listening to because of background noise, particularly in a room with a lot of echo. Noise should be reduced in classrooms to the extent possible but can also be reduced by FM systems such as an auditory trainer or loop system.

In FM systems, teachers wear small microphones that amplify and transmit the teachers' voices to students who wear small receiving units. Students can hear the teachers' voices even though the teachers are speaking in normal tones, not looking at the students, or moving around their classrooms. Microphones can be moved easily to students in the classroom or other sound sources.

Students learn how to use and take care of their hearing aids, although some will need assistance keeping them in working order. Teachers can quickly and discreetly assess whether hearing aids or systems are working by using students' names and asking them questions that require sentences and not simply yes-or-no responses.

Students with normal hearing but who have problems attending to spoken information for any length of time can use tape recorders and listen to recordings in a less distracting environment. Other types of devices related to listening are those used primarily in daily-living activities such as text telephone (TTY, the preferred abbreviation for a teletypewriter for persons with hearing or speech difficulties), closed captioning for televisions, flashing lights to indicate telephones or doorbells ringing, and video monitors to show the activities of children in adjacent rooms. Several of these devices and others are useful in classrooms and schools.[23]

Access to computers and on-screen information Computers have become a critical part of many students' academic and personal lives and are playing a more prominent role in music classrooms. Almost all students engage in learning activities that require access to music information found on the Internet and engage in a wide range of music learning activities using computers.

Multiple strategies and individual adaptations will enable all students to participate in computer-related activities, but information presented on computer screens must be accessible, and students must be able to operate desktop and portable computers as independently as possible. I can only scratch the surface here, but several examples will give you some idea of the possibilities for your students.

As a result of Section 508 of the Tech Act of 1998, federal agencies are required to make a range of their electronic and information technology accessible, including software applications and operating systems, Web-based information or applications, desktop and portable computers, among others.[24] Agencies (including schools) in states that receive federal funds under the Tech Act are to be in compliance with Section 508, although it is safe to say that most are not. The technologies in schools have not yet caught up with the requirements.

Most school districts have individuals who serve as consultants for the development of websites that are accessible with options for large print and assistive devices for access.[25] Music teachers may want to recruit interested students in a project to design and develop accessible websites for their music programs and activities. This may be a first in your district.

Information presented on computer screens is accessible because of the original design and program (following Section 508 standards) but also when simple AT adaptations for vision are used, such as magnifications from larger-screen monitors, large type size, or specially designed software that magnifies and reads the text on the screen (screen readers).

For sound, headphones may help a student concentrate on the information. For screen readers, many different programs are available, and you will want to consult your special educator or school technical consultant about programs that are used by some of your students. Essentially, a synthetic or computerized voice "speaks" the information on the screen, although quality and intelligibility vary depending on the software.

Adaptations can also be made to keyboards and other mechanically operated controls. Several software programs will alter operations on the standard keyboard by changing the layout, providing different types of visual or auditory cues for actions, or increasing or decreasing the number of keystrokes required for an action (e.g., using the shift or cap-lock key with another key). Also, for individuals who press too many keys at one time, key guards (metal frames that fit over keyboards) provide more separation between keys for more accurate typing. A few examples of alternative keyboards include on-screen keyboards, mini-keyboards that require less range of motion and an easier touch to operate, programmable keyboards, and keyboards with speech feedback to let students know what they have entered.

As you may imagine, there are many alternatives to the traditional mouse. Examples include touch screens, trackballs, switches, and joysticks (discussed in the next section) and pointing devices such as mouth sticks and head pointers. Also, voice recognition programs can be used to type; words spoken into the microphone appear on the screen, and text can be edited with spoken commands.

Switches and similar devices Electronic and battery-operated devices and equipment can be controlled with body movements (including eye movements and puffs or sips of air using the breath), sounds (voice and other types of sounds), light beams, and switches. Switches and similar devices such as joysticks and slides are perhaps the most flexible, simple, accessible, and inexpensive. Almost all students use these types of devices in games and to operate other equipment, and although you may select a particular device based on some of your students' needs, most likely everyone can use it.[26]

Equipment can be on, be off, or change in degree after activation (e.g., dimmer light switches, volume controls, metronome markings, variable speed or pitch controls on keyboards and recorders). Individuals who operate switches in their homes and classrooms are making choices and manipulating their own environments. Imagine not having the physical capacity to control many aspects of your environment. There are instances when we want to control the CD, the lighting, the air-conditioning system, or the TV remote. AT switches allow individuals to experience more autonomy, make choices, and express preferences—all self-determined behaviors.

Teachers regularly use switches as a way to input a signal to a computer or sound system or to record and play back speech and music. Switches can be of any material or shape (e.g., button, slide, knob, joystick). One commonly used simple switch allows students or teachers to record any sound, voice or music, for playback at the touch of the switch (length of record times can vary). For example, a student will touch the switch for a prerecorded response when it is her turn to sing a phrase, answer a question, indicate a preference, and so on. Although often used by students with multiple disabilities, classmates no doubt can find creative ways to use these switches in activities and for performances.

Position and seating As I am writing this book, I sit in a comfortable, padded, ergonomic chair that is positioned on a mat for easy rolling. Underneath the desk is a foot rest that takes the strain out of my back and helps circulation. I still need to get out of my chair and change position from time to time. Devices and materials for seating and positioning are intended not only to help students be more comfortable but to give them more control over movements, let them perform tasks more easily and independently, and prevent further injury. Remaining in one position for any period of time is problematic for anyone.

When students are physically comfortable in a seated position, they will have longer attention spans and work more efficiently and effectively on the task at hand. For students with limited use of trunk and leg muscles who are unable to use wheelchairs, mobile standers will help them approximate a seated position and face forward in their classrooms. Also, students who cannot stand for long periods of time in a performance or rehearsal may benefit from specially designed chairs that attach to risers.[27]

The design of chairs and wheelchairs should consider students' physical sizes and needs. As mentioned, bolsters, foam cushioning, and other materials can be used for positioning and can help students feel more comfortable. You may want to keep some of these materials in your room. Many of us have found beanbag chairs a welcome change for younger students who use a wheelchair throughout the day; it's a comfortable change for them physically and a way for them to look at other classmates who are sitting on the floor. Of course, more than one beanbag is desirable, not only to "normalize" the environment, but also to make more children happy.

Throughout class sessions, observe your students carefully to see when they are experiencing discomfort and what changes of position will help them continue to work and participate more easily. You will need to know how to transfer students from one position to another and may need the assistance of your paraprofessional. Through collaboration and careful observation of students, you will know when it is time to assist the student, how to assist, and if and when you need to ask another adult for help.

AT adaptations need not be expensive, electronic, or complex. As you have read, several technologies are inexpensive, off-the-shelf items or can be made easily. When appropriate, engage the student and all of your class members in problem solving—to think of ways to turn pages more quickly, carry both music and an instrument, introduce music to the audience at a performance, all as independently as possible. Consultants, particularly music therapists, occupational therapists, and physical therapists, are invaluable resources regarding AT devices and adaptations, but we should not ignore the creativity and wisdom of our own students.

Support from Others (Classmates, Paraprofessionals)

Almost everyone benefits socially and emotionally when supported by others. For some students, personal support is imperative (e.g., interpreters, healthcare professionals, counselors, therapists). Professionally trained adults who provide this support are invaluable resources for teachers, parents, and, of course, the students they serve. I focus in this book on support provided by classmates for one another and, as needed, support from paraprofessionals. These topics were discussed in depth in chapter 3's Principle 2 (peer interactions) and Principle 4 (collaboration). They are reviewed here briefly, since they are also elements for consideration in the design of learning environments to meet students' needs.

When music teachers develop a culture of inclusion in their programs, classmates become natural supports for one another, and the practice of support becomes natural, a part of the regular classroom routine. In some cases, support can come from tutoring and cross-age tutoring. Support from same-age classmates helps to build friendships and a social network, but there are also positive benefits when support comes from older typical students who can serve as models for their classmates and for younger students.

You've read about the benefits that positive peer interactions have for students' overall academic, social, and emotional development. Based on students' needs and characteristics, use partners and small groups as the instructional format for some activities. As students accomplish music goals with supportive partners or in groups, they will develop feelings of competence, self-efficacy, and self-esteem. Also, carefully structured and extended positive peer interactions can lead to more positive attitudes of classmates toward peers who are often isolated or ignored. Seat assignments, group assignments, and assignment of peer assistants need to be considered carefully, since students differ in their ability to remain on-task when they are next to classmates with disabilities, and they also differ in their attitudes and types of interactions with them.

Call on paraprofessionals only when necessary. In some situations, only knowledgeable adults should provide support and assistance (e.g., repositioning a child in a wheelchair, calming a student experiencing extreme anxiety), although to the extent possible and appropriate, peer support is preferred.

Whether support is provided by classmates or paraprofessionals, music teachers need to define their roles; they need to know when and how to help and when and how to fade support. To do this to the degree appropriate and as the situation demands, classmates and paraprofessionals must have relevant information regarding students' specific needs along with pertinent information about students' musical preferences, skills, and knowledge.Sensitive, wise teachers will know what information should be given to classmates and also whether the teacher or the student is the best source of that information. Remember the student who learned to play steel pan in high school? After graduation, in his role as an assistant to a music teacher in another school, he felt it was important to meet with the students in the band and talk with them about his disability. He wanted them to have an understanding of some of the ways he could help them and when he might encounter some problems and need their help. What courage. He was a hero to his classmates, his teachers, his parents.

Thinking Ahead

As you rightly assume, this section has to do with future actions—ways to think about universal strategies and adaptations that you have developed and implemented. As you have read in the section on assessment, important questions need to be asked about each individual student. Is the student making progress? Why or why not? Did these specific strategies or adaptations contribute to the student's progress? What needs to be done next? In thinking ahead, you will want to:

- Use authentic assessments to determine the students' progress and the effectiveness of strategies and adaptations; make changes as necessary.

- Share and discuss outcomes with parents or guardians, team members, and students, as appropriate.
- Continue collaboration and develop, implement, and assess new strategies and adaptations.
- Focus on the degree to which students develop musically and experience meaningful musical lives in and beyond school.

Assessment keeps us honest about what teaching should be about; it keeps us focused on students' learning and progress and guards against the idea that being busy in the classroom is teaching. Teaching occurs only when students learn what was intended to be taught. That's real teaching.

Almost all teachers ask hard questions about their own effectiveness, and most are willing to accept failures and make appropriate changes based on their observations and feedback from knowledgeable and caring individuals. The following outlines a broad plan to approach assessment:

- Observe students engaged in the activity or task; observe frequently and in different contexts (with other students, materials, etc.).
- Make notes (keep data) on successes and problems.
- Invite music therapists, special education teachers, paraprofessionals, or students from local colleges or universities to observe and collect data.
- Consult regularly with music therapists, special education teachers, and parents.
- Continue, revise, or discontinue strategies and adaptations based on learning outcomes (data).
- Present and discuss outcomes at meetings and in informal discussions with teachers, parents, and, as appropriate, the individual student.

For more specific ideas, I've constructed a list of questions that you can use to assess your students' progress and the effectiveness of your strategies and adaptations (see box 4.10). Many of these questions can also be used to head off problems, to ask yourself before developing new ideas. For quick and frequent assessments of individual students, you can always ask yourself the short questions presented much earlier in this book:

> Where is the student?
> What is the student doing?
> With whom is the student interacting?
> How is the student feeling?

Box 4.10

ASSESSING EFFECTIVENESS OF STRATEGIES AND ADAPTATIONS

If universal strategies and/or adaptations are necessary for students to perform music tasks and activities successfully, the questions below can be used to help guide decisions for their development and to assess their effectiveness.

TASK AND/OR ACTIVITY

- What is the rationale for selecting this task or activity?
- What is the purpose of the strategy or adaptation?
- Is the task or activity a priority for the student?
- Will the student be motivated by this task or activity?
- Is the performance standard appropriate?
- If the task or activity requires a modification of a music goal, will the modified task or activity be meaningful for the student?

OUTCOMES AFTER IMPLEMENTATION

- Is the student successful when the strategy or adaptation is implemented?
- Will successful outcomes transfer to other situations and environments?
- Is the student participating in meaningful ways and as fully and independently as possible?
- Are there additional positive outcomes for the student when the task or activity is completed successfully? Social outcomes? Outcomes associated with self-determination?
- Can this strategy or adaptation be used successfully in other tasks or activities?

COLLABORATIONS

- Do other individuals have useful information about the effectiveness of this strategy or adaptation?
- How does the student feel about the outcomes, and what suggestions does the student have regarding this or other strategies or adaptations?

Every meaningful, successful learning outcome for students contributes to their quality of life. I hear the excitement in teachers' voices when they tell me stories about their students who are learning to sing, play instruments, interact with their peers, smile, and show pride in their accomplishments. These are accomplishments for their teachers, too!

Although the bar must continue to be raised for students to reach important long-term goals, we cannot underestimate the importance of any achievement, no matter how small it may seem initially.

In inclusive music programs, learning differences are considered along a continuum, expectations are high for all students, and diversity is valued. The degree to which all students develop musically and experience meaningful musical lives in and beyond school is influenced greatly by their music teachers. The goal for inclusive music education classes is for all students to participate happily and successfully. Achieving that goal becomes possible when teachers design accessible, effective music programs by (1) creating a quality music program and a culture of inclusion; (2) gathering information about their students, their music teaching environment, and activities; (3) planning and implementing flexible, effective instructional strategies in a universal approach to meet students' diverse needs; and (4) assessing students' progress. I realize the magnitude of the challenge I present, but teachers can meet this challenge with the understanding that much of what we know about learning and teaching applies to students across the spectra of abilities.

It is appropriate that this chapter ends with a theme that frames the opening of this book. We view children as members of multiple groups defined by any number of factors and also view them as individuals with unique characteristics and needs. The principal features of learning experiences that effectively prepare children for meaningful musical lives beyond school are not differentiated among age and ability levels; they are universal, in the sense that they engage diverse groups of children in common experiences and yet recognize the unique needs of individual students. How can this be done? Teachers make this possible—individual teachers who recognize the tremendous potential for including everyone, every day.

APPENDIX A

Historical Timeline

SELECTED FEDERAL LAWS, PROGRAMS, ACTIONS, AND EVENTS PERTINENT TO INCLUSION PHILOSOPHY AND PRACTICES

1642, 1647 The Massachusetts School of Law of 1642 gives community leaders the authority to ensure that children would learn to read and understand religious principles and the law of the land, and the 1647 law requires townships of fifty or more households to hire a teacher for their children.

1700s The concept of educating persons with disabilities is introduced by physician Benjamin Rush, who would be designated the "Father of American Psychiatry" by the American Psychiatric Association in 1965. Among his contributions are reforms for the care of people with mental illness at the Pennsylvania Hospital and as a teacher at the medical school of the College of Philadelphia.

The singing school movement and singing schools begin with itinerant singing teachers (masters) who teach for a fee. This movement will last well into the late nineteenth century.

1776 Articles of Confederation (the first Constitution of the United States) formally unites the thirteen colonies under one government with articles concerning representation, taxation, and the disposition of lands. Submitted to the Second Continental Congress (1776), adopted (1777), and ratified by the thirteen states (1781). It will be in effect until the Constitution becomes the law of the land in 1789.

Declaration of Independence, drafted in writing by Thomas Jefferson, is officially adopted by the Second Continental Congress, July 4, and is signed by almost all members by August 2. The Declaration justifies a break with Britain and includes statements regarding the necessity for government to have consent of its people and the responsibility of government to its people. The second paragraph begins, "We hold these truths to be self-evident, that all men are created equal, that they are endowed by their Creator with certain unalienable Rights, that among these are Life, Liberty, and the pursuit of Happiness."

1779 The first plan for a state-supported school system is proposed by Thomas Jefferson to educate the poor; the plan is rejected because of the refusal of well-to-do citizens to pay taxes to educate the poor.

1783 End of the American Revolution, a rebellion against acts of Britain imposed on. the thirteen colonies and a war for the rights of the individual and for the establishment of a democratic government.

Formation of philanthropic societies to protect mainstream values held at the time against marginal societal groups; societies would lead to the development of public schools and segregated rehabilitative institutions, training institutions, and schools for people with disabilities. Early schools and training institutions are structured similarly to asylums in Europe. Segregated institutions of persons with disabilities will continue to grow in number and size during the late nineteenth century until the middle of the twentieth century.

Samuel Gridley Howe advocates for educational programs for children with disabilities and not simply social assistance and control under the organizational structure of asylums where they reside.

1787 George Washington is elected president of the Constitutional Convention, meeting at Independence Hall in Philadelphia. State delegates adopt the document known as the Constitution of the United States. The first ten amendments, known as the Bill of Rights, would be added in 1791 to provide additional rights to individuals beyond the seven articles, and the last amendment would be added in 1971, for a total of twenty-seven.

Northwest Ordinance authorizes land grants for the establishment of educational institutions.

1789 The first-known publication in America, author anonymous, on the relationship of music to health and healing appears as an article in the *Columbian Magazine*. The article is entitled "Music Physically Considered." Dissertations on the topic of music in therapy are written by Edwin Atlee and Samuel Mathews, students of physician Benjamin Rush.

1806 Jean-Marc-Gaspard Itard's book describing the use of music to develop auditory discrimination skills with a child found in the wilderness is published. The book is called *The Wild Boy of Aveyron*.

1817 One of the first special programs of education for persons with disabilities is established by Thomas Gallaudet at the American Asylum for the Education and Instruction of the Deaf and Dumb in Connecticut.

1829 The New England Asylum for the Education of the Blind is established in Massachusetts.

1838 Lowell Mason, church musician and music teacher, persuades the School Committee in Boston to include music as a regular subject in the curriculum, justified on the basis of its intellectual, moral, and physical benefits for children.

1841 Dorthea Dix advocates for the separation of people with disabilities from others who reside in penitentiaries and poorhouses. Her efforts helped lead to the establishment of state institutions in the United States.

1846 The Experimental School for Teaching and Training Idiotic Children is established in Massachusetts.

1847 *American Annals of the Deaf* is first published. William Wolcott Turner and David Ely Bartlett will advocate for music education for persons with hearing impairments in an article published in the *Annuals* in 1848.

1848 Horace Mann, secretary of the Massachusetts Board of Education, argues for a public school system and presents his twelfth annual report with cardinal principles of public school education to the board. His reports are the first documents to urge standardization of schools through purpose, curriculum, libraries, training of teachers, and so on.

1849 The Massachusetts School for Idiotic and Feeble-Minded Youth is established around this time as a result of the efforts of humanitarian Samuel Howe, director of the Perkins School for the Blind. 1849 The Massachusetts Supreme Court rules that segregated schools are permissible under the state's constitution.

1852 The Massachusetts Compulsory Attendance Act is the first compulsory school attendance act and requires children between ages eight and fourteen to attend school during at least twelve weeks, six weeks to be consecutive.

1852–1918 Compulsory schooling is legislated in all states by 1918. The government appropriates funding for the growth of public "common schools" for most children to attend. Segregation continues, with separate schools and institutions for African Americans, American Indians, and students with visible and significant disabilities. Separate schools are established for students who are blind or deaf or who have physical disabilities; students with developmental disabilities reside in large state hospitals. By 1905, most states have at least one residential institution for children and adults with disabilities.

1855 Kentucky sets up a printing house for people who are blind; this will eventually become the American Printing House for the Blind.

1857 The US Supreme Court upholds slavery in *Dred Scott v. Sandford*. The decision is regarded as significant among the causes of the American Civil War.

1861–1865 The American Civil War

1863 The Emancipation Proclamation goes into effect.

1865 The Thirteenth Amendment to the US Constitution is adopted, abolishing slavery in the United States.

1866 The Civil Rights Act of 1866 grants citizenship to freed slaves, passes over President Andrew Johnson's veto, and is the first of several Civil Rights Acts.

John Langdon Down publishes the first clinical description for what is now known as Down Syndrome.

1867 The Department of Education Act authorizes the establishment of the US Department of Education. 1868 The Fourteenth Amendment to the US Constitution requires due process and equal protection of the laws. Section 1 grants citizenship to all persons born in the United States and further states: "No State shall make or enforce any law which shall abridge the privileges or immunities of citizens of the United States; nor shall any State deprive any person of life, liberty, or property, without due process of law; nor deny to any person within its jurisdiction the equal protection of the laws."

1869 First named Little's Disease, the British surgeon William Little changes the name to cerebral paralysis, now cerebral palsy.

1870 The Fifteenth Amendment to the US Constitution grants the right to vote to all citizens regardless of "race, color, or previous condition of servitude."

1875 Congress passes the Civil Rights Act of 1875, which bans racial discrimination in public accommodations.

1883 The Supreme Court strikes down the Civil Rights Act of 1875; discrimination in public accommodations is deemed constitutional.

1896 The *Plessy v. Ferguson* Supreme Court decrees that racial segregation is constitutional, leading to the phrase "separate but equal."

1900–1930 The eugenics movement encourages public acceptance of segregation, special classes, tracking, and even sterilization.

Separate classes within schools are taught by special education teachers; general education and special education teachers are perceived to be different in training and in interest; separate administrative models support segregated, parallel teaching environments, curricula, and instructional models. Enrollment in special classes increases dramatically as children with disabilities are identified. Special classes will remain the preferred system well into the 1960s.

1906 Eugen Blueler identifies behaviors he defines as autistic. Leo Kanner will identify the syndrome of autism in 1943.

1907 The Music Supervisors Conference is founded, now known as the National Association for Music Education (NAfME).

1909 The first in a series of conferences hosted by Presidents of the United States (conferences currently called White House Conferences on Children and Youth), the White House Conference on the Care of Dependent Children under Theodore Roosevelt opposes the institutionalization of dependent and neglected children.

1910–1930 The movement of children from institutions to separate classes in public schools increases, and separate special education classes are the social norm. Rapid increases in placements in schools leads to increased services, state appropriations, and, in 1930, the largest federal conference on the welfare of children.

1913 The American Association of Social Workers is formed, and by 1920, social work will be a well-established profession.

1918 The Soldier Rehabilitation Act, also known as the Smith-Sears Veterans Rehabilitation Act of 1918, is the first legislation to provide vocational rehabilitation as a means to assist veterans with disabilities to return to daily living and employment. The Smith-Fess Citizens Vocational Rehabilitation Act of 1920 will provide vocational rehabilitation assistance to nonveterans with disabilities.

1920 The American Civil Liberties Union (ACLU) is founded. Among the founding members is Helen Keller (1880–1968).

Helen Keller forms the American Foundation for the Blind.

1924–1979 The eugenics movement brings forced sterilization to more than sixty thousand individuals. The Supreme Court decision in *Buck v. Bell* (1927) upholds Virginia's 1924 sterilization law. More than thirty-three states participate in the sterilization of individuals thought to be undesirable.

1928–1929 Willem van de Wall, musician, scholar, and professor of music education at Louisiana State University, advocates for a music curriculum for all children, including those with disabilities. His articles and books (including *Music in Institutions* in 1936 and *Music in Hospitals* in 1946) will provide a foundation for music therapy theory, practice, and training.

1930 By this time, legislation has passed in sixteen states for the preparation of special education teachers; most are certification programs consisting of supplementary training beyond the elementary degree. The enthusiasm for the teacher preparation and the quality of services seen during the 1920s begins to decline. Apathy is attributed in part to the economic conditions of the Great Depression. Conditions in special education classrooms are reported to be deplorable, and stigmatization and social rejection of children with disabilities increase.

President Herbert Hoover calls for a White House Conference on Child Health and Protection. The largest conference on child welfare to date, it results in the Children's Charter, speaking to the therapeutic and educational needs of exceptional children for the first time. 1931–1936 Advancements take place in production and distribution of braille reading materials and textbooks through the National Institute for the Blind and the American Printing House for the Blind.

1932 When Frankin Roosevelt is elected President of the United States, he and his advisors hide his disability; he contracted polio in 1921.

1935 The Social Security Act is passed and makes grants available for states to assist children and adults with disabilities.

1944 Michigan State University is the first university to offer a music therapy degree program.

1947 *Mendéz, et al. v. Westminster School District of Orange County* upholds that segregated schooling for Mexican American and Mexican students in California is unconstitutional and establishes an important precedent for *Brown v. Board of Education* in 1954.

1950 The National Association for Retarded Children (now called the Arc) is founded. Advocacy groups of the association will challenge restrictions of segregated institutions, schools, and classrooms during the 1950s and 1960s.

The National Association for Music Therapy (NAMT) is founded. When NAMT merges with a younger organization in 1998, the name of the organization will be changed to the American Music Therapy Association (AMTA).

1954 In a unanimous decision, the Supreme Court holds in *Brown v. Board of Education* that separate schools are "inherently unequal," thus overturning *Plessy v. Ferguson* and the "separate but equal" doctrine.

1957 The Soviet Union launches Sputnik. Responses from local, state, and federal US governments focus policy and educational practices on school reform and basic skills—reading, writing, and mathematics.

1958 The Captioned Films Act of 1958 (P.L. 85-905) and the amended act in 1961 (P.L. 87-715) support the production and distribution of accessible films.

1959 The Training of Professional Personnel Act of 1959 (P.L. 85-926) provides grants to prepare teachers of children with intellectual disabilities.

1960s Egalitarianism and humanism are fervent in the actions of organizations and individuals fighting against discrimination of blacks, women, Latinos, and persons with disabilities. With the deep questioning of the mistreatment of groups of citizens by the public along with state and federal agencies, some of the injustices are addressed, and slowly, positive changes are seen in policies and financial support. In part, the actions of President John F. Kennedy and Senator Hubert Humphrey (both who had a family member with an intellectual disability) lead to federal and state assistance to expand special education services and humanitarian support, actions that are continued during the Lyndon Johnson administration.

1961 The Teachers of the Deaf Act of 1961 (P.L. 87-276) provides grants to prepare teachers of children who are deaf or hard of hearing.

1962 President Kennedy appoints a twenty-six-member panel to examine issues and solutions related to people with intellectual disabilities. The report and recommendations from the Panel on Mental Retardation signal the beginning of a series of actions by the federal government with programs in the areas of disabilities, civil rights, and education.

1963 The first bilingual education program in public schools is offered through a grant from the Ford Foundation.

Cesar Chavez and Dolores Huerta found the United Farm Workers (UFW) in Delano, California. The social justice movement gains momentum for farm workers in the United States. The grape boycott lasts five years and calls international attention to the plight of Mexican American workers.

President Kennedy forms the Division of Handicapped Children and Youth, the first government agency dedicated to the education of children with disabilities and gifted children. (Services are currently provided by the Office of Special Education and Rehabilitation Services, OSERS, and the Office of Special Education Programs, OSEP, which administers the Individuals with Disabilities Education Act, IDEA.)

The Mental Retardation Facilities and Community Mental Health Centers Construction Act of 1963 (P.L. 88-164) provides early assistance for persons with intellectual disabilities and, when amended, is renamed the Developmental Disabilities and Bill of Rights Act (DD Act).

Samuel A. Kirk introduces the term *learning disabilities*.

1964 The Civil Rights Act of 1964 (P.L. 88-352) prohibits discrimination based on race, color, religion, sex, or national origin. Funding is provided for in-service programs for assisting instructional staff at schools to solve issues related to desegregation.

1965 The Elementary and Secondary Education Act of 1965 (P.L. 89-10) provides the first authorized federal grants for elementary and secondary school programs for children of low-income families; resources, textbooks, instructional materials; educational centers and services; and educational research and research training.

The Voting Rights Act of 1965 (P.L. 89-110) is passed, and its language loosely follows the language of the Fifteenth Amendment prohibiting the denial or abridgment of the right to vote based on literacy tests.

Willowbrook State School, the largest institution in the United States houses over 6,000 children with disabilities. After his visit, Senator Robert F. Kennedy describes it as a "snake pit." The deinstitutionalization movement and negative public opinion about state schools leads to its closing, but not until 1987.

1966 The Elementary and Secondary Education Act of 1966 (P.L. 89-750) provides the first federal grant program for children and youths with disabilities. It is repealed with the passage of the first Education of the Handicapped Act of 1970.

1965–1966 The National Technical Institute for the Deaf Act (P.L. 89-313) and the Model Secondary School for the Deaf Act (P.L. 89-694) provide for operations for a postsecondary education and technical training of individuals who are deaf and authorize the establishment and operation, by Gallaudet College, of a model secondary school.

1967 The Tanglewood Symposium, a MENC-sponsored event, results in the publication of the Tanglewood Declaration. Among the agreed-upon statements from participants from a wide range of disciplines is the call for a "greater emphasis on helping the individual student fulfill his needs, goals, and potentials" and music education as a means to assist children with social problems and children in the "inner city" or "other areas with culturally deprived individuals."

1968 The Elementary and Secondary Education Act Amendments of 1968 (P.L. 90-247) authorize grants to states for programs for children with disabilities, model centers for deaf blind children, recruitment of personnel, and bilingual education.

The Handicapped Children's Early Education Assistance Act (P.L. 90-538) authorizes preschool and early-education programs for children with disabilities.

Latino students in Los Angeles engage in walkouts protesting discriminatory actions and unequal treatment in schools.

The Supreme Court orders states to dismantle segregated school systems, "root and branch."

1969 The Indian Civil Rights Act of 1969 prohibits state governments from assuming jurisdiction over lands owned by American Indians (Native American lands) and extends American Indians the same rights held by whites since the addition of the Bill of Rights to the Constitution.

1970 The Education of the Handicapped Act (P.L. 91-230), the first of the EHA acts, includes a grant program to stimulate states to develop special education resources and prepare special education teachers.

1971 The *Swann v. Charlotte Mecklenburg Board of Education* decision by the Supreme Court upholds busing of students to achieve integration, and establishes magnet schools.

1972 *Pennsylvania Assn. for Retarded Children v. Commonwealth of Pennsylvania,* a class action law suit, establishes rights of all children labeled as mentally retarded to a free and appropriate education.

Mills v. Board of Education of District of Columbia, a class action law suit, establishes rights of all children labeled as having a disability (in this case, children labeled as having behavioral problems, mental retardation, emotional disturbance, or hyperactivity represent interests of similar children in D.C. schools) to a free and appropriate education to meet the individual needs of children, regardless of the severity of the disability.

Title IX of the Educational Amendments of 1972 prohibits sex discrimination in any educational program that receives federal financial assistance.

1973 Section 504 of the Rehabilitation Act of 1973 (P.L. 93-112), a civil rights act, prohibits discrimination against people with disabilities under any program or activities receiving federal financial assistance. It is the first federal act to make discrimination against individuals with disabilities illegal and contributes to the beginning of the disabilities rights movement. Although passed in 1973, it will not be implemented officially until 1977, following pressure from activist and advocacy groups. It will be amended in 1992 (P.L. 102-469).

1974 The Family Educational Rights and Privacy Act of 1974 (P.L. 93-380) is passed. FERPA gives parents and eligible children the right to review and copy educational records, to have records explained, and to request that records be changed if they believe they are in error; records may not be destroyed by any agency if they are requested to be reviewed by eligible parents and children.

The Education of the Handicapped Children Act Amendments (P.L. 93-330) substantially increases aid for states that began with EHA 1970. States are required to establish a timetable to show when children with disabilities would achieve full educational opportunities in schools, in addition to other procedural safeguards. Within a year, EHA will be amended again, resulting in the landmark Education of All Handicapped Children Act of 1975 (P.L. 94-142).

People First, the first national organization for self-advocacy is founded.

1975 The Education of All Handicapped Children Act (P.L. 94-142) provides for a free appropriate education (FAPE) in the least restrictive environment (LRE) for all children with disabilities (ages three through twenty-one). The law requires an individualized education program (IEP), nondiscriminatory testing, and due process procedures.

TASH is established as the first organization advocating for human rights and inclusion for people with significant disabilities and support needs—those most vulnerable to segregation abuse, neglect and institutionalization.

The Indian Self-Determination and Education Assistance Act (P.L. 93-642) provides for increased participation of American Indians in the establishment and conduct of their educational programs and services.

1983 The Education of the Handicapped Act Amendments of 1983 (P.L. 98-199) creates parent training and information centers through federal funding and expands financial initiatives for transition services and to expand services for children from birth to three years of age.

A Nation at Risk: The Imperative for Education Reform is published. The report, one of the first in a series from governmental commissions, criticizes the poor quality of American education. The arts are identified as important to personal, educational, and occupational goals.

1986 The Education of the Handicapped Act Amendments of 1986 (P.L. 99-457) (Early Intervention Amendments), Part B of IDEA, requires all states electing to participate (all did) to begin serving children by age three by October 1991. Part H develops a program for infants, toddlers, and families. An individualized family service plan (IFSP) is required for each child served.

The Handicapped Children's Protection Act of 1986 (P.L. 99-372) allows parents of children with disabilities to collect attorney's fees in cases brought under the Education of the Handicapped Act (EHA) and provides that the EHA does not preempt other laws, such as Section 504 of the Rehabilitation Act of 1973.

1987 The Developmental Disabilities Assistance and Bill of Rights Act Amendments of 1987 (P.L. 100-146) authorize grants to support planning, coordination, and delivery of services to people with developmental disabilities. They provide for the establishment of university-affiliated facilities (UAFs) to address the needs of persons with developmental disabilities. Developmental disabilities councils coordinate and integrate the provision of services in the least restrictive environment. Additional amendments in 1990,

1994, and 2000 will strengthen provisions to promote independence, productivity, and integration and inclusion into the community given adequate support.

1988 The Technology-Related Assistance for Individuals with Disabilities Act (P.L. 100-407), the Tech Act, authorizes funding that permits states to develop programs and systems for assistive technology (e.g., motorized wheelchairs, computer systems for communication) and technological assistance to facilitate independence. Assistive technology (AT) can be included as a related service in the IEP.

1990 The Americans with Disabilities Act (P.L. 101-336), ADA, extends provisions of Section 504 to include access and reasonable accommodation in employment and services to private and public sectors, including transportation and telecommunications.

The EHA is reauthorized and renamed the Individuals with Disabilities Education Act of 1990 (P.L. 101-476); includes many provisions from earlier laws. IDEA defines AT devices and services and makes them available as part of the IEP; it requires transition plans for employment or postsecondary education.

1990–1991 The Carl D. Perkins Vocational and Applied Technology Education Act (P.L. 101-392 and P.L. 102-103) requires individuals with disabilities to have equal access to recruitment, enrollment, and placement activities in vocational education and equal access to a full range of vocational education programs available to other students. This law is closely interwoven with IDEA for youth who receive special education and related services. Students' IEPs are to provide educational goals and programs leading to work in a technologically advanced society.

1992 The Rehabilitation Act Amendments of 1992 (P.L. 102-469) strengthens the 1973 Act by increasing opportunities for individuals with disabilities to be actively involved in their vocational rehabilitation program by exercising choice related to the selection of their employment goals, services, and service providers.

1997 With the Individuals with Disabilities Education Act of 1997 (P.L. 105-17), IDEA amendments strengthen the principles of the 1975 law by emphasizing postschool outcomes and including the following: participation in general education and the regular classroom as documented on the IEP; regular education teacher added to the IEP team; age for transition plan no later than fourteen with process to begin no later than age sixteen; assessment of academic progress through state and district assessment programs with AT provisions for assessment and instruction; inclusion of provisions for homeless children with disabilities; discipline of students addressed.

The National Assessment of Educational Progress (NAEP) publishes its *1997 Arts Report Card* showing an overall poor performance of eighth-grade students in the area of music—creativity, responding, and performance. Low percentages of participation are seen for school ensembles. An assessment will be conducted in 2008 at a smaller scale, but few meaningful comparisons can be made; ensemble participation will remain low.

1998 The Assistive Technology Act of 1998 (P.L. 105-394) replaces the original 1988 Tech Act and addresses further the AT needs of individuals with disabilities with increasing focus on policy changes, the removal of systemic barriers that impede the acquisition and use of AT devices, and advocacy.

An amendment to Section 508 of the Rehabilitation Act of 1973 requires the federal government to purchase and deploy new instructional technology and other electronic products that are accessible or compatible with AT used by people with disabilities.

2000 The Development Disabilities Assistance and Bill of Rights Act of 2000 (P.L. 106-402) provides for adult community services, individualized supports, and other forms of assistance focusing not only on independence, productivity, integration, and inclusion (prior law) but also on self-determination (new law) in culturally competent programs. Among the provisions regarding access to community-based living options, child care, and transportation is access to and use of recreational, leisure, and social opportunities in the most integrated settings in order to enrich participation in community life.

The Children's Health Act of 2000 (P.L. 106-310) contains provisions for federal research into several specific disabilities and provisions for pediatric research initiatives at the National Institutes of Health.

Vision 2020: The Housewright Symposium on the Future of Music Education is published. Based on the model of the Tanglewood Symposium of 1967, this project results in the Housewright Declaration, which includes a statement that "All persons, regardless of age, cultural heritage, ability, venue, or financial circumstances deserve to participate fully in the best music experiences possible."

2001 The No Child Left Behind Act of 2001 (P.L. 107-110) results in comprehensive reauthorization of the Elementary and Secondary

Education Act of 1965, with focus on testing, accountability, parental choice, and early reading. NCLB is subject to reauthorization which may result in amendments.

Following the terrorist attacks on September 11, Arab Americans and others of Middle Eastern descent experience increasing discrimination in the United States.

2004 The Individuals with Disabilities Improvement Education Act of 2004 (P.L. 108-446), still known as IDEA, emphasizes access to general education and experiences with typical children in regular classrooms and nonacademic activities; emphasis is on qualified personnel and inclusion of students in state and local assessments.

2005 Rosa Parks dies at the age of ninety-two. Parks was the catalyst for the Montgomery Bus Boycott of 1955, and her ill treatment—being jailed for refusing to give up her seat to a white rider—helped point to the injustices of discrimination.

2006 The Combating Autism Act of 2006 (P.L. 109-416) authorizes almost $1 billion through 2011 in federal funding for autism-related research, early detection, and intervention. Reauthorized in 2011 for three years and renamed Autism CARES, on August 8, 2014, President Obama signs the bipartisan bill authorizing $1.3 billion over the next five years.

The American Association on Mental Retardation changes its name to the American Association on Intellectual and Developmental Disabilities (AAIDD). Although *intellectual disability* is the preferred term, AAIDD points to the important fact that intellectual disability and mental retardation definitions should be considered synonymous, since *mental retardation* continues to be used in some laws and public policy to determine eligibility for state and federal programs.

2008 The Americans with Disabilities Act Amendments Act of 2008 (P.L. 110-325), originally enacted in 1990, continues to prohibit discrimination and ensure equal opportunity for persons with disabilities in employment, state and local government services, public accommodations, commercial facilities, and transportation. The ADAAA (still known as ADA) also mandates the establishment of TDD/telephone relay services. Amendments make major changes to the way the definition of disability was interpreted in the past and apply to both the ADA and the Section 504 of the Rehabilitation Act of 1973.

2010 Rosa's Law (P.L. 111-256) officially changes language in federal laws from "mental retardation" to "intellectual disability" and an "individual with an intellectual disability." Signed into law by President Barack Obama, it is named after Rosa Marcellino, a young girl who attended school in Maryland and whose parents challenged her school's labeling of their daughter. They worked to pass state legislation to that effect, and after passage at the state level, Senator Barbara Mikulski introduced the same bill at the federal level.

2013–2014 The Keeping All Students Safe Act is introduced in the House in May 2013 (H.R.1893) and in the Senate (S.2036) in February, 2014. If passed by Congress, the law would establish the first federal standards to protect students from misuse of physical restraint and seclusion of student in schools and ensure the safety of everyone in the classroom. To read more about the bill, see the website for TASH at tash.org, and track the latest developments of this and other bills at the website for the Congress, congress.gov.

2014 In a court decision involving a person with an intellectual disability, the US Supreme Court ends their use of the term "mental retardation." After Rosa's Law altering language in federal documents, the Supreme Court is the last major national institution to adopt language that self-advocates and organizations have been urging for decades.

Note: Find updates about laws at the website for the US Department of Education, www.ed.gov, and the government's official web portal, www.usa.gov

APPENDIX B

From Exclusion to Inclusion

History gives us perspective. It gives us a picture of the past and provides some way for us to predict and even determine the future. Where have we been? Where are we now? Where do we want to be?

You remember history classes and the seeming importance teachers gave to events with dates in time. People were a part of those past events, but most became known to us only as the French, the soldiers, the women, the Congress, the workers, and so on. Because of talented teachers, pictures, and videos, we began to understand the interactions of events and ordinary people and how they survived, or did not survive, during the American Civil War, the Great Depression, the forced slavery and internment of Americans, the civil rights marches, and many more. Our emotional response was stronger to events when we knew more about the individuals who, through selfless acts of courage, improved the lives of future generations of men, women, and children.

Think of yourself in time now, as you read this page. Today has a date, and events are occurring as you read. Are they significant events in your life? Are they significant in the lives of others? If history is to become alive, we must think of it in human terms. We must think of the lives of people in times past and the actions, the drama, and the human emotion attached to those extraordinary times. The timeline in appendix A gives you some sense of history as it relates to the struggles of individuals to improve quality of life.

Quality of life, no matter how conceptualized, is the driving force behind sociopolitical changes that have positively influenced the lives of generations of individuals, their education, employment, living environments, and day-to-day activities. Overall, we can say that no particular educational system and no systematic teaching of music was in place before the early nineteenth century, segregation dominated the nineteenth century and much of the twentieth century, and civil and educational rights for persons with disabilities began with advocacy and legislation throughout the latter part of the twentieth century and continues to the present.

For many who were marginalized by society, improvements in their lives were a result of protections granted by laws—constitutional and new laws. On a smaller scale, the lives of children were improved by the day-to-day efforts of parents, teachers, and unsung heroes. Whether on a large scale affecting millions of individuals or a smaller scale affecting the life of one child, history is being made. The essay in this appendix discusses some of these events as a story of people and times leading to our present-day inclusive music classrooms.

EARLY PRECURSORS TO SEPARATE EDUCATIONAL SERVICES

Widespread segregation in living conditions began after the Revolutionary War and with the development of philanthropic societies whose members were the affluent and powerful citizens of the new nation. As a means of social and political control, many marginal groups were forced to live in segregated institutions, where the "less desirable" members of society could remain out of public view.

Philanthropic societies were formed in 1783 for the sole purpose of protecting mainstream values against marginal societal groups. The development of public schools was one way of passing on these values to citizens deemed worthy. Public schools for some children existed before the Revolutionary War, as documented by two Massachusetts School Laws, one in 1642, which gave community leaders the authority to ensure that children would learn to read and understand religious principles and laws of the land, and another in 1647, which required every township of at least fifty households to hire a teacher for their children. By the early 1700s, children were also attending "singing schools" led by itinerant singing masters. The public, intent on improving the poor singing in their churches, supported teachers of singing well into the late nineteenth century. Education and music education (singing) was valued, at least for some.[1]

From the founding of this country and for more than one hundred years after that, education for children with disabilities was nonexistent. This was a time of massive neglect. During the 1700s, prominent physician Benjamin Rush, educator and humanitarian, advocated for a free public education for every child, including those with disabilities. His efforts, at least for persons with disabilities, were largely unsuccessful, as were the efforts of Thomas Jefferson in 1779, when he put forward his plan to educate the poor. Well-to-do citizens saw no need to pay taxes that would go toward educating people who were poor or who had disabilities. Even though values were put forward in 1776 exalting "Life, Liberty, and the Pursuit of Happiness," some groups were disenfranchised.

During this period, the quality of life for people with disabilities depended capriciously on the favors and goodness of others. Fortunate children were cared for and informally educated by family members and members of their communities, although they still were not considered worthy of a public education. Less fortunate children and adults were on the streets, imprisoned in different types of institutions (mostly under horrible conditions), and they often died untimely deaths. It would not be until the nineteenth century that states began to take the responsibility of providing an education for children with disabilities through residential schools.

RESIDENTIAL SCHOOLS OF THE NINETEENTH CENTURY AND PIONEER TEACHERS

We know and respond warmly to the word *home,* and for many, we also have happy positive responses to the word *school.* Home is, for most of us, that place where we lived as a child with a few other people, parents and perhaps siblings and even a grandparent or two at times. It is the place we came to after school, where we snacked, played with friends, ate meals, talked with family, and enjoyed privacy in our own rooms, with our stuff (which we may have shared with a sibling). We finished school, got a job, and began our independent lives as adults. Even as independent adults, we may still find ourselves telling others about "going home" and may begin reminiscing about school days and old friends. For many adults, childhood homes and childhood school experiences have special places in memories.

Now, think of home as a place where you live with several hundred other people of all ages in a large building. There is no school, only a few "classes" where you may learn basic living or academic skills. Classrooms are in the same building where you live. Think of this place as where you will live your entire life until death. You will have little privacy and few choices of significance. Days follow a strict schedule. There is a scheduled time to wake, bathe or be bathed, eat all of your meals, do work for which you receive no pay, go to "class" for which there is no graduation, play or be entertained, and sleep, often with many others in the same room. There are hundreds of people but very little communication among people.

Everyone is very busy with routines. There are some friendships and kindnesses from workers, but workers and volunteers come and go in your life. There is little variety, except for holidays, when people seem exceptionally generous and kind and when there are many special activities and music, but this does not last. Although institutions became more humane across several decades, as the line goes, "There's no place like home," a real home. There's also no place like a *real* school, not just a few classes but a real school with all of its diversity and opportunity.

A BRIEF OVERVIEW OF THE FIRST RESIDENTIAL SCHOOLS, TEACHERS, AND ADVOCATES

By the beginning of the nineteenth century, pressure from the public, educators, and humanitarians led to significant advances in education, including provisions for children with disabilities. In keeping with a "philosophy of separation," states established residential schools, primarily for children who were deaf or blind or who had intellectual disabilities. These schools followed the models of European asylums in physical and organizational structure and were initially more custodial than educational in practice, although several had music education programs. In attempts to make institutions more humane, state and local governments created separate, parallel communities complete with schools. Into the twentieth century, when smaller schools were built on the grounds of large institutions, the school grounds were often referred to as "campuses" in an attempt to parallel environments in the outside world. Children lived on the grounds and attended school in a separate building located on the "campus."

There are many unknown individuals behind the struggle to change public policy for those with disabilities, but the names of several dedicated pioneer teachers are particularly notable. Several of these pioneers were music teachers at the first residential schools. You will undoubtedly know the names of some of them from books, movies, and plays about their lives. Knowing that biographical documentaries of these dedicated teachers are easily available, I will limit my discussion to only a few paragraphs about their personal histories, but I would be remiss if I did not include their names, a few stories, and several of their contributions in this essay. Perhaps a brief account of their lives will inspire you to learn more about these courageous, tenacious teachers and humanitarians, pioneers who demonstrated to their communities, states, and country that children with disabilities were indeed worthy of an education—and one that included music instruction.

The very first residential school, a residential school for the deaf, was established in Hartford, Connecticut, in 1817 and named the American Asylum for the Education and Instruction of the Deaf (now the American School for the Deaf). The individual most associated with its organization and founding is Thomas Gallaudet (1787–1851), who served as its principal. As the story goes, Gallaudet's interest in deaf education began through playful interactions while teaching a neighbor child, a deaf girl named Alice Cogswell. His methods were crude—words written in the dirt with a stick—but would be replaced by his knowledge of a manual method of communication that he learned from faculty at a school for the deaf in Paris, France. One of the teachers at the school, Laurent Clerc (1785–1869), was deaf. He returned with Gallaudet to America to raise funds for the first school for the deaf in America. Once the school was established, Gallaudet's young neighbor Alice enrolled as one of its first residents. Students were taught using the French signs and methodology from Paris. Modifications over time led to the American Sign Language (ASL), which is prominent in today's education and in the culture of the deaf community.[2] You may be interested to know that Gallaudet's youngest son, Edward, was the first president of the newly founded and first deaf college in the world. This college, first known in 1857 as the Columbia Institution for the Education of the Deaf and Dumb and Blind, was renamed in 1954 to honor Thomas Gallaudet. Gallaudet University currently educates deaf, hard-of-hearing, and hearing students on its campus in Washington D.C.

The first residential school for the blind, established in 1829 as the New England Asylum for the Blind, was later renamed the Perkins School for the Blind for a wealthy nineteenth-century merchant. The school still exists in Watertown, Massachusetts, and provides residential and day programs for several hundred individuals.

The pioneering work of Samuel Howe (1801–1876), who served as the first director of the Perkins School, was well known to the public, primarily because of his highly publicized work with Laura Bridgeman, the first individual who was deaf and blind to be documented as learning a language. His methods with Bridgeman became the foundation for techniques that were used at the Perkins School for the Blind under his directorship. As an interesting aside, Julia Ward Howe (1819–1910), Samuel Howe's wife, was famous in her own right. She was a humanitarian, poet, teacher, and political activist for women's rights, and she was the first to proclaim "Mother's Day." You may know of her as the poet whose "Battle Hymn of the Republic," published in the *Atlantic Monthly* in 1862, became the lyrics for the famed song of the American Civil War.

Samuel Howe's teaching methods influenced one of the more famous alumni of Perkins, Anne Sullivan (1866–1836), the beloved teacher of Helen Keller. Sullivan had a serious visual impairment and for most of her childhood lived in deplorable conditions in one of the "poor houses." When she entered the Perkins School as a young teen, she was unlike many of the wealthy, sheltered girls living there. Known to be extremely intelligent but a nonconformist regarding school rules, she excelled in her studies. From her friendship with Laura Bridgeman, who was living at the school, and from her observations of methods used by Howe, she became the skillful teacher who was recommended to travel to Alabama to teach the seven-year-old Helen Keller (1880–1968). The inspirational story of Sullivan and Keller has been the topic of plays, movies, and books and needs no further elaboration here.

One of the earliest and most widely publicized and dramatic "education" cases at the turn of the century is described by Gaspard Itard (1774–1838) in *The Wild Boy of Aveyron*.[3] Itard documented his work with the boy for the five years they lived together in a school for the deaf in Paris. This twelve-year-old boy, named Victor by Itard, was found abandoned and "wild" in the forest of Aveyron. Victor did not walk (he ran), lacked all social conventions, and had no language. Itard was largely disappointed with the outcome of his work, since the boy did not acquire language but learned only a few basic skills (eating, sleeping, walking). Itard's teaching, however, gave credibility to the growing concept that children with disabilities were capable of learning. Itard's work inspired Edouard Sequin (1812–1880), a French psychologist who studied with Itard and developed methods to teach self-reliance and independence to individuals with intellectual disabilities—worthy goals and far ahead of the thinking of his time. The work of Itard and Sequin supported the idea of schools for children with intellectual disabilities, and in 1859, the first was established in the United States: the Massachusetts School for Idiotic and Feeble Minded Youth. The labels of "idiot" and "feeble minded" were perfectly acceptable in the nineteenth century. What will the citizens of this country think about our labels and descriptions of individuals with disabilities decades from now?

MUSIC IN THE FIRST RESIDENTIAL SCHOOLS, TEACHERS, AND ADVOCATES

Since institutions during the nineteenth century were infamous for their inhumane treatment of residents, it seems ironic that music was present in those same settings. Most likely, the inclusion of music in residential schools was influenced by the idea put forward by the ancient Greeks, along with philosophers, physicians, and educators, that music has beneficial properties. When positive outcomes were observed and reported, the idea of music either for therapy or for education gained momentum in state hospitals and schools.

Much of the support for music in hospitals and schools came from the belief, now scientifically supported, that music can be used for diagnostic purposes and for therapy. Heller presented an interesting study of the growth of music in therapy during the period from 1789 to 1848 and suggested that the press introduced the idea as early as 1789 in a publication by an anonymous author in the *Columbian Magazine* entitled "Music Physically Considered."[4] The cases of Itard (with Victor) and Seguin (with children with intellectual disabilities) were widely publicized in the early nineteenth century, and both reported using music to help children develop auditory skills. Heller also reports another case, although undocumented, that appeared in a 1796 article in the *New York Weekly Magazine.* The title of the article was "Remarkable Cure of a Fever by Music: An Attested Fact." In this account, a French music teacher, who suffered from severe symptoms of delirium, recovered during a concert performed for him at his request. He regressed at the end of the concert. It was a "Remarkable Cure" for a short time, anyway.

Reports of case studies were the modus operandi of doctors and psychologists at this time in history. Interest in the stringent scientific study of the psychological and physical effects of music and its application in therapy increased during the twentieth century with the founding of the music therapy profession in 1950 and particularly with the establishment of the *Journal of Music Therapy*, the premier research journal of the American Music Therapy Association. You can read more about the music therapy profession and music therapy research throughout this book.

The earliest writings tended to emphasize music's palliative uses, but with the establishment of residential schools came reports of music instruction and case studies of musical accomplishments. The idea of the extramusical benefits of music instruction, however, was never abandoned. In 1838, Lowell Mason (1792–1872), prominent educator, music teacher, and church musician, successfully argued to the School Committee in Boston that music should be included as a regular subject in the curriculum, since it has intellectual, moral, and physical benefits for all children.[5] Whether outcomes were for educational or therapeutic purposes, music was becoming a regular part of the curriculum, not only for children attending public school but also for children confined to residential schools. In fact, there is extensive evidence of music instruction at the first residential schools.

A careful reading of articles by Solomon, Darrow and Heller, and numerous current articles by Darrow and Gfeller[6] will dispel doubts you may have regarding the participation of deaf individuals in music experiences. For a historical perspective, Darrow and Heller provide a fascinating study of William Wolcott Turner and David Ely Bartlett, faculty at the American Asylum for the Deaf during the mid-1800s. Although documentation of music programs at the American Asylum is scanty, Darrow and Heller report that it is likely that music instruction was present at the school, as evidenced by Turner and Bartlett's 1847 article "Music among the Deaf and Dumb," published in the *American Annals of the Deaf and Dumb*, now the *American Annals of the Deaf*.

Turner and Bartlett's article is significant not only because of their position on teaching music to deaf individuals, a position considered radical at the time, but also because of the methods these early pioneers report. Darrow and Heller convey the contents of the article: a case study of the accomplishments of August Avery, a young woman who was deaf from infancy. Bartlett was one of her piano teachers. After she mastered some basic skills with her parents and a friend as teachers, at her request for additional instruction, the parents brought her to study at the New York School for the Deaf (established by Bartlett in 1832 after he left his position at the American Asylum). She performed at the American Asylum and gave demonstrations of her sight-reading skills.

Darrow and Heller conclude that, although she was not a gifted musician, Avery's musical accomplishments contributed to a change in the attitudes of the skeptics and inspired other schools to provide music instruction for deaf and hearing-impaired students. Solomon provides photographic documentation of musical instruments in classrooms at the Clarke Institution for Deaf-Mutes, founded in 1867 in Massachusetts, and gives evidence of music teaching in the Kindergarten and Primary School for Hearing and Deaf Children founded in 1883 in Washington, D.C., by Alexander Graham Bell. Almost thirty years ago, Darrow and Heller wrote that Turner and Bartlett's article "provides evidence that the history of music instruction for the deaf extends at least 137 years; yet, the very idea of music and the hearing impaired continues to meet with surprise, if not suspicion."

The music education program at the Perkins School for the Blind began in 1829, when the school was established, and was developed by none other than Lowell Mason. At the same time as Mason advocated that music be included as a regular subject in the public school curriculum, he developed a music education curriculum for Perkins, taught voice and piano at the school, taught music in his community, and performed as a church musician. His prominence in the community as a musician and educator gave credibility to the idea that children with disabilities benefit from a music education.

Although the early history of music teachers in American residential schools is the focus of this section, Louis Braille (1809–1852), who was born in France, must be included because of his significant contributions: the braille alphabet and music notation. Around the same time that the Perkins School for the Blind was established in Boston, Braille was at work in Paris developing his alphabet. Blinded by an accident at the age of three, he first attended his local community school with neighborhood children, and because of his intellect and music talents, he had several successful years in this regular community school. At the age of ten, he received a scholarship to the Royal Institution for the Blind in Paris, one of the first schools of its kind in Europe. He would eventually serve as one of its teachers. As with all institutions around this time, conditions at the school were deplorable, but Braille distinguished himself through his intellect and musicianship; he was a talented pianist and organist. He published his first book on the alphabet system at the age of fifteen and in 1834 published his music notation system, *Method of Writing Words, Music and Plain Song by Means of Dots, for Use by the Blind and Arranged by Them*. The braille alphabet was not officially recognized in France until a few years after his death, and shortly afterward, it was introduced to residential schools for the blind in America. Although the alphabet is integral to the education of children with visual impairments or blindness, braille music is less well known, but a growing number of music scores are available, as are services for transcriptions and instruction.[7]

Little is known of music instruction at the first residential school for individuals with intellectual disabilities, the Massachusetts School for Idiotic and Feeble Minded Youth. Kraft, in his article "Music for the Feeble-Minded in Nineteenth Century America," reported that in 1869, the school had three pianos valued at $262.50.[8] From this information, he concluded that music must have been an important part of the curriculum, since the total value of all of the school furniture and "apparatus" (this term is not defined) was $420.44, and the school's horse (yes, a horse) was valued at $150.00. It appears that this school, and other residential schools that followed, valued pianos for religious and patriotic occasions in addition to exercise programs. Residents marched to the beat of a drum and possibly to piano music. The purchase of pianos for residential schools may have been influenced by the work of Edouard Seguin, who recommended marching to the piano as a form of musical and rhythmic exercise and whose wife taught piano to several students at the school.

Unlike his wife, Seguin is reported to have valued the piano only for the exercise program and not for education purposes. Seguin viewed music primarily for therapeutic purposes, and in Seguin's book, *Idiocy and Its Treatment by the Physiological Method*, Kraft found evidence that Seguin stressed the functional nature of listening to "appropriate selections" (undefined) but only for the purpose of helping children develop speech. He appears to have developed an elaborate method related to listening, the classes of sounds, and the physiological aspects of music. Kraft suspected that his methods were applied in tutorial conditions and not with groups of residents—groups were, no doubt, marching.

Although Seguin was not optimistic about the ability of individuals with intellectual disabilities to play the piano or to participate in music ensembles, superintendents at other residential schools supported the idea. The Ohio State Asylum for the Education of Idiotic and Imbecile Youth formed an orchestra for "mental discipline and training" in 1878, and its success led to the formation of a band at the Pennsylvania Training School and one at the Illinois Asylum for Feeble-Minded Children. The success of these performing groups led to enthusiastic support for music in residential schools, although the concept of marching continued to be the prominent application of music at the schools. The positive attitude regarding this type of activity is reflected in a quotation that Kraft found in an 1874 report of the US Commission of Education regarding music at the Kentucky Institution for the Education of Feeble-Minded Children. Calisthenic exercises, "of the most graceful character, and to the measure of the sweetest music, are daily engaged in."

THE RISE AND FALL OF STATE INSTITUTIONS IN THE TWENTIETH CENTURY: DEINSTITUTIONALIZATION AND RIGHT TO TREATMENT

Throughout the 1800s and early 1900s, separate institutions and residential schools continued to grow in number and in size. By the middle of the twentieth century, hundreds of thousands of individuals, many of them children, were residing in state institutions. To give you some idea of the public sentiment in the earlier and later part of the twentieth century, I have two samples of the types of headlines that were appearing in the papers at those times. Both are from articles in the *New York Times*, one on July 8, 1917, and the other on September 4, 1988.[9] The headlines read: "Number of Insane at Large Now Less" and "After 30 Years, Mental Institutions May Be as Empty as They'll Ever Be." Most of the public was dismayed at this decrease, since increasing the numbers of individuals in institutions was thought to be a good thing.

Overall, the number of individuals institutionalized in the 1900s increased rapidly. The 1917 article reports data from the federal census and the National Committee for Mental Hygiene, which showed an increase in one year from 187,791 to 234,055 for "insane" individuals, an increase of almost 25 percent. Separate tables present figures for the "feeble-minded" (37,220), "epileptics" (10,801), and "inebriates and drug addicts" (4,891). In describing the rapidly increasing numbers of institutions and residents, the concluding statement summarizes the general sentiment of the times: "The number of insane and feeble-minded at large, with the evils associated therewith, is consequently lessening."

By the mid-1960s, state institution populations were at their highest. In November 1964, a census of all state institutions found 91,592 children and youths twenty-one years or younger among state institution populations (47.6 percent of all residents). Forty years later, on June 30, 2004, the number of children and youths in state institutions had decreased to an estimated 1,641 (4.1 percent of all state institution residents), with sixteen states having no children or youths in state institutions.[10] The decrease is significant; however, the situation remains that hundreds of children are still placed in institutional settings despite the years of research showing the detrimental effects of these unacceptable actions. Disability organizations, advocates, and educational agencies continue to work toward the elimination of congregate placements for children, facilities with sixteen or more residents such as large state institutions, and the increase of home and community care and inclusion in regular classrooms.[11]

For many parents, state institutions or state schools, sometimes located several travel days away from the family residences, were their only choice. Private schools were costly, their children were prohibited from attending public schools, and the sentiment was that many, particularly those with intellectual disabilities, could not learn but could only be "trained." Family life was nonexistent for most children in institutional settings. Although there were, as there are today, people of goodwill who reached out with kindness to those in institutional settings and provided compassionate comfort, conditions in many state facilities were undeniably horrible. This was a time of dehumanization, particularly in institutions for persons with intellectual, behavioral, emotional, or multiple disabilities.

Although the establishment of residential schools showed a bare tolerance of children with disabilities, when these children were segregated in poorly funded schools, many under deplorable conditions with limited educational services and no appropriate models, positive behavior change was improbable. With few positive changes known to the public, myths regarding the behavior of persons with disabilities and the source of their behavior propagated. Misinformation about genetics led to the widely held belief that a disability was a hopeless condition and that these individuals were likely to be criminals and socially uncontrollable. This thinking, which lasted well into the twentieth century, led to one of the more shameful periods of our history: the eugenics movement.[12]

Starting in 1924 and for more than forty years, thirty-three states forced the sterilization of thousands of their residents who were thought to have undesirable and hereditary shortcomings. This atrocity was viewed by some as a way to relieve, in part, the tax burden experienced with the rapid growth of institutions. In 1907, Indiana enacted the first sterilization law on the foundation of eugenics, and with the advocacy of the American eugenics movement, more states followed. Carrie Buck, a seventeen-year-old, was selected to be the first person forcibly sterilized under Virginia's Eugenical Sterilization Act of 1924, a decision eventually upheld in 1927 by the US Supreme Court. The family with which she lived committed her to the Virginia Colony for Epileptics and Feebleminded (her mother also lived there) shortly after Carrie became pregnant; she claimed her pregnancy was the result of a rape.

By the mid-1960s, more than sixty-five thousand forced sterilizations had been conducted across thirty-three states, in part a result of the US Supreme Court's 1927 decision in *Buck v. Bell,* a law that upheld the challenged Virginia law. Oliver Wendell Holmes, the chief justice, wrote in the majority ruling: "It is better for all the world, if instead of waiting to execute degenerate off-spring for crime or let them starve from their imbecility, society can prevent those who are manifestly unfit from continuing their kind." He declared that "three generations of imbeciles are enough."[13] *Buck v. Bell* continues to stand (as of the writing of this book), but on its seventy-fifth anniversary (May 2, 2002), on the occasion of the placement of a historical marker in Buck's honor, Virginia's then-governor Mark Warner expressed profound regret and offered a public apology. He wrote that the marker "will serve as a constant reminder of how our government failed its citizens and how we must always strive to do better."[14] Oregon, North Carolina, South Carolina, and other states have also offered their apologies.

Carrie Buck was sterilized by Dr. John H. Bell at the colony on October 19, 1927, after the birth of her child, and she was released from the colony shortly afterward. She was not permitted to raise her child, even though some of the reports of this incident suggest that Carrie Buck was of normal intelligence.

The deplorable conditions at many state hospitals led to journalistic exposés, testimonials from professionals and parents, and visits from political figures during the mid-1960s. Senator Robert Kennedy visited New York state institutions, and the public was aware of the fact that he and President John F. Kennedy had a sister, Rosemary, who had an intellectual disability. The public's attitude toward disabilities was also softened as a result of returning soldiers from wars conducted during the twentieth century and the many who were in need of rehabilitation programs, vocational training, and job counseling.

One of the more shocking exposés at the time was published by Burton Blatt, an advocate for deinstitutionalization and a leader in special education, and his colleague Fred Kaplan, a talented photographer. They were among the first to chronicle the blatant inequities of physical and social segregation of individuals with intellectual and developmental disabilities. Blatt and Kaplan used a hidden camera to record and then publish the shocking photographs in their book *Christmas in Purgatory*.[15] Their startling photographic essay on life in institutions had a dramatic impact on its readers. The contrast between the beginning of the book, with its stark black-and-white photographs of children and adults with intellectual disabilities in institutions, and the second part, in color, showing children and adults in natural settings of their homes and communities, was shocking to many who were unaware of living conditions in institutional settings. Some of these inequities were and continue to be resolved through the courts.

During the 1970s and 1980s, public awareness, several highly visible programs for disabled veterans, and, in particular, decisions from two class action suits, *Wyatt v. Stickney* and *Halderman v. Pennhurst*, fueled the arguments for right-to-treatment laws and the deinstitutionalization movement and subsequent transfer of residents to community group homes and foster families.[16] When the courts began to define "right to treatment" by specific criteria such as staffing and living conditions, state hospitals began to close.

The admission of children to institutions was also scrutinized more closely as a result of *Parham v. J.R.* in 1979.[17] Two adolescents (J.R. and J.L.), committed to state mental hospitals in Georgia by their parents, brought a class action suit claiming that these actions violated the due process clause of the Fourteenth Amendment. The due process clause relates to states ("nor shall any state deprive any person of life, liberty, or property without due process of law") and protects both children and adults. After this case, no child younger than eighteen could be committed by a parent or guardian without stringent observations, testing, and confirmation by independent mental health physicians.

The children involved in these consequential cases—Ricky Wyatt (at Bryce Hospital in Tuscaloosa, Alabama), Terri Lee Halderman (at Pennhurst State School and Hospital, Pennsylvania), and J.R. and J.L. (at Georgia State Hospitals)—were a part of monumental changes that led to more humane psychological and physical care and treatment plans by qualified staff. As a result of right-to-treatment and other reforms in the 1970s, physical living spaces and standards of care were significantly changed. Environments were made to be more "homelike," with smaller rooms for recreation and leisure, and limits were placed on the number of individuals per unit. Although right-to-treatment laws were in effect in the early 1970s and actions were being taken to keep people out of institutions with placements and services in communities, the struggle for these outcomes continued for decades, and cases were still being heard at the turn of the twentieth-first century.

The closing of state hospitals and schools and the transfer of individuals to the community were problematic for years; community services were few in number and poorly funded. As hospitals closed, new laws and policies gradually brought about a systemic change. Funding increased for local, state, and federal agencies and organizations providing supports, services, assistance, and opportunities for individuals to live, attend school, and work in their communities.

A right to treatment, a right to education—you can see the connection between these two ideas. Treatment implies services for residential and medical care, and a right to treatment was interpreted by education advocacy groups, and eventually the courts, to mean a right to an education. The actions of deinstitutionalization during the middle of the twentieth century supported in full the eventual passage of laws to ensure appropriate education for children with disabilities.

EARLY FEDERAL ASSISTANCE (RESIDENTIAL, MEDICAL, SCHOOL)

Apart from providing state institutional care, there was little activity from the federal government to assist persons with disabilities until it was prompted into action by the creation of programs to assist the disabled veterans of World Wars I and II. Although assistance was at first exclusively for those in the military, over time, Congress enacted a number of laws that extended programs, services, and treatment to other persons with disabilities, including children. These laws and others related specifically to disabilities are still in effect today (Social Security Act, Medicare and Medicaid, Social Security Supplementary Act, Developmental Disabilities Assistance and Bill of Rights Act).

Through federal grants, funding was made available to states to educate children with disabilities beginning in the mid-1960s, most of whom still lived and went to school in institutional settings. Along with legislation to secure medical assistance came a number of legislative acts designed to improve educational programs for children with and without disabilities. For example, the Elementary and Secondary Education Acts of 1965 and 1966 and the Education of the Handicapped Acts of 1970 and 1974 provided the foundation for the Education of All Handicapped Children Act of 1975, now IDEA.

Although education incentives were put in place in the 1960s and early 1970s, children and adults were still being admitted to state institutions (before *Parham v. J.R.*, 1979), and conditions within the institutions were still not subjected to reform (before *Wyatt v. Stickney*, 1972). Improvements to educational programs for children through grant initiatives were slow in coming, and cases were building against the states' institutional model considered by advocates as a violation of the constitutional rights of persons with disabilities. The widespread acceptance of segregated educational practices for children with disabilities, by law, by place, and by tradition, were to come to an end.

PRECURSORS LEADING TO LEGISLATED INCLUSIVE SERVICES

From the eighteenth century until well into the twentieth century, as hundreds of thousands of children with disabilities were living in residential institutional settings far from their families and as most were receiving far less than an adequate education, other children were attending neighborhood schools in accordance with the compulsory school attendance laws. Separate education of children with disabilities and of African American children was in accordance with state and local laws, not necessarily by choice of the families but by law. Some background is necessary to understand the laws that eliminated legislated segregation and mandated a free appropriate education for all children. The foundation for these laws began early in US history, with the Constitution of the United States of America.

"We the People"

Men who were members of an elite group in America chose the words of the Preamble of the US Constitution carefully. In their choice of language, the framers of the Constitution conveyed the idea that common people were the creators of the Constitution and that the Constitution was crafted to serve all of its citizens. In case you haven't read it for some time, I present these inspiring words for you:

> We the people of the United States, In Order to form a more perfect Union, establish Justice, insure domestic Tranquility, provide for the common defence, promote the general Welfare, and secure the Blessings of Liberty to ourselves and our Posterity, do ordain and establish this Constitution for the United States of America.[18]

Completed on September 17, 1787, and adopted by state representatives at the Constitutional Convention in Philadelphia, the new form of government took effect in 1789 only after fierce debate and eventual ratification. With the many engaging books, movies, and television programs about the American Revolutionary War (1775–1781) and the personalities involved, we have some idea of the human drama of those times. At the end of the war for independence from Britain, the first US government was formed, although it was weak by all standards. Under the Articles of Confederation, Congress essentially had no power. Concerned that too much power would rest with one body of government, as it did with imperialist Britain, and in keeping with the ideals of "we the people," the framers of the Constitution designed a federalist system of government with responsibility and power given to three parallel governments (federal, state, local) and with three separate branches of government (executive, legislative, judicial). The federalist system was designed to promote freedom of thought and promote discourse. That it did.

Each of the three governments—federal, state, and local—represents different sources of authority, with the highest source of law at the federal level and with the federal Constitution. Although all share in the responsibility and power that affect the education of children, federal constitutional law (in accordance with the federal Constitution and all its amendments) and statutory law (in accordance with laws created by Congress and state legislatures) are the ultimate authority. Although we would like to believe that state and local governments are following a particular educational policy (e.g., educating children with disabilities) because it is the right thing to do, the federal funding source is a strong contingency. Given that all states, and subsequently local districts, receive federal funds for the education of children, all education laws of states and local districts must comply with federal constitutional law and statutory law. When disputes arise among individuals or groups at any level, the judiciary functions to resolve the disputes.[19]

Battles were fought for many of the laws against discrimination in education, housing, employment, and so on. It takes individuals with courage, tenacity, and intelligence to make and challenge laws that oppress or violate individual freedoms and rights. For example, consider the following landmark laws and the conflicts that must have occurred among legislators and ordinary citizens before laws were passed and lives were changed:

- The Thirteenth Amendment to the US Constitution, ratified in 1865, abolished slavery in the United States.
- The Fourteenth Amendment to the US Constitution, ratified in 1868, granted citizenship to persons born or naturalized in the United States and granted due process and equal protection of the laws to its citizens.
- Compulsory school was legislated by states beginning as early as 1842. The federal government appropriated funds to states that legislated compulsory schooling, and all had passed such a law by 1918.

Consider two of these laws in particular: the Fourteenth Amendment and compulsory schooling (state laws with government funding), along with the fact that, by state laws, based on race and disabilities, children were required to attend separate schools. How in the world could a mandated segregated education become legal? It's unimaginable to us today. Here's the story of the courts, unconstitutional laws regarding segregation, and the major impact that Supreme Court rulings on segregation had for future education laws.

THE ROLE OF THE SUPREME COURT

In its early history, the US Supreme Court was not as active as it is today, and in fact, it had little power until the landmark case of *Marbury v. Madison* in 1803.[20] This case defined the Supreme Court as the arbiter of the Constitution. At issue was whether the Supreme Court could interpret the constitutionality of a law or statute passed by Congress. The law at issue was the Judiciary Act, which set the policies and procedures for government appointments by presidents. Under this act of Congress, appointments were determined to be official when notices, "commissions," were officially delivered by the president's secretary of state to the appointee.

The two political parties at the time were the Federalists and the Jeffersonians. William Marbury was one of many appointments made by President John Adams, a Federalist, shortly before he left office. All appointments were made to members of the Federalist party, including the one to Marbury. Before these appointments became official, the new president, Thomas Jefferson, a Jeffersonian, of course, was in office and ordered several appointments withheld, Marbury's among them.

Jefferson's actions fueled the political dispute between the Federalists and the Jeffersonians.

The Supreme Court heard the case of Marbury, who sued James Madison, the secretary of state under Jefferson. Marbury's petition to force Madison to deliver the commission under the Judiciary Act was denied by the Supreme Court as unconstitutional. Chief Justice John Marshal authored the decision and stated that the Supreme Court was not bound by an act of Congress that was "repugnant to the Constitution."

With *Marbury v. Madison*, the Supreme Court was defined as the judicial body with the responsibility and power to judge acts of Congress and acts of members of the executive branch as unconstitutional if these acts violated constitutional law, a practice known as judicial review. The Supreme Court ruled against Congress again in 1857 in a landmark case that upheld the practice of slavery, *Dred Scott v. Sandford*.[21] By the mid-1800s, the Supreme Court had established its role as the arbiter of the Constitution and was poised to rule on cases that would dramatically change educational practices for all children in the United States.

LEGALIZED SEGREGATION: SEPARATE BUT EQUAL

Racial segregation was the norm for schools in the 1950s and was determined constitutional by the precedent set by *Plessy v. Ferguson*, a case first heard before Judge John H. Ferguson in Louisiana courts, appealed to the Supreme Court of Louisiana, and finally heard by the Supreme Court of the United States in 1896.[22] As the story is reported, Homer Plessy, whose great-grandmother was black, was active in a civil rights group, the Citizens' Committee of African Americans and Creoles. As a protest against Louisiana's Separate Car Act of 1890, which required "separate but equal" trains for blacks and whites, Plessy rode on the "whites-only" car of the East Louisiana Railroad and declared himself to be seven-eighths white and one-eighth black to the conductor who was collecting tickets. He was promptly arrested and jailed. Plessy lost his argument that the Louisiana law violated the Thirteenth Amendment (which abolished slavery as a legal institution) and the Fourteenth Amendment (which granted citizenship to and protected the civil liberties of recently freed slaves and thus provided equal protection of the law to all citizens). The case was lost before Ferguson in Louisiana, the Supreme Court of Louisiana, and finally the US Supreme Court. The decision in *Plessy v. Ferguson* established segregation as constitutional in many of life's activities, whether riding on trains, eating at restaurants, or attending public schools. Segregation was constitutional as long as "separate" was "equal."

Segregation was the modus operandi for the country, under law and at all levels of government, for almost sixty years. It would not be until 1954, in a unanimous decision by the US Supreme Court, that the "separate but equal" doctrine was struck down as it applied to the arena of public school education.

Brown v. Board of Education

Linda Brown was a little girl in Topeka, Kansas, who had a long walk through unsafe railroad yards to get to the bus that would take her to her third-grade classroom in a segregated school, one presumed by the state to be a school with "equal" educational opportunities. Seven blocks from her home was a school for white children, where she was denied enrollment. Her father, Oliver Brown, filed suit against the Board of Education in Topeka, Kansas.

The US Constitution does not guarantee a right to education for any of its citizens, including Linda Brown. And in fact, there is no language referring to education in the Constitution. *State* constitutions guarantee the right to education for their residents, and states comply with their constitutions by providing education for students. States were in compliance with the supreme law of the land by providing "separate but equal" schools as established by *Plessy v. Ferguson*. Arguments for Linda Brown's case were lost at all levels, in trial courts and appeals courts, because of the precedent of the *Plessy* decision. It was the court of last resort, the US Supreme Court, that finally ended "separate but equal" in education law.

The importance of *Brown v. Board of Education* in education law cannot be overstated. It was the first successful case to overturn racial segregation in schools, and it laid the foundation for other challenges to discrimination in education against groups of children of school age, whether on the basis of gender, race, or disability.[23] The decision was justified on the basis of the importance of education throughout the nation, on the negative outcomes of stigmatization of those segregated under the sanction of law, and on the negative effects of segregation on the educational and mental development of students deprived of opportunities, even beyond tangible factors such as buildings, curricula, and teacher salaries.

Chief Justice Earl Warren read the Supreme Court's decision on May 17, 1954. Think about the dramatic consequences of this decision for hundreds of millions of children's lives:

> "Today, education is perhaps the most important function of state and local governments. Compulsory school attendance laws and the great expenditures for education both demonstrate our recognition of the importance of education to our democratic

society. It is required in the performance of our most basic public responsibilities, even service in the armed forces. It is the very foundation of good citizenship. Today it is a principal instrument in awakening the child to cultural values, in preparing him for later professional training, and in helping him to adjust normally to his environment. In these days, it is doubtful that any child may reasonably be expected to succeed in life if he is denied the opportunity of an education. Such an opportunity, where the state has undertaken to provide it, is a right which must be made available to all in equal terms.

> We come then to the question presented: Does segregation of children in public schools solely on the basis of race, even though the physical facilities and other "tangible" factors may be equal, deprive the children of the minority group of equal education opportunities? We believe it does. . . . To separate from others of similar age and qualifications solely because of their race generates a feeling of inferiority as to the status in the community that may affect their hearts and minds in a way unlikely ever to be undone. The effect of this separation on their educational opportunities was well stated by a finding in the Kansas case by a court which nevertheless felt compelled to rule against the Negro plaintiffs."

At this point, Justice Warren quotes from the decision of the Kansas State Supreme Court, whose judges, given the precedent of *Plessy v. Ferguson*, felt "compelled" to rule in favor of the Board of Education and then continues with personal comments and says:

> "Segregation of white and colored children in public schools has a detrimental effect upon the colored children. The impact is greater when it has the sanction of the law; for the policy of separating the races is usually interpreted as denoting the inferiority of the Negro group. A sense of inferiority affects the motivation of a child to learn. Segregation with the sanction of the law, therefore, has a tendency to [retard] the educational and mental development of Negro children and to deprive them of some of the benefits they would receive in a racial[ly] integrated school system."

Returning to of the US Supreme Court's decision, Warren reads:

> We conclude that in the field of public education the doctrine of "separate but equal" has no place. Separate educational facilities are inherently unequal. Therefore, we hold that the plaintiffs and others similarly situated for whom the actions have been brought are, by reason of the segregation complained of, deprived of the equal protection of the laws guaranteed by the Fourteenth Amendment.

This was an incredible time in history. The relationship of this monumental ruling to special education law is vividly clear on a second reading with the substitution of the words "students with disabilities" for "Negro or colored students" and "typical students" for "white students." Try it. The transfer of right-to-education laws for children with disabilities from *Brown* is obvious, although it would be another eighteen years before courts would review cases concerning the appropriate education of children with disabilities.

PARC, MILLS, AND THE RIGHT TO ATTEND NEIGHBORHOOD SCHOOLS

Recall that although the 1960s brought with it some funding for state programs, educational standards for children with disabilities were far from adequate. Children with a range of disabilities were systematically excluded from public schools, so they had no access to a free, public school education. Many advocacy and parent groups were pressed to turn to the courts. This brings us to the two landmark cases in 1972 that, with the precedent of *Brown*, led directly to the first federal law mandating a free, appropriate education for children with disabilities: the Education of All Handicapped Children Act of 1975.

Pennsylvania law, similar to laws in most states, excluded children with disabilities from attending public schools. Pennsylvania laws allowed for this exclusion if children were assessed and certified by psychologists as "uneducable and untrainable." With a psychologist's certification, public schools were "relieved of the obligation of providing education or training for such a child." The Pennsylvania law of exclusion was challenged as unconstitutional by parents of seventeen children with intellectual disabilities. And it was found to be the case as decreed by the federal district court in *Pennsylvania Association for Retarded Children (PARC) v. Pennsylvania*.[24]

Laws to exclude did not provide appropriate due process measures before exclusion (e.g., notice to parents and subsequent hearings). Children were denied equal protection of the laws by being assessed without parental agreement, and the laws violated the state constitution, which guaranteed education for all children. The Pennsylvania Association for Retarded Children (now the Arc of Pennsylvania) argued the case as a class action lawsuit that, in the decree, mandated to every "retarded person between the ages of six and twenty-one years" access to a free, appropriate public education program.

PARC specified that children with intellectual disabilities had a right to attend school and a right to a free, appropriate education. Following with the same arguments of unconstitutional exclusionary practices, *Mills v. Board of Education of the District of Columbia*[25] had substantial notoriety, perhaps because of its location in the nation's capital. As reported in the decree, eighteen thousand children with disabilities went without a public education during the 1972–1973 school year. The challenge of seven of these children, with disabilities varying in type and level of severity (Peter Mills was one of the plaintiffs), was upheld. As a class action lawsuit, *Mills* provided a free appropriate public school education to all school-age children, regardless of the type or level of severity of disability, and a right to due process with a fair hearing regarding their assessment and placement.

The notoriety of *PARC* and *Mills* fueled emerging cases in other states, and soon thereafter, Congress moved to bring about federal legislation that would apply to all children with disabilities between the ages of three and twenty-one and, as amended in 1986, to include children from birth through two years of age. The long history of unconstitutional laws excluding children from their right to education under the due process clauses of the Fifth and Fourteenth Amendments and the equal protection clause of the Fourteenth Amendment[26] was drawing to a close, ending with the passage in 1975 of the Education of All Handicapped Children Act.

Brown, PARC, and *Mills* established legal precedents for IDEA and provided safeguards against discrimination toward some of the most vulnerable citizens in our country. There were several other early education laws that provided the foundation for some of IDEA's premises and even its name. Read about these early laws and the premises of IDEA in appendix C.

APPENDIX C

IDEA: History, Premises, Interpretations

There is a reason law books are massive, so massive that law students use rolling suitcases to transport their books. Laws must be excruciating in detail, and interpretations must be substantiated by evidence. Box C.1 gives you some idea of the complexity of the process of passing and reporting new laws. So it is with justified trepidation that I approach writing a brief description of the law that has transformed the lives of so many children: the Individuals with Disabilities Education Improvement Act (IDEA).

Volumes have been written about IDEA and its evolution from its early beginnings as the Education of All Handicapped Children Act of 1975. This appendix provides only brief summaries of the law's major premises since its passage in 1975 and summaries of several significant amendments through the latest version at the time of this writing, IDEA 2004. Music teachers will want to know about the basic structure and civil rights guarantees of the law and how to use this information to plan and develop meaningful music experiences for their students.

In order to keep this appendix at a reasonable length and readable, only selected material is presented. You will no doubt have many questions about the information presented here and the interpretations of statutes. In addition to conferring with knowledgeable individuals, there are several reliable and informative resources where you can find information about IDEA, its history, premises, and interpretations, and the latest updates.[1]

Box C.1

STATUTES, REGULATIONS, AND CODIFICATION OF LAWS

The sequence of events that occur when Congress passes laws:

1. Congress passes laws (statutes) that are compiled annually in the US *Statutes at Large*, the official chronological compilation of all laws and resolutions enacted during each congressional session. When a law is published in the *Statutes at Large*, it is referred to as an "act." The Individuals with Disabilities Education Improvement Act of 2004 begins with Section 600 in the *Statutes at Large*.
2. Laws in the statutes that apply to the general population are known as public laws (P.L.). As an example, "P.L. 108-446" indicates that the 108th Congress passed public law number 446.
3. Laws are then entered into and published in the *United States Code* (U.S.C.), the official compilation of codified laws. Fifty different titles are used to codify laws. In the U.S.C., IDEA appears as Title 20 and begins with Section 1400 (20 U.S.C. § 1400).
4. Agencies, in the case of IDEA the US Department of Education, develop regulations for special education laws that are then published in the *Federal Register* (F.R.) for commentary from citizens. IDEA appears in the *Code of Federal Regulations* (C.F.R.), Volume 34, Part 300 (34 C.F.R. § 300). A description of the comments received from the public and comments to clarify and explain the statutes are included in a section entitled "Analysis and Commentary."

Note: IDEA is published in the Statutes at Large, *the* United States Code, *and the* Federal Register *and all use different numbering systems. Organizations and numbering systems vary in official compilations resulting in different citations for the same subject (e.g., purposes, definitions, individualized education programs). Citations for IDEA usually reference the* United States Code *(20 U.S.C.) or the* Code of Federal Regulations *(34 C.F.R.). When citations include the Latin abbreviation* et seq. (et sequential*), meaning "and the following ones," the reference is to a page and the next following pages (e.g., 20 U.S.C. §1400* et seq.*).*

You've read about the importance of *Brown v. Board of Education* (1954), a landmark discrimination case in which the US Supreme Court ruled that separate education of people of difference races was not equal education. This case was the catalyst for two class action suits in 1972 concerning discrimination against children with disabilities. *Pennsylvania Assn. for Retarded Children (PARC) v. Commonwealth of Pennsylvania* resulted in a consent decree specifying that children with "mental retardation" (the term used in 1972) must have access to a free public education and that states had to identify and provide a free public education to all those children who had been excluded in the past.[2] *Mills v. Board of Education of District of Columbia* specified that the District of Columbia must provide a free public education for all children with disabilities, regardless of the severity of their disabilities.[3]

The *PARC* and *Mills* cases led to a congressional investigation of the education of children with disabilities in the United States. Overwhelmed by statistics, with estimates of millions of children without an appropriate education, and long-term financial implications for their care as dependent children and adults, Congress passed the Education of All Handicapped Children Act of 1975 (P.L. 94-142). This landmark law provided the long-awaited safeguards against discrimination for all children with disabilities throughout the country and educational opportunities for their living more meaningful, productive lives. EHA 1975 guaranteed a free, appropriate public education to all children with disabilities regardless of the severity or type of disability, ensured rights and due process, and provided financial support for state efforts to education the children. EHA 1975 has been reauthorized, amended, and renamed several times since its inception.

With the reauthorization in 2004, the law became known as the Individuals with Disabilities Education Improvement Act (P.L. 105-446). Although the word "improvement" was added to the law's name, the law states, "This title may be cited as the 'Individuals with Disabilities Education Act,'' (U.S.C. § 1400). In this book and other publications, current law is referred to as the Individuals with Disabilities Education Act or simply IDEA.

EARLY FEDERAL SPECIAL EDUCATION LAWS

Court rulings in *Brown, PARC,* and *Mills* established legal precedents for IDEA as a law to address inequalities of educational opportunities for children with disabilities. There were, however, several other early education laws that provided the foundation for some of its premises and even its name (see box C.2). These early laws provide a good look at the values of the country, how these values were changing, and how they resulted in practices that led to improvements in educational services for children.

IDEA's most direct past began with the historically important Elementary and Secondary Education Act of 1965 (P.L. 89-10).[4] The Civil Rights Act of 1964 and President John F. Kennedy's initiatives to improve education laid the groundwork for this law, which was brought to Congress by President Lyndon B. Johnson. The Elementary and Secondary Education Act of 1965 (ESEA) provided the statutory basis for special education law

Box C.2

EARLY EDUCATION LAWS: THE EDUCATION OF CHILDREN WITH DISABILITIES

1965 ELEMENTARY AND SECONDARY EDUCATION ACT (P.L. 89-10)

Provided the statutory basis for special education law. Title 1 designated funding through states for schools with high percentages of "poor" children. Sweeping revisions were made when ESEA was reauthorized in 2001 and renamed the No Child Left Behind Act (P.L. 107-110).

1966 ELEMENTARY AND SECONDARY EDUCATION ACT (P.L. 89-750)

First federal grant program specifically targeting funding for children and youths with disabilities. Repealed in 1970 with the passage of the Education of the Handicapped Act.

1970 EDUCATION OF THE HANDICAPPED ACT (P.L. 91-230)

Grant programs offered to stimulate states to develop programs, provide special education resources, and prepare special education teachers. The preparation of teachers was a priority.

1974 EDUCATION OF THE HANDICAPPED ACT (P.L. 93-380)

In order to receive grants, states must establish a timetable to show when children with disabilities would achieve full educational opportunities in schools that would accommodate them and how states would provide procedural safeguards for identification, evaluation, and placement (equal protection guarantees).

1975 EDUCATION OF ALL HANDICAPPED CHILDREN ACT (P.L. 94-142)

First federal law mandating a free appropriate public education (FAPE) for children with disabilities in the least restrictive environment (LRE), with a fair evaluation, an individualized education program (IEP), and a guarantee of due process of the law when disagreements arise over decisions about placements, the educational program, or other school actions. The LRE occurs when, to the maximum extent appropriate, children with disabilities are educated in regular classrooms and removed only when the nature or severity of the disability is such that education in regular classes with the use of supplementary aids and services cannot be achieved satisfactorily. This act, renamed in 1990 as the Individuals with Disabilities Education Act and in 2004 as the Individuals with Disabilities Education Improvement Act, is referred to as the Individuals with Disabilities Education Act or IDEA.

by designating funds through states for schools with high percentages of "poor" children. ESEA constituted the most important educational component of the "War on Poverty" launched by President Johnson and continues to provide funds for a number of programs (e.g., Title 1, Head Start). Sweeping changes to ESEA came when it was revised in 2001 and renamed the No Child Left Behind Act (P.L. 107-110).

ESEA 1965 was revised several times in the 1960s, including in 1966, when for the first time, a law provided a federal grant program specifically targeted for children and youth with disabilities. ESEA 1966 was repealed in 1970, but grants were continued with the passage of the Education of the Handicapped Act (P.L. 91-230) in the same year. EHA 1970 offered grant programs to stimulate states to develop programs, provide special education resources, and prepare special education teachers. For the first time, the phrase "education of the handicapped" was used in a law.

In spite of the grants to states to educate children with disabilities, progress was slow. The *PARC* and *Mills* cases were providing fuel for additional discrimination cases throughout the country, and advocacy organizations were putting pressure on state and federal agencies for increased leadership and assistance. Congress responded in 1974 with amendments to the Education of the Handicapped Act (P.L. 93-380), which substantially increased aid for states. In order to receive funds, however, states were required to establish a timetable to show when children with disabilities would achieve full educational opportunities in schools that would accommodate them and how they would provide for procedural safeguards for identification, evaluation, and placement (equal protection guarantees). Within a year, EHA was amended again. This time, the amendment was significant; Congress passed the landmark Education of All Handicapped Children Act of 1975 (P.L. 94-142).

MAJOR PREMISES SINCE EHA 1975

EHA 1975, now IDEA, guaranteed a free, appropriate public education to children with disabilities from ages three through twenty-one in every state and locality across the country. The law authorized financial incentives to enable states and local school districts to comply. This law does not expire, although changes may occur during reauthorization. Although IDEA has been amended throughout its history, many premises of the early 1975 law have continued.

There also continue to be questions about the interpretation of many of the main ideas of the law. Many questions you may have about the major premises presented in this section are not easily answered. States, schools, and even schools in the same state differ in their interpretation of terms such as "appropriate public education," "maximum extent appropriate," "least restrictive environment," and others. States' statutes and regulations must provide the same rights as federal law, but they often vary in language, terminology, definitions, and interpretation. As long as states and schools are not found to be in conflict with federal statutes and regulations, state interpretations may vary. Conflicts of interpretations, however, may arise between parents and schools.

At the school level, based on each child's needs, members of IEP teams determine what is meant by "appropriate public education," "maximum extent appropriate," and "least restrictive environment" and make other interpretations and decisions for the child's educational program. A parent is also a member of the IEP and may offer ideas for the child's program. Ultimately, the child's IEP cannot be implemented without written consent from the parent. When disagreements arise over decisions about placements, the educational program, or other school actions regarding interpretation of the language of the law, IDEA gives children and parents a guarantee of due process of law. As you may well imagine, procedures to protect children and parents and requirements related to mediation and litigation are described in great detail in IDEA.

In every version of IDEA, beginning with the landmark law of 1975, you will find major premises. Even with revisions during reauthorization, these main ideas from the 1975 law have endured:

- Free appropriate public education (FAPE), due process, and procedural safeguards.
- Least restrictive environment (LRE) and supplementary aids and services.
- Fair evaluation and parental consent.
- Individualized education program (IEP) and IEP team.

Because of the length and complexity of the statutes and citations, the four major premises are presented briefly below in citations from IDEA 2004. Italics do not appear in the original citation and are used here only to emphasize important words.[5]

Free Appropriate Public Education (FAPE), Due Process, and Procedural Safeguards

"The Purpose [of the law] is . . . to ensure that all children with disabilities have available to them a *free appropriate public education* that emphasizes special education and related services designed to meet their unique needs and *prepare them for further*

> *education, employment and independent living* . . . [and] to ensure that the *rights of children with disabilities and parents of such children are protected.*" (U.S.C. § 1400)
>
> [Parents are] "guaranteed procedural safeguards with respect to the provision of a free appropriate public education." (U.S.C. § 1415)
>
> [Parents and children are given a] "*guarantee of due process of law when disagreements arise over decisions about placements, the educational program, or other school actions.*" (U.S.C. § 1414)

The law has as its foundation individual rights guaranteed by the Fifth and Fourteenth Amendments of the US Constitution. Any state agency or local education agency (LEA) that receives assistance under this law is required to "establish and maintain procedures to ensure that children with disabilities and their parents are guaranteed procedural safeguards with respect to the provision of a free appropriate public education." All children who are eligible for services under IDEA from the ages of three through twenty-one, including children who have been suspended or expelled from school, are entitled to a free appropriate public education (FAPE). FAPE is defined in IDEA to mean special education and related services that (1) have been provided at public expense, under public supervision and direction, and without charge; (2) meet the standards of the state educational agency; (3) include an appropriate preschool, elementary school, or secondary school education in the state involved; and (4) are provided in conformity with the IEP.

Types of procedural safeguards include rights of parents to view records regarding their children and all actions related to evaluations, placements, and programs. Children without parents and without homes are protected under this statute, and procedures are specified for notifications, complaints, responses, and, if need be, legal actions.

The emphasis on special education and related services designed to meet their unique needs and prepare students for further education, employment, and independent living was not present in past law. The idea of transition services for preparing children for a meaningful adult life (future education, employment, and independent living) became increasingly prominent in the statutes beginning with the reauthorization of IDEA in 1990.

Least Restrictive Environment (LRE) and Supplementary Aids and Services

> "To the *maximum extent appropriate, children with disabilities,* including children in public or private institutions or other care facilities, *are educated with children who are*

> *not disabled*, and special classes, separate schooling, or other *removal* of children with disabilities from the regular environment occurs *only when the nature of the disability or severity of the disability of a child is such that education in regular classes with the use of supplementary aids and services cannot be achieved satisfactorily*. (U.S.C. § 1412)

Federal regulations clarify that requirements for a least restrictive environment (LRE) also apply to nonacademic settings. The "public agency is to ensure that each child with a disability *participates* with nondisabled children in the extracurricular services and activities *to the maximum extent appropriate* to the needs of that child" and "ensure that each child with a disability has the supplementary aids and services determined by the child's IEP Team to be appropriate and necessary for the child to participate in nonacademic settings" (C.F.R. § 300.17). "The term 'supplementary aids and services' means aids, services, and other supports that are provided in regular education classes or other education-related settings to enable children with disabilities to be educated with nondisabled children to the maximum extent appropriate" (U.S.C. §1401).

Fair Evaluation and Parental Consent

> [Parents or educational agencies may initiate a request for an initial evaluation to determine] "if the child is a child with a disability." [*Before an initial evaluation is conducted* to determine the eligibility of a child for services under IDEA,] "the agency must obtain *informed consent from the parent of the child*." [Assessment and evaluation materials] "are to be selected and administered so as *not to be discriminatory on a racial or cultural basis*." (U.S.C. § 1414)

> [If the child is eligible and receives services, and if parents or the agency determines that the educational or related services needs, including improved academic achievement and functional performance of the child, warrants a reevaluation, with *informed parental consent, reevaluations* can be conducted] "*not more frequently than once a year*, unless the parent and local educational agency agree . . ." [and] "*at least once every 3 years*," [unless the agency and parent agree it is unnecessary. Agencies must] "use *a variety of assessment tools and strategies to gather relevant functional, developmental, and academic information, including information provided by the parent*." (U.S.C. § 1414)

"Parent" is used throughout IDEA 2004 to mean any natural, adoptive, or foster parent, guardian, or other adult legally responsible for the child. The *Federal Register* clarifies that parental consent for an initial evaluation must not be construed as consent for services. Informed consent must be obtained from the parent before the initial provision of special education and related services to the child (C.F.R. § 300.300).

IDEA 2004 requires that the initial evaluation must "be conducted within 60 days of receiving parent consent" and that the assessment be comprehensive assessments to "identify all of the child's special education and related services needs" (C.F.R. § 300.301). The movement away from single-measurement instruments or assessment to a "variety of assessment tools and strategies," including information from the parent, is new with IDEA 2004. Also new is the emphasis on a comprehensive initial evaluation to determine not only eligibility but also the "content of the child's IEP" (C.F.R. § 300.304). Significant changes were made in IDEA 2004 regarding evaluation requirements to determine whether a child has a specific learning disability (U.S.C. § 1414 and C.F.R. § 300.307).

Individualized Education Program (IEP) and IEP Team

[The] "determination of whether the child is a child with a disability . . ." "and the educational needs of the child shall be made by a team of qualified professionals and the parent of the child." [The team develops an individualized education program or IEP to meet the educational needs of the child. The IEP is a written statement for each child with a disability that is developed, reviewed, and revised in a meeting in accordance with provisions specified in sections of the law.] "In developing each child's IEP, the IEP Team must consider—

The *strengths* of the child;

The *concerns of the parents* for enhancing the education of the child; The *results of the initial evaluation or most recent evaluation* of the child; and

The *academic, developmental, and functional needs of the child*."

[In cases when the child's behavior] "impedes the child's learning or that of others [when developing the IEP, the team must] consider the use of *positive behavioral interventions* and other strategies, to address that behavior"[6] [and also consider the needs] "of a child with *limited English proficiency*," "a child who is *blind or visually impaired*," [a child who has] "*communication needs*," "a child who is deaf or hard of hearing," [and a child who] "needs *assistive technology and devices*" (C.F.R. § 300.324).

[Agencies must ensure that] "one or both of the parents of a child with a disability are present at each IEP Team meeting," [and that] "*parents are members of any group that makes decisions on the placement of their child, and informed parental consent is required prior to the implementation* of services in the IEP." [Also, public agencies must ensure that the] "child's *IEP is accessible to each regular education teacher*, special education teacher, related services provider, and any other service provider who is responsible for its implementation [*and be informed* of his or her] *specific responsibilities* related to implementing the child's IEP" [*and* the] "*specific accommodations, modifications, and supports* that must be provided for the child in accordance with the IEP" (C.F.R. § 300.323).

There are many provisions and details in the statutes regarding the IEP, the IEP team, and the development of the IEP. Several of the provisions in the statement above are new with IDEA 2004, although many of the requirements for an IEP and an IEP team were present in the 1975 law. Although the format for the written IEP varies across school districts, the basic components must adhere to federal law. The team consists of parents, at least one regular education teacher and one special education teacher, a representative of the local education agency (LEA), an individual who can interpret the instructional implications of evaluation results who may be one of the other members mentioned, other individuals (chosen at the discretion of the parent or agency), and, whenever appropriate, the child with a disability (C.F.R. § 300.321). Components of the IEP (C.F.R. § 300.320) must include the following:

- Present levels of academic achievement and functional performance.
- Measurable annual goals (academic and functional).
- A description of how progress will be measured and when periodic reports on progress will be provided.
- Special education and related services and supplementary aids and services, based on peer-reviewed research to the extent practicable, and statements of modifications or supports toward goals, progress in the general education curriculum along with participation in extracurricular and other nonacademic activities, and education and participation with other children with disabilities and children without disabilities.
- An explanation of the extent, if any, to which the child will not participate with children without disabilities in classes and activities.
- Accommodations necessary to measure academic achievement and functional performance of the child on state- and district-wide assessments or statements about why the child cannot participate or why an alternate assessment will substitute for the regular tests.
- Dates for the beginning of services and other specifics related to frequency, location, and so on.
- Transition statements to be in effect by the age of sixteen, or younger if determined appropriate by the IEP team, and updated annually. Appropriate measurable goals to be based on age-appropriate transition assessments related to postsecondary goals training, education, employment, and, where appropriate, independent living skills; transition

> services needed for the child to meet those goals; and a statement that the child has been informed of his or her rights under this law on reaching the age of majority. (In most states, the age of majority is eighteen.)

Related services are numerous and include transportation and such developmental, corrective, and other supportive services as are required to assist a child with a disability to benefit from special education. The list of related services has been expanded significantly as a result of amendments during reauthorization. In 1975, related services were listed as transportation, speech-language pathology, audiology, physical therapy, psychological services, physical therapy, occupational therapy, and others. A statement in the Senate version of the 1975 law stated that the list of related services was not intended to be exhaustive and may include other developmental, corrective, or supportive services (such as artistic and cultural programs, art, music, and dance therapy) if they are required to assist a child with a disability to benefit from special education. Although you will not find reference to music therapy after the 1997 revision of IDEA, music therapy is still considered a related service.[7]

Although the major premises put forward in 1975 had a significant impact on the education of children with disabilities, many critical issues were not addressed. For example, the law covered ages three through twenty-one but not infants and toddlers younger than three. The issue of qualifications for teachers and other professionals was not considered. And although the 1975 law required goals and objectives for the IEP, requirements for assessment of progress were minimal (and usually came with the annual review of the IEP). There were also no requirements for goals, transition programs, and assessments related to children's quality of life as adults. These critical issues and others were addressed in amendments to the law.

AMENDMENTS

Through the process of reauthorization, review, and public opinion, the EHA of 1975 (P.L. 94-142) has been amended six times, as of this writing, the last being in 2004. Amendments have occurred in all parts of IDEA, from definitions to implementation, some more significant than others. Amendments have occurred as a result of new knowledge about learning, supports, and resources (e.g., curricular priorities, transitioning to adult life, paraprofessional assistance, assistive technology devices) and assessments of its implementation. What went right? What went wrong?

Amendments in 1986, 1990, 1997, and 2004 were particularly significant, and several are summarized here.[8] Don't consider these summaries as direct quotes, even though I use language from the amendments to the degree possible; reading may be a bit awkward. I've added additional requirements, information, and comments in brackets for clarification.

The Education of the Handicapped Act Amendments of 1986 (P.L. 99-457) expanded the 1975 law to include children from birth through five years of age. Age three was covered by the 1975 act, but even with this amendment, programs for preschool children were not well developed. Research during the 1970s and 1980s increased awareness of early-intervention programs for children's success in future school years. The 1986 amendment improved services for three-year-olds and extended services to birth through age two with two programs: (1) a required free appropriate education in public schools for children with disabilities between the ages of three and five and (2) a discretionary grant program known as the Handicapped Infants and Toddlers Program to serve children from birth through age two.[9] EHA 1986 continued many statutes of the 1975 law, assessment, IEP team, and planning and included the following amendments specific to infants and toddlers:

- Assessments to identify a child with a disability:
  A comprehensive and multidisciplinary assessment of the child conducted by professionals and parents.
- Individualized program and transition:
  An individualized program that regards the family as the focus of services.
  Services identified on an individual family service plan (IFSP) designed by parents and professionals. The IFSP includes many of the components of the IEP and takes into account the unique needs of infants and toddlers and their families (delivered in the home or other settings as appropriate).
  An employed case manager who is designated on the IFSP and is responsible for the implementation of the program and coordination with other agencies and professionals.
  A plan for the transition of the child to preschool services at three years of age.

The Individuals with Disabilities Education Act of 1990 (P.L. 101-476) renewed the provisions of previous laws but also included several significant changes:

- Name of the law:
  - Person-first language replacing "education of the handicapped" with "individuals with disabilities."
- Definition of a "child with a disability":
  - Includes two new categories: autism and traumatic brain injury.
- IEP and transition:
  - A statement of transition services in the student's IEP no later than age sixteen for purpose of focusing on postschool outcomes (e.g., living, employment, recreation).
  - AT devices and services defined and to be made available if required as part of the child's educational program.

The Individuals with Disabilities Education Act of 1997 (P.L. 105-17) was the first significant change to occur after more than twenty years of observing the progress of students during their school years and into their adult lives. IDEA 1997 strengthened the law by mandating participation in general education classrooms and state assessment programs to the maximum extent possible. Children were to be educated with children without disabilities to the extent possible, but with the 1997 law, focus was on the curriculum, academic and functional goals, and students' progress. Curriculum and measurement of success were to be included in planning and implementing transition services.

Overall, performance expectations were higher beginning with this new law because of requirements for students' access to the general curriculum to the maximum extent possible and the measurement of their achievements. Parents were included more in transition planning and implementation. Special education began to be viewed as a service rather than a place (e.g., special education rooms or special schools), and the delivery of special education and related services were to be in the regular classroom whenever appropriate. IDEA 1997 required training of personnel such as teachers, providers of related services, and paraprofessionals to ensure appropriate education and put forward statutes concerning the discipline of children with disabilities. Several changes included:

- Definitions:
  - A "child with a disability" includes, at the discretion of states and the LEAs, a child from ages three through nine who is experiencing developmental delays.
  - A "parent" is a natural, adoptive, or foster parent of a child, a guardian, or an individual acting in the place of a natural or adoptive

parent with whom the child lives, or an individual who is legally responsible for the child's welfare.

- IEP and transition:
  - Increased participation in the general education curriculum and the regular classroom must be documented in the IEP.
  - The IEP must provide a statement of special education, support services, and other resources that will advance the student toward reaching annual goals.
  - Students are to be involved and progress in the general curriculum, participate in extracurricular programs and other nonacademic activities, and be educated and participate with other children with and without disabilities in activities; a separate statement must explain reasons the student will not participate with children without disabilities in regular classes and activities [services to be coordinated to provide access to the general curriculum].
  - Transition services defined as a coordinated set of activities that are within a results-oriented process and with a focus on academic and functional achievement. Requires a statement of transition *service* needs in the IEP beginning at age fourteen and updated annually [age sixteen was indicated simply for transition needs in the 1990 law], and beginning at age sixteen (or younger), a statement of transition services focusing on employment and other postschool adult living objectives, including a statement of interagency responsibilities or needed linkages [in previous versions, agencies other than schools were not required to participate].
  - An expanded IEP team to include the regular education teacher [who would be the individual who can interpret the instructional implications of evaluation results] and, at the discretion of the parent or the agency, other individuals who have knowledge or special expertise regarding the child, including related services personnel [individuals may be those outside of the school and are in addition to those required for the IEP team].
- Assessments and accountability:
  - IEP plans describe goals and short-term objectives and how those goals would be met.
  - Progress reports to parents on the same schedule as for parents of children without disabilities.
  - Children with disabilities to be included in general state- and district-wide assessment programs and modified and/or alternate assessments may be developed.

- Discipline:
  - School must determine if behavior is a result of the disability before removing the student from school, and if removed, services continue [no student is denied services].
  - An interim alternative education setting (IAES) to be determined by the IEP team and selected to enable continuation of education and services; the IAES or suspension cannot be more than ten school days ["Stay Put Rule" applies.][10]
  - School can remove a student to an IAES for forty-five days [without questions] if a student brings a gun, bomb, or drugs to school.
  - If behavior is not a result of the disability, educational placement does not change [student is "disciplined" consistent with school policies].
- Teachers, other personnel, and preparation:
  - Personnel development programs (through grants) to be offered by state and local agencies to ensure a sufficient number of adequately trained special education teachers, related services personnel, and general education faculty (trained to accommodate students in the least restrictive environment).
  - Paraprofessionals may be used but must be appropriately trained and supervised.

The Individuals with Disabilities Education Improvement Act of 2004 (P.L. 108-446), the current law at the time of this writing, preserves the basic structure and civil rights guarantees of IDEA 1997 but with several important changes.

IDEA 2004 places greater emphasis on learning outcomes and accountability and focuses on alignment with the No Child Left Behind Act (e.g., participation in state- and district-wide tests, "highly qualified teacher" requirements). Importance is given to access to the general education curriculum and instruction, academic performance, evaluation of students' progress, and highly qualified personnel. In several places throughout the law, language denotes both "academic" and "functional" (daily living) performance goals.

In IDEA 2004, services are also extended to children with disabilities who are homeless or who are otherwise members of highly mobile populations, such as migrant workers. Significant changes are made regarding the evaluation of children who are suspected of having specific learning disabilities. Transition services are to be "results-oriented," facilitate transition from school to employment and continued education, and take into account the students' interests and participation. "Early intervening services" are new in IDEA 2004. Schools may use a percentage of IDEA funds to provide services to students who need assistance in school but who are not evaluated as needing special education services under IDEA. Several changes are made regarding discipline. Significant changes to provisions include the following:

- Definitions and eligibility assessment:
    - Regarding eligibility assessment of children who are suspected of having specific learning disabilities (SLD), local education agencies (LEAs) are to use "technically sound instruments that may assess the relative contributions of cognitive factors"; states may not require the use of a single instrument, such as one to measure a severe discrepancy between achievement and intellectual ability, as the only criterion to determine whether a child has an SLD; a public agency must use the state criteria in determining whether a child has an SLD and discuss the role that the child's response to scientific research-based interventions plays in a comprehensive evaluation process.[11]
    - Extensive provisions for special education and related services for children with disabilities who are homeless or who are otherwise members of a highly mobile population.
    - Definition of "parent" substitutes "biological" for "natural." "Parent" includes an adoptive or foster parent, guardian, or individual legally responsible for the child, and language clarifies under this definition that a "guardian" must be a person generally authorized to act as the child's parent or authorized to make educational decisions for the child.
- IEP (programs and services) and transition:
    - Statement of child's present levels of academic achievement and functional performance [academic achievement is addressed for the first time].
    - Measurable goal statements that include academic and functional performance related to the child's present level and assessment of progress; benchmarks and short-term objectives required for children who take alternate assessments [separate academic and functional goals and assessment and alternate assessments are addressed for the first time].
    - IEP must specify how progress will be measured and when periodic reports on the child's progress are to be provided to the parents.
    - Statements of special education and related services and supplementary aids and services designated in the IEP to be based on peer-reviewed research to the extent practicable.

Clarification that supplementary aids and services can be provided in extracurricular and nonacademic settings to enable children with disabilities to be educated with children without disabilities to the maximum extent possible.[12]

Each regular education teacher (and other individuals as specified) has access to the child's IEP, and is to be informed of specific responsibilities for implementation and specific accommodations, modifications, and supports that must be provided in accordance with the IEP.

Interpreting services and school nurse services added to the list of related services.

States must make instructional materials accessible to children with disabilities in accordance with the National Instructional Materials Accessibility Standard (NIMAS)[13] and with reasonable steps to provide instructional materials in accessible formats to children with disabilities at the same time as children without disabilities receive their instructional materials.

Transition services defined to mean a coordinated set of activities [involving other agencies such as Vocational Rehabilitation] designed to be within a results-oriented process focused on improving the academic and functional achievement of a child with disabilities to facilitate movement from school to postschool activities. Services to be based on the individual child's needs, taking into account the child's strengths, preferences, and interests. Transition *process* for the student begins at age sixteen (or earlier) and is not merely a plan for transition [IDEA 1990 and 1997 required only plans of needs and services; agencies were not required to participate; the student's interests were not previously part of this process].

Measurable postsecondary goals must be developed for each student, and the child is to be involved in discussions regarding postsecondary goals and transition services, or, if the child is not in attendance, interests must be considered [again, the student's interests were not previously part of this process].

Other methods in addition to meetings can be used for schools and parents to develop and change IEPs and/or transition plans (e.g., conference calls).

- Assessments and accountability (also see IEP and transition, above):

All children with disabilities to be included in *all* general state- and district-wide evaluation programs. A detailed explanation must be provided for children who require individual appropriate accommodations and for those who take alternate assessments of progress.

Using universal design,[14] assessments to be developed for typical students that, if necessary, can be modified without invaliding the result.

Major changes in compliance monitoring focusing on student performance, not only compliance with IDEA policies and procedures [monitoring of compliance previously did not include student performance and participation in state and district testing].

- Teachers, other personnel, and preparation:

  Requirements that all special education teachers be highly qualified; qualifications expanded for related services personnel and paraprofessionals in addition to special education teachers[15] [establishment of standards was not required in previous laws].

- Early intervening services:

  Early intervening services (EIS) can be provided for students not identified as needing special education but who require academic or behavioral support to succeed in regular education classes.

  LEAs may use up to 15 percent of their local IDEA funds for "early intervening services" aimed at reducing or eliminating the future need for special education among children who do not currently qualify for services through IDEA [services and funding were not previously identified in the law and are intended to prevent students from having future problems in school].

- Discipline:

  If behavior is not a result of the disability, services continue, but the educational placement may be changed; parents may appeal the decision [the responsibility is now placed on the parents to appeal any decision by the school].

  Students can be removed for causing serious bodily injury [in addition to the previous law specifying bringing a gun, bomb, or drugs to school].

PROTECTION AGAINST DISCRIMINATION: SECTION 504 AND ADAAA

A number of laws are considered disability rights laws and primarily affect adults; however, two protect both children and adults and have important implications for children with disabilities and their education: Section 504 of the Rehabilitation Act of 1973[16] and the Americans with Disabilities

Act Amendments Act of 2008 (ADAAA, but still referred to as ADA).[17] Both have been discussed in different chapters of this book but will be reviewed briefly here as they relate to IDEA.

Section 504 and ADA reinforce the purposes of IDEA and emphasize postschool outcomes for daily living, employment, and recreation or leisure. Under 504, children and adults with disabilities must have access to all public programs and services that receive federal funds, whether these programs and services are in their schools or in their communities. Under ADA (first passed in 1990), children and adults with disabilities must have access to all programs and services that are public and private. Section 504, however, is the more familiar law regarding access to educational programs and services. Overall, the three laws (IDEA, 504, ADA) provide nondiscriminatory practices for children with disabilities who now have a guarantee of a free appropriate education, access to public services and accommodations, and employment without discrimination.

The Rehabilitation Act of 1973 prohibits discrimination on the basis of disability in programs conducted by federal agencies, in programs receiving federal financial assistance, in federal employment, and in the employment practices of federal contractors. There are several sections concerning affirmative action and employment in the Rehabilitation Act, but it is Section 504 that has direct implications for educational programs and services.

Section 504 states that "no qualified individual with a disability in the United States shall be excluded from, denied the benefits of, or be subjected to discrimination" from programs and activities that receive federal financial assistance. The requirements of Section 504 fueled the disabilities movement and the barrier-free movement that began in the 1960s. Observable changes were first made to the architecture of buildings receiving federal funds, but this was viewed only as a "prerequisite" to full participation in the public programs and services housed in buildings. These topics are discussed in chapter 4 as background related to designing universal strategies for teaching.

Section 504 is wide-sweeping when you consider that individuals with disabilities, both children and adults, must have access to buildings (e.g., schools and classrooms) that house programs and activities receiving federal funds (e.g., teaching and instruction). Access to both programs and activities are accomplished for some children through different types of adaptations as needed, in instruction, assessment, physical environment of the classroom, and so on.

If a child is defined as having a disability under IDEA, that child will also have protections of Section 504 and ADA. You will recall that IDEA defines a child as having a disability using disability categories (e.g., traumatic brain injury, intellectual disability). In both Section 504 and ADA, a person with a disability is defined as someone who:

- Has a physical or mental impairment that substantially limits one or more major life activities (major life activities are expanded substantially from those in ADA 1990).
- Has a record of such an impairment.
- Is regarded as having such an impairment.

If a child is assessed and defined as having a disability using the broad criteria above but does not meet the definition for a child with a disability using criteria stipulated by IDEA, this child can still receive appropriate educational services and protections under Section 504. For example, if a child is assessed as having a substantial limitation in thinking, reading, and/or writing but does not qualify for services under IDEA, 504 protections and services most likely will apply.

You can see the value of Section 504 for those children who do not quality for services under IDEA but still require some types of changes in their educational program to be successful in school. In these cases, children do not have an IEP but do have a "504 plan." A 504 plan is developed by parents, teachers, and other professionals to meet the needs of the child (e.g., changes to instructional procedures, behavioral strategies). It is not uncommon for children with behavioral characteristics associated with attention deficit disorder (ADD), attention deficit hyperactivity disorder (ADHD), or an auditory processing disorder (APD) to have 504 plans. In more severe cases of these same disabilities, the broad category "other health impairments" may be applicable, allowing children to receive instructional and medical services under IDEA.

Using amended language from ADA, Section 504 also states that mitigating measures, including assistive devices, auxiliary aids, accommodations, medical therapies, and supplies, other then eyeglasses and contact lenses, have no bearing in determining whether a person has a disability and qualifies for protections under the law. For example, a student may communicate effectively when using an alternative communication system, may navigate the school building successfully with a walker, or may read without problems when the print is larger. Even though this student may not be eligible for services under IDEA, the student may still be defined as having a disability using 504 criteria. If defined under 504 as having a disability, this student would be eligible for a 504 plan and any services determined as necessary for his or her success in school.

The protections and/or accommodations guaranteed by Section 504 apply equally to public and private educational institutions and agencies related to educational services (e.g., K–12 schools, colleges, universities, and testing agencies), although ADA is a broader law and extends to both the public and private sectors. (e.g., businesses, transportation, recreational facilities). The major premises of ADA 2008 are unchanged from the earlier 1990 act, although the definition of disability (major life activities) is expanded.

ADA prohibits discrimination on the basis of disability in employment (e.g., recruitment, hiring, promotions, training, pay, social activities, and other privileges of employment), state and local government activities (e.g., public education, employment, transportation, recreation, healthcare, social services, courts, voting, and town meetings), public accommodations (e.g., concert halls, restaurants, retail stores, hotels, movie theaters, private schools, dry cleaners, convention centers, doctors' offices, homeless shelters, transportation depots, zoos, funeral homes, day-care centers, and recreation facilities including sports stadiums and fitness clubs), public transportation (city buses and public rail transit), and telecommunications (telephone and television access for people with hearing and speech disabilities).

You can see the breadth of this law in providing safeguards against discrimination in a variety of settings and activities and how, in many cases, it overlaps with Section 504. There can be exceptions to the statutes, and questions regarding violations are ultimately defined in courts of law. From time to time, you will see newspaper stories and court cases about violations (e.g., access to a particular chain of video stores and car rentals comes to mind).

Given the legal safeguards against discrimination related to education, employment, housing, and participation in many activities beyond school, we can be hopeful for the future of children with disabilities. However, laws are just the beginning, and without vigilance from parents, teachers, and advocates, laws can be (and are) violated. Advocacy is the responsibility of all knowledgeable and caring adults. Music teachers who are knowledgeable about the major premises of IDEA, Section 504, and ADA can be invaluable supports to parents, professionals, and advocates to ensure protections for their students. Also, with knowledge of the law and a spirit of advocacy, competent music teachers are more likely to develop and implement music programs that will lead to their students' participating more successfully, fully, and happily in a variety of music experiences throughout life.

APPENDIX D

Significant Changes in Practices: 1970s to the Present

1970s AND 1980s: FUNCTIONAL, CHRONOLOGICAL AGE-APPROPRIATE CURRICULA WITH COMMUNITY-REFERENCED PRACTICES

- A developmental model dominates special education practices for children and adults; many reside in institutional settings with separate schools on institutional grounds.
  - Curricular and instructional decisions are based on practices used in infant and preschool programs; a multitude of age-inappropriate prerequisite skills and knowledge are required in curricula for children and adults with significant disabilities.
  - The concept of "mental age" is prominent.
  - Research and assessments of outcomes show slow educational progress and poor quality-of-life outcomes.
  - The model is eventually deemed ineffective and for the most part, eliminated from special education practices.
- Groundbreaking ideas emphasize a model focusing on quality-of-life outcomes.
  - Curricular and instructional practices are chronological age-appropriate, are community-referenced, and focus on functional outcomes (e.g., domestic and social knowledge and skills, vocational skills).
  - The concept of "chronological age" is prominent.
  - The concept of "partial participation" allows for greater participation in a variety of activities.

Research and assessments of outcomes show positive quality-of-life outcomes.

A model developed initially for individuals with significant disabilities, many of whom reside in institutional settings, gains recognition in special education practices in school settings.

- Focus on independence to the maximum extent possible and access to programs and facilities continues to gain ground as a result of laws—Section 504 of the Rehabilitation Act, IDEA, and the Technology-Related Assistance for Individuals with Disabilities Act (Tech Act). Sweeping advances are seen in technology.

1990s: SOCIAL INCLUSION, SELF-DETERMINATION, AND THE PROMINENCE OF ASSISTIVE TECHNOLOGY

- Practices focus on social justice and inclusion as a civil right.

  Increase in civil rights activities by individuals with disabilities, self-advocacy groups, and supportive individuals and professional organizations, all working for full membership of people with disabilities in their schools, neighborhoods, and communities.
- Professionals produce a wealth of articles on social inclusion, social interactions, and self-determination.
- IDEA 1997 mandates access to the general curriculum to the maximum extent possible and also participation in the general curriculum, extracurricular activities, and other nonacademic activities, all to be documented in the IEP; participation in state and district tests is required, or alternate tests if necessary. Special education begins to be viewed as a service rather than a place where children receive instruction.
- Transition requirements from IDEA 1990 and IDEA 1997 strengthen the importance of postschool adult-living objectives in education programs.
- Greater access and opportunities for participation in all aspects of life in the public and private sectors are a result of Section 504 of the Rehabilitation Act of 1973 and the passage of the Americans with Disabilities Act of 1990 (ADA amended in 2008).
- Technological advancements continue with amendments in 1999 to the Tech Act and increase access to academic learning and activities of daily life.

2000s: ACCESS TO THE GENERAL CURRICULUM AND ASSESSMENT OF STUDENT PROGRESS

- Earlier priorities and effective practices of the 1980s and 1990s are prominent; the biggest thrust is access to academic subjects in the general curriculum and assessment of students' progress.
- IDEA 2004 continues to focus on access to the general education curriculum and instruction, academic performance, and assessment of students' progress.
    - Both academic and functional (daily-living) goals are included, assessed, and integrated into regular education practices to the degree possible.
    - Scientifically based instructional practices and services based on peer-reviewed research are used to the extent possible.
    - Access to instructional materials and assistive technology (AT) devices and services is required.
- The concept of universal design introduced in IDEA 2004 specific to assessment practices gains prominence as an instructional approach.
- Response to Intervention (RTI) emerges from language in IDEA 2004 and develops into a schoolwide, multitiered instructional model that receives much attention in general education at all levels, particularly as a proactive process designed to identify and meet diverse learning needs of students with disabilities and those at risk.

For more information about these and other changes that added significantly to progress in education and civil rights for individuals with disabilities, see appendix B. Current curricular and instructional practices are discussed in depth in chapter 4.

LEARN MORE: INDIVIDUAL AND GROUP ACTIVITIES

Activities presented here are organized by chapters and by historical material in the appendices, but they are not meant to be exclusive. As you work with an activity, individually or as a group, to the degree possible, incorporate ideas from other chapters. For example, the governing principles in chapter 3—ideas about culturally normative experiences and social value, peer interactions, self-determination, and collaboration and cooperation—can be incorporated into many of the activities.

Some activities can be done on your own, but many involve others, including people with disabilities, parents, teachers, therapists, other professionals, and your classmates if you are a student. Several are designed to stimulate personal reflections about your experiences and attitudes and for you to think about and discuss issues related to freedom and social justice, laws and education policies in different states and communities, and attitudes toward people who are marginalized in society. Many have been developed to help you create ideas for designing inclusive music programs, where you will implement effective strategies and adaptations, where students will accomplish music goals, and where they will learn how to interact with one another, enjoy one another's successes, and feel proud of their accomplishments. Enjoy learning more.

CHAPTER 1. WHO'S HERE?

1. Describe yourself by making a list of some of your physical characteristics, preferred music activities, other preferences and interests, skills and knowledge, and so on. Compare descriptions of yourself with those from other individuals who have done this activity. What kinds of similarities and differences do you find? What kinds of groups could be created among several individuals participating in this activity? What groups do you find yourself in, and to which do you not belong? Is it possible for you to be in a group to which you do

not now belong? What would it take for this to happen? Discuss issues of group identity and those that can be socially and/or politically consequential and those that do not or should not matter.

2. Think of a child you know well, any child, and engage in the same type of activity described above. Look at your list, and think about different types of groups to which this child would belong. If you know a child with a disability or one who is struggling in school, compare your list with the list for gathering information about students (in chapter 4, box 4.3). What do you know and not know about this child? About his or her music interests, preferences, and capabilities? Would knowing more about any of the items on the list change the nature of your interactions with the child? If yes, in what way?
3. Find examples of negative stereotyping or the lack of person-first language in written or spoken language. When appropriate, work to bring about positive change. For example, write or call the newspaper regarding an inappropriate use of language, and provide positive alternatives; privately inform a student, family member, or friend about person-first language.
4. Using online resources, find several definitions for children at risk for school failure. Compare definitions, and find common factors among them. Using reports from the US Census Bureau, discuss how the percentages of children living below the poverty level have changed in the past several years. What types of services are available for these children and their families, and does your state provide these services? Talk with music teachers who work in low-income school districts about their programs, their students, their communication with students' families, and the benefits of music in the lives of students, families, and communities.
5. Examine the Disabilities Information Pages at the website for the Center for Music Learning (CML), cml.music.utexas.edu. Choose one disability, and learn about it in more depth from these pages and other resources. Using these and other resources, examine the various types of disabilities found in the category "other health impaired," and search for information that suggests reasons for increases in the numbers of children categorized as having a health impairment. Search also for information related to increases in the numbers of children with autism. What does the latest research say about causes for these increases?
6. Some parents and their children with disabilities are comfortable talking informally about their music education experiences. Children and adults can provide important information about ways to make music more accessible in schools and communities. Ask adults to talk

about accessible music experiences in and outside of school and their suggestions for music teachers and community music programs.

7. Professionally made videos of children and teachers can be a valuable resource. Disability organizations in communities often have videos for loan, and others can be obtained through disability organizations online (e.g., TASH and CEC). AMTA sells a CD of children with disabilities and their teachers in inclusive music settings. You can also find well-done video clips at sites for professional organizations and even on YouTube (screen these carefully). When watching videos of children with disabilities, discuss the content related to guidelines discussed in this book. How are the children portrayed? What skills do the children have, and can you visualize possibilities for these children to participate in meaningful music experiences in their homes, schools, and communities? What would be required to make this happen?
8. Schools and local organizations present talks and events designed to inform the community of educational services for people with disabilities. Learn about events sponsored by local chapters for national organizations (e.g., autism, intellectual disabilities), "Very Special Arts" organizations, and special education departments in school districts. Share these events with colleagues, and attend those of interest.
9. "Very Special Arts" organizations often sponsor outdoor events in communities. Learn about these events, the age groups involved, and if any include typically developing children. Attend these events, interact with attendees as appropriate, and discuss some of your impressions and observations. You may want to collaborate with this organization and provide live music performances.
10. Go to the home page for *Healthy People* (www.healthypeople.gov) and examine the topics and objectives pages (new topics continue to be added). Find facts and data reporting disparities in health among different populations and for school-age populations. Children living with low-income families or who are living in poverty are highly likely to have health conditions that will affect their success in school and throughout life. What measures are being taken by your school, school district, and state to provide the support and services they may need?

CHAPTER 2. WHAT'S THE POINT?

1. Think about a young child you care about, and then visualize this child as an adult at the age of thirty, forty, or fifty. What musical life would you wish for this child as an adult?

2. In small groups, brainstorm as many ideas as possible regarding music activities that can be performed by adults (who are not music professionals) in their homes, local schools, and communities. All activities should be considered valid, even singing in the shower. You may want each group to focus on one environment and then share ideas. Identify those you consider priorities. If your ideas are seen as goals for an adult life, how do they compare with goals, objectives, and standards found in national and state curricula? How do they differ?
3. Transition services for children with disabilities are defined to mean a coordinated set of activities designed to be within a results-oriented process focused on improving the academic and functional achievement of the child to facilitate movement from school to postschool activities. If students are to learn to transfer skills and knowledge, transition plans for music learning and participation must begin early. Students must also know about their communities and have ongoing music experiences in the communities. Identify specific music and music-related groups and businesses in your community that can work with you to develop an ongoing connection with your students and your music program. Perhaps music businesses can sponsor music programs, in spirit and not necessarily with money, and community ensemble members can be regular visitors for live performances in classrooms. Make a list of stores, ensembles, and other possibilities for ongoing collaborations.
4. What national and state music curricular goals do you consider priorities, and in what ways do they fit into your list of curricular priorities for an adult musical life? Choose any national or state objective, and add contexts. Vary the physical environment, people involved, materials, and so on. Discuss ways to facilitate transfers of skills and knowledge by making contexts more like the real world.
5. In what ways are the ideas of transition and transfer related? Describe how you could apply these ideas in your own work as a music teacher. Give many examples to explain your thinking.
6. Choose any of the transfer principles discussed in this chapter, and provide examples in music learning situations and other types of activities in school and daily life. You may want to choose examples of your own learning and also when you did not learn what you wanted to. Why did learning occur or not occur as you intended? What was necessary to ensure the transfer of your learning to a new situation?
7. Examine the research literature for articles on transfer of learning. What other principles are evident in the literature? Describe music teaching and learning examples for these principles.

8. Choose a preferred adult music activity, and examine all of its component parts (refer to examples in the chapter). What functional prerequisites are required? Create age-appropriate experiences for lower- and upper-grade-level students. Experiences should be as close as possible to the adult experience.
9. Interview adults who were in music ensembles in school and/or who studied an instrument and adults who had no additional music study beyond elementary school. What are their attitudes regarding their experiences, their perceptions of their music skills and abilities, and their interest in continuing music study in their adult lives? Do these adults still participate in music activities? Beyond the verbal information they provide, what general effect can you observe from their descriptions of past and current music experiences?
10. Read articles about adult music experiences and the development of adult music programs and ensembles. Several successful music programs have been developed for older adults. If you have such a group in your community, ask the director and members to talk about their ideas for recruiting adults and how they provide positive experiences for them. What ideas do they have to connect school students with their members and to keep students involved as adults?

CHAPTER 3. WHERE DO I START?

1. The concept of "natural proportion" is useful in estimating the number of children with disabilities who should be included in regular classrooms. It is not a law, but using this concept as a guideline for placements guards against unnecessary segregation of services and resources or the placement of too many children with disabilities in any classroom. Discuss how the type and severity of the disabilities of children would influence the numbers of students in a classroom. Are there situations in school and in life where diversity populations are generally accepted and others are not acceptable? What protections do you recall from the US Constitution or other laws for individuals who are from diverse groups and/or who have "diverse" ideas?
2. Make a list of "roles" in society that are valued by a large majority of the population. What are some possible factors that led to individuals being in those roles, and are there opportunities for many others to perform those roles? Make a list of roles that are valued in school—in music classrooms, rehearsals, and performances. Are there opportunities for everyone to perform these roles? Should

everyone perform the same role? How can you, as a teacher, enhance the value of any given role, assignment, or task performed by a student?

3. Preserving confidentiality, ask music educators and music therapists to show you examples of 504 plans, IEPs, and RTI interventions and to discuss their experiences in the development of these plans and how meetings are conducted. Ask music therapists to discuss their assessment procedures to determine whether a child with a disability will benefit from music therapy services. Ask teachers to talk about the decision-making process when a child is identified at Tier 1, indicating that the child needs support and an intervention plan. How is the child assessed throughout the process? If you were to attend one of these meetings, how would you prepare, and what brief, succinct statements would you make regarding broad goals and music goals for all of your students? Verbalize your values clearly and succinctly to another person.
4. Talk with any parent about the goals that parent has for his or her child—goals for school and adult life. What kinds of music experiences do parents want for their children? Had they thought about their children having music experiences outside of school? What do they know about their children's music interests and capabilities? Preserving confidentiality, compare and discuss answers. For parents of children with disabilities, compare answers with those from parents of typically developing children. What values do they have in common?
5. Watch for examples in the media of negative stereotyping and prejudice regarding different groups of individuals. Keeping your thoughts private, examine your own biases regarding people who are from other countries, who belong to different organizations, or who are from different backgrounds from yours. Have you had positive experiences that have resulted in changes in your attitudes and/or actions toward these individuals? How can you go about changing any negative thinking you have learned? Have you seen examples of negative stereotyping in schools and any positive measures that were taken to try to alleviate this problem? Under what circumstances have you seen individuals from disparate backgrounds unite? Discuss these examples.
6. Examine various resources on social development and social skills. Make a list of several activities you have gleaned from these resources. If possible, implement classroom activities designed for social interactions and music learning, or simulate them in a college classroom. Examine different types of activities in classrooms and rehearsals,

and design ways for these activities to be accomplished, or enriched, using small groups or partners. What criteria would you use for the selection of group members and partners? What short, upbeat activities using small groups will you implement early in the school year and/or on the first day of class that will result in positive interactions among students?

7. Design various types of activities that your students can perform in their classroom, school, and community as a way to build a sense of community and giving. How can you involve students and members from community service organizations in these activities? What types of contacts and decisions can be made by the students, and what responsibilities and tasks are appropriate for them to complete independently or with minimal assistance?
8. Self-determined acts are volitional acts by an individual. Make a list of the many decisions, substantive and trivial, that you have made and subsequent actions that suggest that you are a self-determined individual. What are your perceptions of your own capabilities (self-efficacy), and in what ways do you use self-regulation regarding your actions and thoughts? Have there been times when you felt less secure in interpersonal settings? Discuss how feelings of self-efficacy, self-regulation, and security are learned or not.
9. Discuss various types of classrooms activities for students that involve component elements of self-determined behaviors, such as choice making, decision-making, problem solving, self-observation, self-evaluation, self-reinforcement, and others. Do some activities "naturally" lend themselves to these elements? Alone or in pairs or groups, discuss these activities, and list and develop others for music classrooms of children in different age groups. Discuss what is required for skills associated with self-determination to be internalized, learned deeply and thoroughly, and transferred to new situations.
10. Examine the phrases, problems, and questions from the Self-Determined Model of Instruction discussed in this chapter. Answer the questions for yourself, to the extent possible. Choose music goals or other goals for yourself that you believe are attainable and a time frame, preferably within several weeks. Follow the model to select and reach goals. Discuss some of your actions with others, and get feedback. What have you learned from going through this process? If you are working with a school-age child, typically developing or with a disability, have the student go through the process, and provide assistance and adjustments to individualize the process as needed.

CHAPTER 4. NOW WHAT?

1. University and college campuses typically have assistive technology centers with assistive devices and examples of adaptations. Arrange a visit and orientation at one of these centers. Write a one-page description of your visit, and list at least five ways some of the AT devices can be used for music teaching and learning. Individually or in a group, locate websites related to disabilities, and examine assistive devices on the sites. Use the CML site and others. What are the policies and practices for your state or school district regarding the provision of accessible instructional materials, equipment, and AT devices and services for children?
2. Talk with individuals who use various types of assistive devices. Ask about their experiences and the barriers they find in schools and communities. Discuss types of devices and adaptations that could make music materials, equipment, and environments more accessible.
3. Find and read articles from the *Journal of Research in Music Education* and the *Journal of Music Therapy* related to children and adults with disabilities and other diverse populations. Why was this research conducted? What were the variables of interest? What were the outcomes? If music was used to reach nonmusic outcomes, how can these results apply to the teaching and learning of music or music participation? Why do you suspect there are so few research studies examining music learning and children representing diverse populations?
4. Consider any test you have taken or given to students in the past. Discuss ways to vary the input modality and response modality for different test questions. Are there ways different modalities can be used at the same time with a group as a universal approach? Under what conditions, considering student characteristics and behaviors, would this test need to be administer to a student individually, apart from the group?
5. What music and social goals do you have for yourself? Write these goals in the contexts of environments, people, materials, and so on. Write music and social goals for a typical student you know or whom you may be teaching. Write goals for a student of the same age who has a disability or who is struggling in school (characteristics of the student can be real or hypothetical). What considerations will you need to make, if any, for this student to successfully achieve these goals?
6. Conduct interviews with teachers regarding strategies and adaptations that they use in their inclusive classrooms. Observe classrooms, and note strategies and adaptations that appear to be effective. Could these effective instructional practices be used in different settings and with different age groups?

7. Examine the CML website and other sites for specific strategies and adaptations for children with different types of disabilities. Compile a list that identifies those that could apply to all children in a classroom setting as universal strategies and those that apply only to students with specific characteristics and behaviors as individual adaptations.
8. Examine websites for universal design, universal design for learning, and universal design for instruction. Specifically search for unique contributions from each site and information that can apply to different music environments in schools, classrooms, auditoriums for performances, community music venues, and so on. What sites do you find most helpful, and why?
9. Select specific tasks among the many routines of daily life (e.g., brushing teeth, dressing, tying shoes) and others related to music (e.g., assembling an instrument, buzzing lips, sight-reading a piece). Complete a task analysis with steps specifying component behaviors beginning with an action verb (e.g., "pick up the brush . . ."). Be specific. Compare your list with another person's. Do you both list the same behaviors in the same order? If not, what are the consequences for omitting a behavior or doing the task using a different order of steps? If you were to teach these steps, which steps are essential, and in what order should they be taught?
10. This activity will result in a major project that you can complete in its entirety or in part, alone or in a collaborative group with colleagues in a college and university class, or at in-service workshops for music teachers. It is based on the model for effective, accessible music programs and corresponding activities for the chapter sections on "Gathering Information" and "Planning and Implementing Strategies." The corresponding online examples at the companion website will be useful as you work on this project.

    With college and university students, this project is conceived of as an ongoing process that begins early in the semester. To begin, consider a student with a disability or one who is struggling academically and/or socially in school. You may want to consider a student you are teaching now or a student from your past. If you have no student experiences to draw on for this activity, create a hypothetical student and a plausible teaching environment. You will then develop a profile for your student using characteristics and behaviors of the student and/or characteristics and behaviors for students from the disability pages at the CML site. Collaboration with colleagues in groups is an important part of the process. You may want to work with others who share your interest and expertise in a similar teaching area (e.g., orchestra) and think about all of the students you are considering being in the same classroom together. In a sense, you are creating a real situation where students with diverse learning needs are in the same classroom. As you read more and discuss ideas in class, complete the remainder of the project (analyzing environments and activities, designing strategies) following suggestions in the text and in the online examples. Throughout the process, present your ideas to other members of the class, and benefit from their feedback.

APPENDIX B. FROM EXCLUSION TO INCLUSION

1. Examine the archive at the Disability History Museum's library (www.disabilitymuseum.org/lib). At this site, you will find interesting photographs, several with musicians, and pictures from Blatt and Kaplan's book *Christmas in Purgatory*. Download a free PDF copy of the entire book and read interesting stories about its development with a search for the book title at the website for the Minnesota Governor's Council on Developmental Disabilities, http://mn.gov/mnddc/. When you examine the photographs, think about and discuss the different components (lighting, space, angles, subjects) that Kaplan chose for the photographs so as to create different emotional responses. Find and talk about other examples from magazines, books, videos, and film that elicit different kinds of emotions. You may also want to examine the portrayal of people from different cultures, races, economic status, and disabilities in children's picture and chapter books. Discuss ways media can influence and change attitudes toward diverse populations and how you can use appropriate media examples in music classes.
2. Read articles about the civil rights movements for different groups—African American, American Indian, Asian, Hispanic, Mexican American, Middle Eastern, and others groups, such as those determined by gender and sexual orientation. Discuss laws and events in history that fueled discriminatory practices (e.g., the bombing of Pearl Harbor and the forced internment of Japanese Americans). In what ways were children educated during these times, and in what ways did they participate in boycotts, marches, and so on?
3. Read historical accounts of musicians with disabilities and professional musicians with disabilities in modern society. Discuss their musical, educational, and life experiences. Identify laws, social policies, and attitudes that were factors, positive and negative, in their careers.

4. Examine the goals regarding disabilities put forward at the website for *Healthy People 2010: Disability and Secondary Conditions.* Among the goals for the year 2010 was the elimination of all public and private congregate facilities for children, increasing home- and community-based care, and increasing the proportion of children and youths with disabilities who spend at least 80 percent of their time in regular education programs from 45 percent to 60 percent. Did you find a progress report? Have the goals been met?
5. The disturbing accounts of eugenics have been documented in several books and articles. You may want to read these and think about issues that led to the US Supreme Court's support of such practices. Discuss the attitudes and other prevailing factors that could lead to national and state approval of these practices. What legal and social policies are necessary to prevent similar actions toward any group of people? Investigate the history of the eugenics movement in your state.
6. Read the full text of any of the cases discussed in this appendix. What are some of the stories of the individuals involved in the cases (plaintiffs, family members, lawyers, judges), and what were the decisions of the courts? How have issues changed since these decisions were rendered? Are you able to find current news reports about discrimination of any kind? Based on your readings and experiences, what current issues related to discrimination should be examined in the courts?
7. Read any books about pioneer teachers (Itard, Gallaudet, Braille, Sullivan) and the children they taught. If the children they taught (e.g., the "wild boy of Aveyron" or Helen Keller) were children in modern society, what dramatic differences would we expect to see in their education, and what would be similar?
8. Examine the etymology of the words *asylum, bedlam, institution, handicap, maniacal.* Are there other words in the common vernacular that might have some historic connection to disabilities and practices? How does this connection function regarding attitudes toward persons with disabilities, disability services, and practices? What words specific to other diverse populations would you "eliminate," to the degree possible?
9. Philanthropic societies were developing at the end of the American Revolution (1783) as the country saw dramatic increases in population, a rise in wealth for some, and many adults and children living in poverty. Charities developed shortly afterward to help remedy some of the social problems. Most remedies involved placement in institutional settings. In the first half of the nineteenth century, at the

urging of the general public and charities, a separate school for children who were deaf and another for children who were blind were established. A school for those children determined to be "feeble minded" was established at mid-century. Speculate about why separate schools were established for these three disabilities first. Examine the histories of education for children with other types of disabilities. Where do you think children who were living in poverty were being educated?

10. Look at the timeline in this book (appendix A), and add new significant events and laws. Discuss these new additions and their relevance for improving the quality of life of individuals. If you were to write a historic account of laws, social policies, and educational practices for the beginning of the twenty-first century, from 2000 to the present, what would you highlight for this short period, and why? To the degree possible, consider how this brief historical account would be viewed by people living in poverty, people with disabilities, people from diverse populations, families, educators, and lawmakers. In what ways would the perspectives of these groups be similar or different?

APPENDIX C. IDEA: HISTORY, PREMISES, INTERPRETATIONS

1. Annual reports are presented to Congress on the implementation of IDEA with national and state data. From the website for the Office of Special Education and Rehabilitative Services (OSERS), find the latest report, and compare data for your state to other state and national data. Examine data for race and ethnicity. What observations can you make, and what questions do the data generate?
2. All states have education agencies that make available special education publications of laws, regulations, and resources. Obtain for review copies of state laws, policies, and regulations concerning the operation of special education programs in your state. Find other useful general information at state offices, and ask especially about information for parents and families.
3. Ask someone knowledgeable in school law to talk with you or meet with your class to discuss the concept of due process and the role and responsibility of parents, schools, and lawyers in this process.
4. Definitions of a child with a disability (and the specific type of disability), a child who is at risk, a homeless child, or a child living in poverty may differ in state and federal documents. Whether the child

meets the criteria in the definition may affect the availability of services for that child. Discuss differences among the definitions and also among definitions preferred by organizations (e.g., the American Association on Intellectual and Developmental Disabilities).

5. Examine discipline policies and procedures in your state and school district regarding children with disabilities, homeless children, and children who qualify for free or reduced-cost lunch programs. What questions do you have for parents and teachers who may have had experiences related to disciplinary measures?
6. In the area of discipline, the law specifies that when a child's behavior "impedes the child's learning or that of others [the team must] consider the use of positive behavioral interventions and other strategies, to address that behavior." The law, however, does not define positive behavior interventions. Examine articles and resources for Positive Behavior Support (PBS) at the Center on Positive Behavioral Interventions and Supports (PBIS) through the Office of Special Education Programs and Rehabilitative Services (OSERS). Are there aspects of this approach that can be implemented for all children in the same classroom?
7. Arrange a session with a person who monitors compliance with the Americans with Disabilities Act Amendments Act of 2008. This act, which continues to be called ADA, provides standards for implementation. Ask about implementation of ADA in your building and campus. Using standards from ADA, examine the physical environment of your building, classroom, and campus. Make recommendations for changes and access for persons with different types of disabilities, those who are temporarily disabled, and older adults. For example, are changes required for individuals to attend concerts and classes, go to libraries, use practice rooms, and so on? Consider in your decision-making issues related to culturally normative experiences and self-determination related to all individuals, both children and adults.
8. Ask parents, music educators, and music therapists to talk about their experiences participating in RTI, Section 504, and IEP meetings. What is the process, and what is important to know in preparation for these meetings? Ask about statements of transition services in the student's IEP. Parents, educators, and therapists may also have interesting information regarding their experiences in the development and implementation of any of these plans.
9. Federal regulations include music therapy as a related service. At the discretion of the state, music therapy may be listed as a related service in state laws and/or regulations. Contact your state special

education agency to find out whether music therapy is considered a related service. Ask music therapists who work in schools about the requirements for students to receive music therapy. What is the history of the addition of music therapy as a service in their school districts? Also learn about music therapy as a related service from the American Music Therapy Association (AMTA) at www.musictherapy.org. You may want to work with parents, music educators, and special educators to find ways to add this service in your school district, if it is currently not available, and to have it recognized in state documents. AMTA will be helpful in these efforts.

10. Arrange to observe music therapy sessions and inclusive music education classes. Keep a log of your observations. Describe the physical environment, students in the class, objectives of the therapist or teacher, activities, and outcomes, and provide general impressions of your observations. See the same class more than once, and compare observations. Discuss your observations with others. After your observations, if possible, arrange a session in the schools when you can provide a mini-performance for the students, just for fun. Everyone will be appreciative.

NOTES

CHAPTER 1

1. In December 2004, Congress reauthorized the Individual with Disabilities Education Act (IDEA) (P.L. 108-446), which was signed into law. Reports on the implementation of IDEA have been ongoing for decades, and it takes several years between the collection of data from states and the published report. The most current data are available online from the Office of Special Education Programs (OSEP) (*35th Annual Report to Congress on the Implementation of the Individuals with Disabilities Education Act*, 2009). You will find all annual reports by searching for Annual Report on the Implementation of the Individuals with Disabilities Education Act at the website for the Department of Education, www.ed.gov. (See this book's companion website, www.oup.com/us/includingeveryone, for an overview of the organization and publication of the Individuals with Disabilities Education Act, excerpts related to purposes and definitions, definitions of disability and disability terms, and tables of percentages of children of different ages and with different disabilities who receive services. You will find data for your state in the full report. Also check for the latest updates at the website for OSEP.)

   Since it take several years for data to be gathered and reported, some data in the latest report are presented only through 2011. In 2011, 17.1 percent of children and young adults (infants through age twenty-one) were identified as receiving services under IDEA. Of those receiving services 5,789,884 were ages six through twenty-one, a number that represented 8.4 percent of the population, with 94.9 percent of them being educated in regular classrooms for at least some portion of the school day. More than half of all students ages six through twenty-one were educated *inside* the regular classroom for 80 percent or more of the day. Only 5.1 percent were educated *outside* of the regular classroom in other environments. Tables from the report show percentages in different categories of time outside the regular classroom and trends in percentages and numbers of children served by age groups and by disability category. (See the companion website for tables showing percentages and trends and also information about two other categories, that of infants and toddlers and that of children ages three through five.)

   The definition of a "child with a disability" is found in the statutes (20 U.S.C. § 1401) and regulations (34 C.F.R. § 300.8). A "child with a disability" is a child "with mental retardation, hearing impairments (including deafness), speech or language impairments, visual impairments (including blindness), serious emotional disturbance (referred to in this title as 'emotional disturbance'), orthopedic impairments, autism, traumatic brain injury, other health impairments, or specific learning disabilities; and who, by reason thereof needs special education and related services." The definition of a "child with a disability" also includes children ages three through nine experiencing developmental delays. Again, it is important to note that the school is not required to determine the child's "label" or classification before it provides services, only that assessments show that a child has a disability and would benefit from special education and related services.

The use of the category "developmental delay" is at the "discretion of the State and the local educational agency." Developmental delays, "as defined by the State and as measured by appropriate diagnostic instruments and procedures," include a child experiencing delays in one or more of the areas physical development, cognitive development, communication development, social or emotional development, or adaptive development; and by reason of the developmental delay, needs special education and related services. The category "developmental delay" allows for early services for young children who cannot be assessed appropriately or accurately for other types of disabilities identified in IDEA.

To be eligible for special education and related services under IDEA, all children must be in need of *both* services: special education and related services. In other words, a child who may only need to have physical therapy, a related service, and no other services related to his or her academic educational program (special education) would not quality for any services under the definition of a disability in IDEA but can receive physical therapy through other sources. (See the companion website for definitions of different types of disabilities and disability terms from IDEA, 34 C.F.R. § 300.8, and tables of percentages of children of different ages and with different disabilities who receive services.)

2. These statistics are from a report prepared for the National Center for Children in Poverty (NCCP) and can be found at its website, www.nccp.org. See the report by S. Addy, W. Engelhardt, and C. Skinner, *Basic Facts about Low-Income Children: Children under 18 years, 2011* (New York: Columbia University, National Center for Children in Poverty, 2013). The NCCP reports that in 2011, the federal poverty level was set at $22,350 for a family of four and $14,710 for a family of two. Of the 72 million children younger than eighteen years old in the United States in 2011, 32.4 million infants, young children, and children ages six through seventeen (45 percent) lived in low-income households; nearly half of those, 16.1 million (22 percent) lived in poor families. For more information about demographic, socioeconomic, and geographic characteristics of low-income children and their parents, see the full report and other facts on poverty at the website for the US Census Bureau, www.census.gov.
3. For in-depth descriptions and general information about organizations and agencies that offer a variety of services and support for persons with disabilities, see the Center for Music Learning website, cml.music.utexas.edu. Also see note 5.
4. Student success is one of many factors that influence students' decisions to continue music at the secondary level. Motivation, particularly as it relates to peer influences and school success, is discussed in chapter 2.
5. The National Center for Education Statistics (NCES) regularly reports data on children considered to be at-risk. Although definitions will vary across different sources, most definitions take into account characteristics put forward in NCES research and reports (demographic characteristics, family and personal background, family income, parental involvement in the student's education, academic history, behavioral factors, teacher perceptions of the student, and characteristics of the student's school). Most often, researchers and scholars agree that many factors predict a student's failure in school, factors that can be independent of a student's ethnicity, culture, gender, or native language. For predictors of music participation and issues related to at-risk students, see D. Kinney, "Selected Nonmusic Predictors of Urban Students' Decisions to Enroll and Persist in Middle School Band Programs," *Journal of Research in Music*

Education 57 (2010): 334–350; and K. Elpus and C. R. Abril, "High School Music Ensemble Students in the United States: A Demographic Profile," *Journal of Research in Music Education* 59 (2011): 128–145.

6. See the AAIDD website at, aaidd.org,for definitions, resources, and other support information. For some countries, the term for children with intellectual and developmental disabilities is "learning disability," which in the United States is a term associated with types of "specific learning disabilities" (e.g., dyslexia, dysgraphia, dyscalculia).
7. R. K. Barnhart, *The Barnhart Concise Dictionary of Etymology* (New York: H. W. Wilson, 1988).
8. "Rosa's Law" is the short title of the act passed by Congress in 2010 (P.L. 111-256) that changes references in federal laws from "mental retardation" to "intellectual disability" and from "mentally retarded individual" to "individual with an intellectual disability." Signed into law by President Barack Obama, it was named for Rosa Marcellino, a girl who attended school in Maryland and whose parents challenged her school's labeling of their daughter. They worked to pass state legislation to that effect, and after passage at the state level, Senator Barbara Mikulski introduced the same bill at the federal level. The US Supreme Court adopted the language "intellectual disability" beginning with a 2014 decision involving an individual with a disability.
9. Joseph Shapiro, in his well-regarded book *No Pity* (New York: Random House, 1993, 1994), reminds us of the negative images created in the classics—Shakespeare's Richard III with a hunchback (the real king had no disability); Captain Hook fighting against children and Peter Pan; Captain Ahab losing a leg as a result of his "mad derangement" over Moby Dick; Lenny with an intellectual disability in Steinbeck's *Of Mice and Men*, who "did not know his own strength" and killed a young woman (Lenny lived in the community, and Shapiro suggests that this image fueled negativism regarding group homes). Negative sinister characters with disabilities pervade classic literature and movies, although others are characterized to elicit pity. Remember Tiny Tim?
10. Several examples of reducing bias in written language can be found in the style manual for the American Psychological Association and also online in the "Guidelines for Unbiased Language" section at www.apastyle.org.
11. In 2002, the Centers for Disease Control and Prevention estimated the prevalence of children with autism spectrum disorders (types of ASDs to include autism, Asperger syndrome, and pervasive developmental disorder) to be one child in 150; for 2006, one child in 110; for 2008, one child in 88; and for 2010, one child in 68. Inconsistencies in reports of prevalence by different organizations may be a result of differences in data collection procedures or other methodological factors. Prevalence and other credible information related to autism and ASDs and the latest research are available at the websites for the Autism Society of America, www.autism-society.org, the Centers for Disease Control and Prevention, www.cdc.gov, and the Autism Center of Excellence through the homepage for the University of California, San Diego, www.ucds.edu.
12. The determination of whether a child has a specific learning disability has been a topic of controversy since IDEA was passed in 1975. Assessment tools and procedures have improved, and more have proven to be valid and reliable. Additional requirements for the evaluation and reevaluation of children who may have specific learning disabilities were added to IDEA when it was reauthorized in 2004 (20 U.S.C. § 1414).
13. Children with disabilities are to receive an education in the "least restrictive environment" (LRE), which is described in the statutes as settings with children without disabilities. LRE would apply to settings for music classes and other extracurricular music activities. In part, the law reads "that each public agency must ensure that—(i) To the maximum extent appropriate, children with disabilities, including children in public

or private institutions or other care facilities, are educated with children who are not disabled, and special classes, separate schooling, or other removal of children with disabilities from the regular environment occurs only when the nature of the disability or severity of the disability of a child is such that education in regular classes with the use of supplementary aids and services cannot be achieved satisfactorily" (20 U.S.C. § 1412). For nonacademic settings, in part, the law reads "that each public agency is to ensure that each child with a disability participates with nondisabled children in the extracurricular services and activities to the maximum extent appropriate to the needs of that child" (20 U.S.C. § 1401).

14. See "IDEA: History, Premises, Interpretations" in appendix C for descriptions of amendments and legal citations.
15. Several reliable and informative organizations offer the full text of IDEA, its history, how it is interpreted by organizations for children with different types of disabilities, teaching materials and resources, and updates. I suggest you begin with the full text found at the website for the US Department of Education at idea.ed.gov. For other information, see the following:

    - US Department of Education, Office of Special Education Programs (OSEP).
    - Council for Exceptional Children (CEC).
    - Center for Parent Information and Resources (CPIR).
    - Other professional organizations (e.g., American Association on Intellectual and Developmental Disabilities, Association for Learning Disabilities, Autism Society of America).

16. See appendix C for more information about Section 504 and its protections. The full text for the statute (20 U.S.C. 701 *et seq.*) can be found through the home page of the US Department of Labor, www.dol.gov.
17. This model emerged from IDEA, but it is receiving much attention in general education at all levels, particularly as a proactive process for identifying students who need extra support to succeed in school. Its name comes from language in § 300.307 (a) (2) in IDEA and is in reference to a child identified as having a specific learning disability and the child's *response to* scientific, research-based *interventions*.

    There is a healthy caution that pervades decision-making in this model. The goal is to identify students who require additional instruction, resources, and support and to make decisions based on the collective wisdom of members of the educational team who will recommend no more extra support than is necessary. The idea is to help a student succeed in school, academically and behaviorally, without referring the student for special education assessment and services, unless necessary. Supporters see RTI as a promising approach in that it acts as a safeguard against inappropriate labeling of children as having a disability. Others object that some children who are in need of special education services may not be referred for services in a timely manner. Both arguments could be valid, since the success of the approach rests almost entirely with the intelligence, sensitivity, and diligence of members on schoolwide and grade-level teams who evaluate students' records and make recommendations.

    Teams consult with parents and recommend the intensity (tier) of the intervention. When students make gains, the team may recommend pulling back support. When assessments show that a student is unable to benefit from extra supports and services provided at Tier 3, or if at any point in this multileveled process the team suspects that the student may have a disability, it is the team's responsibility to consult with the student's parents and to make a referral for special education evaluation (which can only be conducted with parental consent). Students with disabilities may have varying levels of support recommended by the team, interventions that are not written on the students' Individualized Education Programs (IEPs) but that provide support for successful participation in classrooms and extracurricular activities.

There are a number of books, articles, and online descriptions about RTI. Organizations and authors vary in their positions and interpretations, particularly in regard to students with specific learning disabilities, but most are consistent in their agreement on the main principles of RTI as a schoolwide instructional model. Several online resources provide information about RTI (e.g., Response to Intervention Action Network).

18. J. A. Jellison and D. M. Taylor, "Attitudes toward Inclusion and Students with Disabilities: A Review of Three Decades of Music Research", *Bulletin of the Council for Research in Music Education* (2007): 9–23. Findings from the few music studies examining direct contact as a research variable are consistent with research from other disciplines showing that intergroup contact with extended, direct, face-to-face interactions positively influences attitudes toward individuals with disabilities and decreases prejudices and that the effects generalize to other situations and individuals in the same group (e.g., disabilities, race, gender, culture).

    Three reviews of music research related to children and youth and specific to inclusion are J. A. Jellison, "A Content Analysis of Music Research with Disabled Children and Youth (1975–1999)," in *Effectiveness of Music Therapy Procedures: Documentation of Research and Clinical Practice*, 199–264 (Silver Spring, MD: American Music Therapy Association, 2000); L. E. Brown and J. A. Jellison, "Music Research with Children with Disabilities and Their Typical Peers: A Systematic Review," *Journal of Music Therapy* 49, no. 3 (2012): 335–364; and J. A. Jellison and E. A. Draper, "Music Research in Inclusive School Settings: 1975–2012," *Journal of Research in Music Education* (in press). Reviews refer to many publications in the *Journal of Music Therapy* and the *Journal of Research in Music Education*. Although not related exclusively to inclusion, some articles of interest can be found at www.kennedy-center.org/education/vsa/programs/special_education.cfm.

CHAPTER 2

1. Ideas in this chapter first appeared in J. A. Jellison, "How Can All People Continue to Be Involved in Meaningful Music Participation?" in *Vision 2020: The Housewright Symposium on the Future of Music Education*, edited by C. K. Madsen, 111–137 (Reston, VA: Music Educators National Conference, 2000); and J. A. Jellison, "It's About Time," MENC Senior Researcher Address, *Journal of Research in Music Education* 52, no. 3 (2004): 191–205. *Vision 2020* is available free online through the National Association for Music Education,www.nafme.org.
2. R. A. Duke, *Intelligent Music Teaching: Essays on the Core Principles of Effective Instruction* (Austin, TX: Learning and Behavior Resources, 2014).
3. More information about the development of national music standards and availability of the documents can be found at www.nafme.org. Also see information from the National Coalition for Core Arts Standards (NCCAS) at nccas.wikispaces.com for background, the framework, and other developments.
4. Duke, *Intelligent Music Teaching*, 74.
5. Several publications with survey findings on arts participation were published in the late 1990s: American Music Conference, *American Attitudes towards Music 1997* (Carlsbad, CA: National Association of Music Merchants, 1997); E. V. Lehman, ed., *Age and Arts Participation with a Focus on the Baby Boom Cohort* (Santa Ana, CA: Seven Locks Press, 1996); A. R. Andreasen, *Expanding the Audience for the Performing Arts,*

National Endowment for the Arts Research Report 24 (Santa Ana, CA: Seven Locks Press, 1996). The National Association for Music Merchants (NAMM) commissioned the 2003 Gallop survey although the website for NAMM is only available to members. I suggest you search for the results online using the words "Gallup Poll 2003 NAMM."

6. Reports on the status of arts education in public elementary and secondary schools for the years 1994–1995, 1999–2000, and 2009–2010 are available through the US Department of Education, National Center for Education Statistics (NCES), nces.ed.gov. Search for "Arts Education in Public Elementary and Secondary Schools: 1999-2000 and 2009-10."
7. The latest report is entitled "The Nation's Report Card: Arts 2008." The NAEP reports for both years, 1997 and 2008, are available at nces.ed.gov/nationsreportcard/arts/.
8. In addition to assessing subject-area achievement, NAEP collects information that serves to fulfill reporting requirements of the No Child Left Behind Act (NCLB). NCLB requires that whenever feasible, NAEP include information on special groups (e.g., information reported by race, ethnicity, socioeconomic status, gender, disability, and limited English proficiency).

   NAEP has an extensive inclusion policy regarding the participation of students with disabilities in national assessments. Current and past reports have included information about students with disabilities and English-language learners participating in assessments. The 2009 report includes information for disabilities and music for the first time since assessments have been conducted. Of the students with disabilities, 88 percent participated in the assessments, 26 percent without accommodations and 62 percent with accommodations. NAEP states that because students with disabilities (SD) and English-language learner (ELL) students "typically score lower than students not categorized as SD or ELL, jurisdictions that are more inclusive—that is, jurisdictions that assess greater percentages of these students—may have lower average scores than if they had a less inclusive policy." The inclusion policy, its history, permitted accommodations, rates of use of accommodations, and research about inclusion can be found at nces.ed.gov/nationsreportcard/about/inclusion.asp.
9. K. Elpus and C. R. Abril, "High School Music Ensemble Students in the United States: A Demographic Profile," *Journal of Research in Music Education* 59, no. 2 (2011): 128–145.
10. Transition planning and identification of services are required by IDEA to begin by the time the student reaches age sixteen, at the latest, and may start earlier. They are required as a part of the development of the student's IEP and must include postsecondary goals and services needed to reach those goals. Goals may be postsecondary or vocational training, employment, independent living, and community participation, and services must take into account the student's preferences and interests. The definition is quite lengthy and can be found in IDEA, 20 U.S.C. § 300.43.

CHAPTER 3

1. Laws, regulations, policy guidelines, fact sheets, and other practical information about various types of discrimination prohibited by law (e.g., age, disability) can be found at the websites for the US Department of Education, www.ed.gov, the US Equal Employment Opportunity Commission, www.eeoc.gov, and the US Department of Housing and Development, www.hud.gov.
2. Some publications by N. Bank-Mikkelsen, B. Nirje, and W. Wolfensberger are difficult to find, although many are reprinted in their original forms in R. J. Flynn and K. Nitsch, eds., *Normalization, Social Integration, and Community Services* (Baltimore: University Park Press, 1980). This book is out of print, but used copies can still be found. An

important 1972 paper by Wolfensberger, "The Principle of Normalization in Human Services," is available through the National Institute on Mental Retardation, Toronto.

3. B. Blatt and F. Kaplan, *Christmas in Purgatory* (Boston: Allyn & Bacon, 1966). Originally published in 1966, the book was reprinted in 1974 by the Human Policy Press, Center on Human Policy, Syracuse University. Pictures and captions from *Christmas in Purgatory* are available at the website for the online Disability History Museum, www.disabilitymuseum.org. Search for the complete book online by its title. At this library you will find fascinating materials dating back to the eighteenth century.
4. The complete texts of IDEA and the original Education of All Handicapped Children Act of 1975, in addition to related programs and services, are available at the website for the Office of Special Education Programs (OSEP). Access the OSEP through the website for the US Department of Education, www.ed.gov.
5. 20 U.S.C. § 1412, State Eligibility, (a) (5) (A): Least restrictive environment, p. 118, Stat. 2677. The quotation defines least restrictive environment, one of several conditions in IDEA 2004 that must be met if states are to receive financial assistance.
6. L. Brown, B. Wilcox, E. Sontag, B. Vincent, N. Dodd, and L. Gruenewald, "Toward the Realization of the Least Restrictive Educational Environments for Severely Handicapped Students," *AAESPH Review* (American Association for the Education of the Severely/Profoundly Handicapped) 2, no. 4 (1977): 195–201. Also see L. Brown, A. Ford, J. Nisbet, M. Sweet, A. Donnelan, and L. Gruenewald, "Opportunities Available When Severely Handicapped Students Attend Chronological Age Appropriate Regular Schools," *Journal of the Association for the Severely Handicapped* 8 (1983): 16–24.
7. W. Wolfensberger, "Social Role Valorization: A Proposed New Term for the Principle of Normalization," *Mental Retardation* 21 (1983): 234–239.
8. Several authors are noted for their work related to cultural diversity, social practices, and the musical development of children. For examples, see M. S. Barrett, ed., *A Cultural Psychology of Music Education* (Oxford: Oxford University Press, 2011); and P. S. Campbell, *Songs in Their Heads: Music and Its Meaning in Children's Lives*, 2nd ed. (New York: Oxford University Press, 2010). Music and social contexts are topics in a number of articles and books by music education scholars (e.g., see works by D. J. Elliott, L. Green, D. Hargreaves, S. O'Neil, R. MacDonald, and J. Sloboda).
9. A. Bandura, *Social Learning Theory* (Englewood Cliffs, NJ: Prentice-Hall, 1977).
10. L. Vygotsky, *Mind in Society: The Development of Higher Psychological Processes* (Cambridge, MA: Harvard University Press, 1935/1978).
11. A review of some of the earliest research on the topic appears in R. E. Slavin, "Cooperative Learning," *Review of Educational Research* 50 (1980): 315–342. In his introduction, Slavin traces the concept of cooperative learning to the 1920s and the writing of J. B. Maller, one of the earliest authors on the topic. See J. B. Maller, *Cooperation and Competition* (New York: Teachers College, Columbia University, 1929). Although only twenty-eight studies were available for Slavin's early review, published articles and books on the topic are now in the hundreds. Slavin, D. Johnson, and R. Johnson are well-known scholars on the topic of cooperative learning, and their studies have included children from diverse cultural backgrounds and children with disabilities. D. Johnson and R. Johnson, *Learning Together and Alone: Cooperative, Competitive, and Individualistic Learning* (New Jersey: Englewood Cliffs), first published in 1975, is widely used in college classrooms today.
12. M. Tomasello, *The Cultural Origins of Human Cognition* (Cambridge, MA: Harvard University Press, 1999).
13. As examples, see P. S. Campbell, *Oxford Handbook of Children's Musical Cultures* (New York: Oxford University Press, 2013); and K. Marsh, *The*

Musical Playground: Global Tradition and Change in Children's Songs and Games (New York: Oxford University Press, 2008).

14. C. A. Rohrbeck, M. D. Ginsburg-Block, J. W. Fantuzzo, and T. R. Miller, "Peer-Assisted Learning Interventions with Elementary School Students: A Meta-Analytic Review," *Journal of Educational Psychology* 95 (2003): 240–257.
15. M. D. Ginsburg-Block, C. A. Rohrbeck, and J. W. Fantuzzo, "A Meta-Analytic Review of Social, Self-Concept, and Behavioral Outcomes of Peer Assisted Learning," *Journal of Educational Psychology* 98 (2006): 732–749.
16. G. W. Allport, *The Nature of Prejudice* (Reading, MA: Addison Wesley, 1954).
17. T. F. Pettigrew and L. R. Tropp, "Interpersonal Relations and Group Processes," *Journal of Personality and Social Psychology* 90 (2006): 751–783.
18. For a current look at concerns of teachers related to discipline and classroom management, see J. N. Killian, K. G. Dye, and J. B. Wayman, "Music Student Teachers: Pre-Student Teaching Concerns and Post-Student Teaching Perceptions over a 5-Year Period," *Journal of Research in Music Education* 61 (2012): 63–79. For other examples, see J. R. Austin and W. P. Vispoel, "Motivation after Failure in School Music Performance Classes: The Facilitative Effects of Strategy Attributions," *Bulletin of the Council for Research in Music Education* 111 (1992): 1–23; D. G. Gordon, "Discipline in the Music Classroom: One Component Contributing to Teacher Stress," *Music Education Research* 4 (2002): 157–165; C. B. Hancock, "Music Teachers at Risk for Attrition and Migration: An Analysis of the 1999–2000 Schools and Staffing Survey," *Journal of Research in Music Education* 56 (2008): 130–144; and C. K. Madsen and K. A. Kaiser, "Pre-Internship Fears of Student Teaching," *Update: Applications of Research in Music Education* 17, no. 2 (1999): 27–32.
19. M. J. Bergee and L. Cecconi-Roberts, "Effects of Small-Group Peer Interaction on Self-Evaluation of Music Performance," *Journal of Research in Music Education* 50 (2002): 256–268.
20. For more recent and earlier overviews of music education in urban schools, see C. Frierson-Campbell, ed., *Teaching Music in the Urban Classroom: A Guide to Survival, Success, and Reform* (Lanham, MD: Rowman & Littlefield Education, 2006); and J. A. Taylor, N. H. Barry, and K. C. Walls, *Music and Students at Risk: Creative Solutions for a National Dilemma* (Reston, VA: Music Educators National Conference, 1997).
21. NCES data for schools in districts with high poverty concentrations were presented and discussed in chapter 2. Several examples from the music research literature concerning characteristics of music programs in urban schools and their teachers and students include V. D. Baker, "Profile of an Effective Urban Music Educator," *Update: Applications of Research in Music Education* 31 (2012): 44–54; E. Costa-Giomi, "Characteristics of Elementary Music Programs in Urban Schools: What Money Can Buy," *Bulletin of the Council for Research in Music Education* 177 (2008): 19–28; E. Costa-Giomi and E. Chappell, "Characteristics of Band Programs in a Large Urban School District: Diversity or Inequality?" *Journal of Band Research* 42, no. 2 (2007): 1–18; K. R. Fitzpatrick, "A Mixed Methods Portrait of Urban Instrumental Music Teaching," *Journal of Research in Music Education* 59 (2011): 229–256; K. R. Fitzpatrick, J. C. Henninger, and D. M. Taylor, "Access and Retention of Marginalized Populations within Undergraduate Music Education Degree Programs," *Journal of Research in Music Education* 61 (2014): 5–25; D. Kinney, "Selected Demographic Variables, School Music Participation and Achievement Test Scores of Urban Middle School Students," *Journal of Research in Music Education* 56 (2008): 145–161; D. Kinney, "Selected Nonmusic Predictors of Urban Students' Decisions to Enroll and Persist in Middle School Band Programs," *Journal of Research in Music Education* 57 (2010): 334–350; and N. R. Robinson, "Preservice Music Teachers' Employment

Preferences: Consideration Factors," *Journal of Research in Music Education* 23 (2012): 1–14.

22. Susan O'Neil has written extensively on the topic of musical engagement in diverse contexts and cultures and adolescents' social identity and self-identity. For an example of her papers on this topic, see S. O'Neil, "Positive Youth Musical Engagement," in *The Child as Musician*, edited by G. McPherson (London: Oxford University Press, 2006), 461–474.
23. Programs for at-risk youth in the United States and globally are discussed in M. L. Cohen, L. H. Silber, A. Sangiorgio, and V. Iadeluca, "At-Risk Youth: Music-Making as a Means to Promote Positive Relationships," in *The Oxford Handbook of Music Education*, Vol. 2, edited by G. E. McPherson and G. F. Welch (Oxford: Oxford University Press, 2012), 185–202.
24. C. Shields, "Music Education and Mentoring as Intervention for At-Risk Urban Adolescents: Their Self-Perceptions, Opinions, and Attitudes," *Journal of Research in Music Education* 43 (2001): 273–287.
25. K. Elpus and C. R. Abril, "High School Music Ensemble Students in the United States: A Demographic Profile," *Journal of Research in Music Education* 59 (2011): 128–145.
26. See music research articles in note 21 above.
27. D. Kinney, "Selected Nonmusic Predictors."
28. C. Adderly, M. Kennedy, and W. Berz, "'A Home away from Home': The World of the High School Music Classroom," *Journal of Research in Music Education* 51 (2003): 190–205; S. Morrison, "The School Ensemble: A Culture of Our Own," *Music Educators Journal* 88, no. 2 (2001): 24–28.
29. Adderly, Kennedy, and Berz, "'A Home away from Home.'"
30. J. A. Jellison and D. M. Taylor, "Students with Disabilities, Inclusion, and Attitudes: A Review of Music Research (1975–2005)," *Bulletin of the Council for Research in Music Education* 172 (2007): 9–23.
31. Three reviews of music research related to children and youth, and specific to inclusion, include the following: J. A. Jellison, "A Content Analysis of Music Research with Disabled Children and Youth (1975–1999)," in *Effectiveness of Music Therapy Procedures: Documentation of Research and Clinical Practice*, (Silver Spring, MD: American Music Therapy Association, 2000), 199–264; L. S. Brown and J. A. Jellison, "Music Research with Children and Youth with Disabilities and Their Typical Peers: A Systematic Review," *Journal of Music Therapy* 49 (2012): 335–364; and J. A. Jellison and E. A. Draper, "Inclusive Music Research in School Settings: 1975–2012," *Journal of Research in Music Education* (in press).
32. M. J. Kostka, "Secondary Music Students' Attitudes toward Atypical Peers," *Update: Applications in Music Education* (Spring/Summer 1999): 8–12.
33. M. Humple, "The Effects of an Integrated Early Childhood Music Program on Social Interaction among Children with Handicaps and Their Typical Peers," *Journal of Music Therapy* 28 (1991): 161–177.
34. P. Kern and D. Aldridge, "Using Embedded Music Therapy Interventions to Support Outdoor Play of Young Children with Autism in an Inclusive Community-Based Child Care Program," *Journal of Music Therapy* 43 (2006): 270–294
35. J. A. Jellison, B. Brooks, and A. M. Huck, "Structuring Small Groups and Music Reinforcement to Facilitate Positive Interactions and Acceptance of Severely Handicapped Students in the Regular Music Classroom," *Journal of Research in Music Education* 32 (1984): 243–264.
36. C. K. Madsen, D. S. Smith, and C. C. Feeman, "The Use of Music in Cross-Age Tutoring within Special Education Settings," *Journal of Music Therapy* 25 (1988): 135–144.

37. L. A. Scott, J. A. Jellison, E. W. Chappell, and A. A. Standridge, "Talking with Teachers about Inclusion: Perceptions, Opinions and Experiences," *Journal of Music Therapy* 54 (2007): 38–56.
38. Although residential and educational opportunities for individuals with disabilities, particularly those with intellectual and developmental disabilities, have increased in most states, some states still have low commitments to ending institutionalization. In these states, residencies in nursing facilities, private institutions, and state institutions are increasing. TASH states on its website, www.tash.org, that it is dedicated to "the full inclusion and participation of persons with disabilities in all aspects of life" and has been at the forefront of promoting self-determination and improving residential services and educational services for people with significant disabilities.
39. Bandura has written extensively on the topics of social learning and self-efficacy. Two books are considered to be classic texts on the topics: A. Bandura, *Social Foundations of Thought and Action: A Social Cognitive Theory* (Englewood Cliffs, NJ: Prentice-Hall, 1986); and A. Bandura, *Self-Efficacy: The Exercise of Control* (Stanford, CA: Stanford University Press, 1997).
40. For a brief summary of self-determination theory, see R. M. Ryan and E. L. Deci, "Self-Determination Theory and the Facilitation of Intrinsic Motivation, Social Development, and Well-Being," *American Psychologist* 55 (2000): 68–78. A comprehensive discussion of the research can be found in E. L. Deci and R. M. Ryan, *The Handbook of Self-Determination Theory* (Rochester, NY: University of Rochester Press, 2002).
41. S. Field, J. Martin, R. Miller, M. Ward, and M. L. Wehmeyer, *A Practical Guide to Teaching Self-Determination* (Reston, VA: Council for Exceptional Children, 1998), 2.
42. D. E. Mithaug, M. L. Wehmeyer, M. Agran, J. E. Martin, and S. Palmer, "The Self-Determined Learning Model of Instruction: Engaging Students to Solve Their Learning Problems," in *Making It Happen: Student Involvement in Educational Planning, Decision Making, and Instruction*, edited by M. L. Wehmeyer and D. J. Sands (Baltimore: Brookes, 1998), 303.
43. Two books explain in detail components for a curriculum for self-determination: M. L. Wehmeyer, M. Agran, C. Hughes, J. Martin, D. E. Mithaug, and S. Palmer, *Promoting Self-Determination in Students with Intellectual and Developmental Disabilities* (New York: Guilford Press. 2007); and M. L. Wehmeyer and S. Field, *Self-Determination: Instructional and Assessment Strategies* (Thousand Oaks, CA: Corwin Press, 2007).
44. See B. Algozzine, D. Browder, M. Karvonen, D. W. Test, and W. M. Wood, "Effects of Interventions to Promote Self-Determination for Individuals with Disabilities," *Review of Educational Research* 17, no. 2 (2001): 219–277; and W. M. Wood, C. H. Fowler, N. Uphold, and D. W. Test, "A Review of Self-Determination Interventions with Individuals with Severe Disabilities," *Research & Practice for Persons with Severe Disabilities* 30, no. 3 (2005): 121–146.
45. Deci and Ryan, *The Handbook of Self-Determination Theory.*
46. M. L. Wehmeyer, S. B. Palmer, M. Agran, D. E. Mithaug, and J. E. Martin, "Promoting Causal Agency: The Self-Determined Model of Instruction," *Exceptional Children* 66 (2000): 439–453. You will also find a list of books, book chapters, and articles on the topic at Wehmeyer's website through the University of Kansas home page, www.ku.edu.
47. R. A. Duke, "Their Own Best Teachers," *Music Educators Journal* 99, no. 2 (December 2012): 36–41.
48. For examples of music studies related to self-determination behaviors with school-age and college-age students, see M. J. Bergee, "Relationships among Faculty, Peer, and Self-Evaluation of Applied Performances," *Journal of Research in Music Education* 45,

no. 4 (1997): 601–612; Bergee and Cecconi-Roberts, "Effects of Small-Group Peer Interaction"; P. Broomhead, "Shaping Expressive Performance: A Problem-Solving Approach," *Music Educators Journal* 91, no. 5 (2005): 62–80; G. E. McPherson, "From Child to Musician: Skill Development during the Beginning Stages of Learning an Instrument," *Psychology of Music* 33 (2005): 5–35; G. E. McPherson and J. McCormick, "Motivational and Self-regulated Learning Components of Musical Practice," *Bulletin of the Council for Research in Music Education* 141 (1999): 98–102; G. E. McPherson and K. S. Hendricks, "Students' Motivation to Study Music: The United States of America," *Research Studies in Music Education* 32 (2010): 201–213; D. Rohwer and J. Polk, "Practice Behaviors of Eighth-Grade Instrumental Musicians," *Journal of Research in Music Education* 54 (2006): 350–362.

49. Shel Silverstein's famous book of poems and drawings, *Where the Sidewalk Ends,* first published in 1974, was published again in 2004 by HarperCollins in a thirtieth anniversary edition. The poem "Helping" appears on p. 101 in all editions.
50. J. A. Jellison, "On-Task Participation of Typical Students Close to and Away from Classmates with Disabilities in an Elementary Music Classroom," *Journal of Research in Music Education* 32 (2002): 228–247.
51. Field-tested curricula, sample lesson plans, and reports from pilot programs fostering self-determination can be accessed at several websites for centers for self-determination at universities (e.g., University of Kansas, University of Minnesota, University of North Carolina, University of Wisconsin) as well as the Council for Exceptional Children (CEC), cec.sped.org.
52. One of the first publications of the model can be found in Wehmeyer et al., "Promoting Causal Agency." Instructional and assessment strategies are provided in Wehmeyer and Field, *Self-Determination.*
53. These keywords emerged from a systematic review of healthcare research literature. See D. D'Amour, M. Ferrada-Videla, M. Rodrigues, and M. D. Beaulieu, "The Conceptual Basis for Interprofessional Collaboration: Core Concepts and Theoretical Frameworks," *Journal of Interprofessional Care* 1 (2005): 116–131. I have not located a systematic review of collaboration in educational research, although the concepts in the healthcare literature are relevant to education. For example, see M. Friend and L. Cook, *Interactions: Collaboration Skills for School Professionals,* 4th ed. (Boston: Allyn & Bacon, 2003); and D. VanGarderen, M. Stormont, and N. Goel, "Collaboration between General and Special Educators and Student Outcomes: A Need for More Research," *Psychology in the Schools* 49 (2012): 483–497.
54. For a review of literature on the topic, see D. D. Cox, "Evidence-Based Interventions Using Home-School Collaboration," *School Psychology Quarterly* 20 (2005): 471–497. Also, for insights into the concerns of parents and guardians, read material at the website of the Parent Advocacy Coalition for Education Rights, www.pacer.org.
55. For historical information and empirical research on the influence of music on behavior in therapy settings, see publications by the American Music Therapy Association, www.musictherapy.org. The premiere research journal is the *Journal of Music Therapy;* clinical papers and research can be found in *Music Therapy Perspectives.*
56. In NCLB schools, a paraprofessional with instructional support duties must have a high school diploma or its equivalent and one of the following: complete two years of education at a college or university, earn an associate degree or higher from a college or university, or pass a formal school paraprofessional state or local test that demonstrates ability to assist in reading, writing, and mathematics. These requirements and updates regarding qualifications can be found by searching "paraprofessionals" at the home page for the US Department of Education, www.ed.gov, or the NCLB page, www.ed.gov/nclb.

57. Much of the writing and research on issues concerning paraprofessionals comes from Michael Giangreco and his colleagues. For more on this topic specific to music education, see E. Bernstorf, "Paraprofessionals in Music Settings," *Music Educators Journal* (2001): 36–40; and A. A. Darrow, "Working with Paraprofessionals in the Music Classroom," *General Music Today* 23, no. 1 (2010): 35–37.
58. Under Part A, 20 U.S.C § 1401, the term *related services* means "services designed to enable a child with a disability to receive a free appropriate public education as described in the individualized education program of the child, counseling services, including rehabilitation counseling, orientation and mobility services, and medical services, except that such medical services shall be for diagnostic and evaluation purposes only as may be required to assist a child with a disability to benefit from special education, and includes the early identification and assessment of disabling conditions in children."
59. Although music therapists can develop their own assessment tools, the Special Education Music Therapy Assessment Process (SEMTAP), developed by Brunks and Coleman, is used widely by music therapists in schools. Read more about their work and assessment in music therapy in B. Brunks and K. Coleman, "Development of a Special Education Music Therapy Assessment Process," *Music Therapy Perspectives* 18 (2000): 59–68. Also see B. Brunks and K. Coleman, "A Special Education Music Therapy Assessment Process," in *Models of Music Therapy Interventions in School Settings*, 2nd ed., edited by B. Wilson (Silver Spring, MD: American Music Therapy Association, 2002), 69–82.
60. See information about AMTA, education and clinical training, practices, and publications at www.musictherapy.org. Also see AMTA publications, including *Music in Special Education* (Adamek and Darrow); *Introduction to Approaches in Music Therapy* (Darrow); *An Introduction to Music Therapy: Theory and Practice* (Davis, Gfeller, and Thaut); and *Models of Music Therapy Intervention in School Settings*, (Wilson, ed.). A few articles on collaboration with special educators and music therapists will be of interest. See K. A. McCord and E. H. Watt, "Collaboration and Access for Our Children: Music Educators and Special Educators Together," *Music Educators Journal* 92, no. 4 (2006): 26–33; and J. Montgomery and A. Martinson, "Partnering with Music Therapists: A Model for Addressing Students' Musical and Extramusical Goals," *Music Educators Journal* 92, no. 4 (2006): 34–39.

CHAPTER 4

1. See online resources at the companion website and the CML site for additional strategies and adaptations. Also, see the website for the Exceptionalities Special Research Interest Group of the National Association for Music Education (NAfME). Search for the exceptionalities research group at www.nafme.org.

   Books that provide additional examples include M. A. Adamek and A. A. Darrow, *Music in Special Education*, 2nd ed. (Silver Spring, MD: American Music Therapy Association, 2010); A. M. Hammel and R. M. Hourigan, *Teaching Music to Students with Special Needs* (New York: Oxford University Press, 2011); and K. Mixon, *Reaching and Teaching All Instrumental Students*, 2nd ed. (Lanham, MD: Rowman & Littlefield, 2011). Also see several relevant articles in *Special Abilities, Special Needs*, part edited by A. Ockelford, in *The Oxford Handbook of Music Education*, Vol. 2, edited by G. E. McPherson and G. F. Welch (London: Oxford University Press, 2012), 5–96.

2 Many ideas in this book are based on the principles of the Universal Design for Learning (UDL) framework developed at the Center for Applied Special Technology

(CAST). Principles in the framework focus on designing multiple and flexible methods at the onset of instruction to accommodate "learner differences" among children. Assistive technology (AT) plays a prominent role in the UDL classroom, particularly in literacy programs. For more information, see articles and books by David H. Rose and Anne Meyer from CAST and other information at the website (www.cast.org).

Also see the Center for Universal Design (CUD) at North Carolina State University (www.ncsu.edu) for interesting information about demographic, legislative, and social changes that brought greater access to individuals with disabilities and the Center for Universal Design for Instruction (UDI) at the University of Washington (www.washington.edu/doit) for information related to postsecondary schools, colleges, and universities.

3 Mace was a devoted advocate for the rights of people with disabilities, an architect, a design pioneer, and a visionary of universal design. His history is available at www.ncsu.edu, the website for the Center for Universal Design. IDEA 2004 refers to the definition of universal design found in the Assistive Technology Act of 1998 (29 U.S.C. § 1401[35]). The Tech Act, as it is called, defines universal design as a "concept or philosophy for designing and delivering products and services that are usable by people with the widest possible range of functional capabilities, which include products and services that are directly accessible (without requiring assistive technologies) and products and services that are interoperable with assistive technologies" (U.S.C. § 3002[19]).

4. Title II of the Americans with Disabilities Act of 1990 (ADA), 42 U.S.C. § 12131 *et seq.*, prohibits state and local governments from discriminating on the basis of disability. Section 504 of the Rehabilitation Act of 1973 protects the rights of individuals with disabilities in programs and activities that receive federal financial assistance, including federal funds. Section 504 provides that "No otherwise qualified individual with a disability in the United States . . . shall, solely by reason of her or his disability, be excluded from the participation in, be denied the benefits of, or be subjected to discrimination under any program or activity receiving Federal financial assistance" (Section 504 of the Rehabilitation Act of 1973, as amended, 29 U.S.C. § 794). The full text of the ADA as amended (28 C.F.R. § 36.104) and other information on disability laws and standards for access is available at www.ada.gov.

5. Many curricular and instructional practices in special education can be traced to the early actions of parents and professionals who questioned the quality of educational services for persons with severe disabilities. In the mid-1970s, Lou Brown, Norris Haring, and Wayne Sailor, along with supportive parents, educators, and advocates, formed a new organization to represent the interests of individuals with significant disabilities, the American Association for the Education of the Severely and Profoundly Handicapped, now named simply TASH (www.tash.org).

A significant challenge to the developmental model was presented in a 1978 grant report by Brown and his colleagues. These groundbreaking ideas are found in a classic article by L. Brown, M. B. Branston, S. Hamre-Nietupski, N. Certo, and L. Gruenwald, "A Strategy for Developing Chronological-Age Appropriate and Functional Curricular Content for Severely Handicapped Adolescents and Young Adults," *Journal of Special Education* 13, no. 1 (1979): 81–90. Summaries of significant curricular changes are presented in appendix D.

6. D. Baumgart, L. Brown, I. Pumpian, J. Nisbet, A. Ford, M. Sweet, R. Messina, and J. Schroeder, "Principle of Partial Participation and Individualized Adaptations in Educational Programs for Severely Handicapped Students," *Journal of the Association for Persons with Severe Handicaps* 7 (1982): 17–27. This is the first publication proposing the principle.

7. IDEA 2004 includes numerous references to scientifically based instructional practices and peer-reviewed research. Also, the IEP must include a statement of special education and related services, and supplementary aids and services, based on peer-reviewed research to the extent practicable, and a statement of the program modifications or supports for school personnel (20 U.S.C. § 1414).

   Evidence-based practice (EBP) is a term in special education referring to the use of interventions, strategies, and supports that have documented effectiveness in the research literature. The term *empirically based (research-based) instruction* has a longer history in the broader field of education. The definition of EBP has stimulated many questions in the field. What are the indicators or sources of evidence? Should evidence include articles, fact sheets, case studies, anecdotal notes along with findings from the research literature or include only findings from peer-reviewed research employing stringent quantitative and/or qualitative methodologies? As you may imagine, opinions vary. Other topics in the literature concern practices for different populations and teacher preparation and education, to mention a few. Useful information on evidence-based practice can be found at the websites for CEC, www.cec.org, and other organizations (e.g., the American Psychological Association, www.apa.org).
8. J. A. Jellison, J. A. "Life Beyond the Jingle stick: Real Music in a Real World," *Update: Applications of Research in Music Education*, 17, no. 2 (1999): 13–19.
9. Selected goals from R. A. Duke, *Intelligent Music Teaching* (Austin, TX: Learning Behavior and Resources, 2014). When discussing what students should learn, Duke proposes a comprehensive list of music and social behaviors that can be performed by musicians at all levels of experience and expertise.
10. D. L. Ferguson and D. Baumgart, "Partial Participation Revisited," *Journal of the Association for Persons with Severe Handicaps* 16 (1991): 218–227.
11. Duke, *Intelligent Music Teaching*, 72.
12. L. Brown, "Learning characteristics of individuals with significant intellectual disabilities," unpublished manuscript, School of Education, University of Wisconsin-Madison, 2013, 10. An online search for "Lou Brown" will lead to papers and talks about curricular and instructional decisions for students with significant intellectual disabilities.
13. 20 U.S.C. § 1412 (c) (16). See additional information on large-scale assessments and assessing students with disabilities at www.osepideasthatwork.org.
14. J. A. Jellison and P. J. Flowers, "Talking about Music: Interviews with Disabled and Nondisabled Children," *Journal of Research in Music Education* 39 (1991): 322–333.
15. Many interesting adaptations for instruments can be found online. See the CML site, the Exceptionalities SRIG site, and sites for companies that focus on instrument adaptations (e.g., ERGObrass, www.ergobrass.com). You might also view and have your students view inspiring stories and performances of musicians with disabilities playing adapted instruments (e.g., YouTube videos of violinist Adrian Anantawan).
16. AT devices and services are defined in IDEA 2004 (devices, U.S.C. § 300.5, and services, U.S.C. § 300.6). There are any number of definitions, readings, and books on the topic online. Also, a visit to www.abledata.com will give you some idea of the hundreds of AT devices on the market.
17. The official website for Section 508,www.section508.gov, provides extensive information for the Assistive Technology Act of 1998, referred to as Section 508, along with other relevant laws and links. Section 504 of the Rehabilitation Act of 1973, which prohibits discrimination based on disability in federally funded and federally conducted programs and activities, was expanded by the Technology-Related Assistance for Individuals with Disabilities Act in 1988 (P.L. 100-407), known as the Tech Act, and the Assistive Technology Act of 1998 (P.L. 105-220), referred to as Section 508 of the Tech Act. These acts resulted in the expansion of programs and systems to provide

assistive technology devices (e.g., motorized wheelchairs, computer systems for communication) and services to facilitate access to technologies (e.g., Web-based sites, software, computers).

18. B. Freedman, *Teaching Music through Composition: A Curriculum Using Technology* (New York: Oxford University Press, 2013), vi.
19. K. A. McCord and E. H. Watts, "Music Educators Involvement in the Individual Education Program Process and Their Knowledge of Assistive Technology,". *Update: Applications of Research in Music Education* 28, no. 2 (2010): 79–85.
20. IDEA provides definitions related to the purchase of and access to instructional materials and requirements for the adoption of NIMAS by states, along with descriptions of the responsibilities of local education agencies for purchasing and providing instructional print materials to individuals who are blind or who have other types of reading (print) disabilities. (34 C.F.R. § 300.172). The website for NIMAC, www.nimac.us, will give you more information about centers, the national standard, and accessible instructional materials.
21. For a full description of all music services, see the NLS website. An online introduction to braille music transcription by DeGarmo is also available at the site, www.loc.gov/nis/.
22. For an interesting discussion of literary braille and braille music, information about teaching braille music, and selected software, see W. R. Siligo, "Enriching the Ensemble Experience for Students with Visual Impairments," *Music Educators Journal* 91, no. 5 (2005): 31–37. Also, the NLS provides brief explanations and in-depth courses on the topic of braille music.
23. If you are interested in knowing more about students who are deaf or hearing-impaired, read publications on this topic by Alice Ann Darrow and Kate Gfeller, experts in the field. I suggest you do an online search for their publications and review the publications lists at the website for the American Music Therapy Association, www.musictherapy.org.
24. The full text of the 1998 Amendment to Section 508 can be found at www.section508.gov. Standards at this site provide criteria specific to various types of technologies, including software applications and operating systems, Web-based information or applications, desktop and portable computers, and others.
25. When websites meet 508 standards, an icon appears on the page: "508 Approved." Most pages that are 508 approved will indicate that they are also "Bobby Approved." Bobby is a Web-based tool that was originally launched by CAST as a free public service; it won several awards for helping novice and professional Web designers analyze and make improvements in their pages. At this time, it is no longer a free service. Software for testing and developing accessible websites is available, although the industry is changing quickly; I suggest you do an online search for the current versions. For some trivial facts, the common icon indicating that a site is Bobby Approved is a bobby, the nickname for the British police, in honor of Sir Robert Peel, the home secretary who established the police force in 1829.
26. There are a number of scholarly articles about switches as AT devices and also manufacturers that can be found on the Internet. If you are interested in seeing pictures of different types of switches and their uses, begin your search at www.ablenetinc.com.
27. A specially designed chair, the Peery Riser Chair is available for singers who cannot stand or have difficulty tanding for rehearsals and performances. The chair is designed to fit Peery and Wenger risers and locks onto the riser for safety. More information is available at www.peeryproducts.com. There may be others on the market by now. Also see www.ablenetinc.com for more examples of devices to support standing and sitting.

APPENDIX B

1. For sources on the history of music education, in addition to articles cited in these notes, I have relied on three books: J. A. Keene, *A History of Music Education in the United States* (Lebanon, NH: University Press of New England, 1982); M. L. Mark, *Contemporary Music Education* (New York: Schirmer, 1996); and M. L. Mark, *Music Education: Source Readings from Ancient Greece to Today*, 2nd ed. (New York: Routledge, 2002).
2. The National Association of the Deaf, www.nad.org, provides helpful information of issues concerning the deaf and hearing-impaired. See Frequently Asked Questions (FAQs) for more information about the use of lowercase "deaf" and uppercase "Deaf." Often, lowercase is used when referring to the audiological condition of not hearing (e.g., a child who is deaf). Uppercase is preferred by individuals who have, throughout their social values and language, American Sign Language (ASL), created a distinct community and culture (e.g., the Deaf community). Individuals who are deaf, however, may differ in their values and may not have a strong association to the Deaf community and culture.
3. J. G. Itard, *The Wild Boy of Aveyron* (Englewood Cliffs, NJ: Prentice-Hall, 1962; originally published 1806).
4. G. N. Heller, "Ideas, Initiatives, and Implementations: Music Therapy in America, 1789–1848," *Journal of Music Therapy* 24 (1987): 35–46.
5. Read Lowell Mason's persuasive arguments for adopting vocal music as a regular subject in the school curriculum in Mark, *Music Education*, 70–75. Scholarly articles pertinent to the life and works of Mason are found in C. M. Colwell and G. N. Heller, "Lowell Mason's *The Song Garden (1864–66)*: Its Background, Content, and Comparison to a Twentieth-Century Series," *Journal of Research in Music Education 51* (2003): 231–244; and P. D. Perrin, "Pedagogical Philosophy, Methods, and Materials of American Tune Book Introductions: 1801–1860," *Journal of Research in Music Education 18* (1970): 65–69.
6. A. L. Solomon, "Music in Special Education before 1930: Hearing and Speech Development," *Journal of Research in Music Education 28* (1980): 236–242; A. A. Darrow and G. N. Heller, "Early Advocates of Music Education for the Hearing Impaired: William Wolcott Turner and David Ely Bartlett," *Journal of Research in Music Education* 33 (1985): 269–279. Use online searches to find articles by Alice-Ann Darrow and Kate Gfeller, widely recognized scholars on the topic of music and individuals who are deaf or hearing-impaired.
7. The National Library Service for the Blind and Physically Handicapped is a free national library that provides braille and recorded materials to eligible borrowers. The library has a large special music collection. For a full description of all music services, see the National Library Service for the Blind and Physically Handicapped website,www.loc.gov/nis. See additional information at the website for the National Federation of the Blind,www.nfb.org, and other websites available through the Center for Music Learning, website, www.cml.music.utexas.edu.
8. I. Kraft, "Music for the Feeble-Minded in Nineteenth Century America," *Journal of Research in Music Education 11* (1963): 119–122.
9. "Number of Insane at Large Now Less," *New York Times*, July 8, 1917, retrieved from www.nytimes.com, August 17, 2014. M. Wines, "After 30 Years, Mental Institutions May Be as Empty as They'll Ever Be," *New York* Times, September 4, 1988, retrieved from www.nytimes.com, August 17, 2014.
10. L. Breedlove, C. Decker, K. C. Lakin, R. Prouty, and K. Coucouvanis, "Placement of Children and Youth in State Institutions: 40 Years after the High Point, It Is Time to Just Stop," *Mental Retardation* 43, no. 3 (2005): 235–238.

11. *Healthy People 2010, Disability and Secondary Conditions* (HP2010). Led by the US Department of Health and Human Services, HP2010 is the ten-year health-promotion program for improving the health of all Americans. Among the goals for disabilities for the year 2010 were elimination of all public and private congregate facilities for children, increasing home- and community-based care, and increasing the proportion of children and youths with disabilities who spend at least 80 percent of their time in regular education programs from 45 percent to 60 percent. In the final report, a downward trend was observed in congregate-care living between 1997 and 2009, although 28,890 children and youths were living in those facilities in 2009, an 11 percent increase. The proportion of children and youths ages six to twenty-one with disabilities who were enrolled in regular education programs increased from 45 percent to 58 percent for the years 1995 to 2008, which moved closer to the goal of 60 percent. See the report for 2010, the latest program for 2020, and other updates at www.healthypeople.gov.
12. The literature on eugenics is vast, in part because of the deep emotional reactions individuals have to this shameful period in our history. In scholarly books and articles, you will find fascinating, if disturbing, accounts of the economic, social, and political conditions that fueled the eugenics movement in the United States. For our purposes here, I will provide only a few cursory facts. The word *eugenics* is derived from the Greek, meaning "well bred," and the term appears for the first time in the writings of Englishman Sir Francis Galton, considered the founder of the eugenics movement in the late nineteenth century. Prominent figures throughout history have supported ideas and practices to control reproduction toward the elimination of "undesirable traits" in future generations, although the names of two scientists appear consistently: Galton and Davenport. Their writings and research, built on the ideas of Galton, gave momentum to the movement in the United States in the 1900s. Davenport wrote widely on the topic and initiated and administered eugenics research activities at the Cold Spring Harbor Laboratory on Long Island, a well-funded facility considered the premier institution for eugenics research under his administration. (Cold Spring Harbor is now a site for cancer research.) Among the eugenics lab activities was the collection of data about individuals determined to be "unfit." The lab was shut down in 1939, after Andrew Carnegie, one of its supporters, denied funding following a scathing committee report on its operations. Sterilizations in the United States continued for almost thirty more years.
13. *Buck v. Bell*, 274 U.S. 200 (1927). See images of documents and pictures at the Cold Spring Harbor Laboratory's Image Archive on the American Eugenics Movement (www.eugenicsarchieve.org/eugenics/). For another interesting historical account with pictures of Carrie and Emma Buck, and Carrie's baby, go to the website for historical collections at the University of Virginia, exhibits.hsl.virginia.edu.
14. Virginia's eugenics law was passed in 1924 and repealed in 1979. On February 15, 2001, the Virginia legislature expressed "profound" regret for the state's involvement in eugenics, which had led to the sterilization of 7,450 Virginians. "Virginia Expresses Regret for Past Sterilizations," *New York Times*, February 15, 2001. Several sources report on Warner's apology and the historical marker. You can see a picture of the marker at the Historical Marker Database, www.hmdb.org, and references to Warner's comments and an interesting account of apologies from governors from other states at the University of Virginia news services, www.virginia.edu/topnews.
15. B. Blatt and F. Kaplan, *Christmas in Purgatory* (Boston: Allyn & Bacon, 1966). Originally published in 1966, the book was reprinted in 1974 by the Human Policy Press, Center on Human Policy, Syracuse University. Pictures and captions from *Christmas in Purgatory* are available at the website for the online Disability History Museum, www.disabilitymuseum.org. Search for the complete book online by its title.

16. *Wyatt v. Stickney*, 344 F. Supp. 373 (M.D. Ala. 1972); *Halderman v. Pennhurst State School and Hospital*, 446 F. Supp. 1295 (E.D. Pa. 1977), aff'd. in part, rev'd. in part, 612 F. 2d 84 (3d Cir. 1979), rev'd and remanded, 451 U.S. 1 (1981). Arguments for "right to treatment" were predicated in part on the Developmental Disabilities Assistance and Bill of Rights Act (DD Act) originally authorized by Congress in 1963. This act, reauthorized in 2007, provides financial assistance to states in their efforts to establish and maintain programs for individuals with developmental disabilities. Participation by the states is voluntary, but no states have forgone funding and therefore comply with the stipulations of the Act. Among the rights in the Bill of Rights section are appropriate treatment, services, and habilitation designed to maximize the potential of the individual and provided in the setting that is least restrictive of the individual's personal liberty. Additional information about the Administration on Developmental Disabilities and the DD Act can be found at the U.S. government's official web portal, www.usa.gov.
17. *Parham v. J.R.*, 442 U.S. 584 (1979).
18. The Preamble and the full text of the Constitution and other charters and federal records are available at the National Archives website, www.archives.gov.
19. The court system of the judiciary branches is complex, particularly since the names of different courts vary among the states, and disputes are heard in state or federal courts depending on whether they involve state or federal laws. Judicial decisions can be made in different types of courts—trial courts, courts of appeal (appellate courts), and supreme courts (state and federal)—and a decision is binding on districts, circuits, states, and throughout the United States depending on which court made the last, and final, decision.
20. *Marbury v. Madison*, 5 U.S. 137 (1803).
21. *Dred Scott v. Sandford*, 60 U.S. 393 (1857). States were given the authority to determine the status of their residents, and Congress had not yet passed the Thirteenth and Fourteenth Amendments when the Supreme Court heard the *Dred Scott* case. Among the issues considered was that of a change of residency from free territories to states where slavery was authorized as legal. After extended residencies in free territories, slaves were freed. After being purchased by John Emerson, Dred Scott moved with his owner to the Wisconsin Territory, where slavery was banned. Having married and had children, Scott worked for Emerson and moved with him across several states. When Emerson died and Scott was left to Emerson's wife, Eliza Sandford, Scott offered to buy his freedom, but Sandford refused. Scott sought freedom through the courts; his fight lasted ten years. Chief Justice Roger Taney delivered the Supreme Court decision declaring that slaves were not citizens of the United States. It was almost another ten years before the *Dred Scott* decision was overturned by the Thirteenth and Fourteenth Amendments.
22. *Plessy v. Ferguson*, 163 U.S. 537 (1896).
23. *Brown v. Board of Education of Topeka*, 347 U.S. 483 (1954).
24. *Pennsylvania Assn. for Retarded Children (PARC) v. Commonwealth of Pennsylvania*, 334 F. Supp. 1257 (E.D. Pa. 1972).
25. *Mills v. Board of Education of District of Columbia*, 348 F. Supp. 866 (D. DC 1972).
26. The due process clauses of the Fifth and Fourteenth Amendments and the equal protection clause of the Fourteenth Amendment read as follows:

> Amendment V (1791). No person shall be held to answer for a capital, or otherwise infamous crime, unless on a presentment or indictment of a grand jury, except in cases arising in the land or naval forces, or in the militia, when in actual service in time of war or public danger; nor shall any person be subject for the same offense to be twice put in jeopardy of life or limb;

nor shall be compelled in any criminal case to be a witness against himself, nor be deprived of life, liberty, or property, without due process of law; nor shall private property be taken for public use, without just compensation.

Amendment XIV (1868). All persons born or naturalized in the United States, and subject to the jurisdiction thereof, are citizens of the United States and of the state wherein they reside. No state shall make or enforce any law which shall abridge the privileges or immunities of citizens of the United States; nor shall any state deprive any person of life, liberty, or property, without due process of law; nor deny to any person within its jurisdiction the equal protection of the laws.

APPENDIX C

1. There are several reliable and informative organizations offering the full text of IDEA, its history, how it is interpreted by organizations for children with specific disabilities, teaching materials and resources, and updates to the law. I suggest you begin by looking at the law found at the website for the US Department of Education at idea.ed.gov. For other information, see the following:

    - US Department of Education, Office of Special Education Programs (OSEP).
    - Center for Parent Information and Resources (CPIR).
    - Council for Exception Children (CEC).
    - Professional organizations (e.g., American Association on Intellectual and Developmental Disabilities, Association for Learning Disabilities, Autism Society of America).

2. *Pennsylvania Assn. for Retarded Children v. Commonwealth of Pennsylvania* (PARC), 334 F. Supp. 1257 (E. D. PA, 1971) and 343 F. Supp. 279 (E. D. Pa. 1972).
3. *Mills v. Board of Education of District of Columbia*, 348 F. Supp. 866 (D. DC 1972).
4. Title I of the Elementary and Secondary Education Act of 1965 (P.L. 89-10) specifically designated funding through states for schools with high percentages of "poor" children. Descriptions of Title I, other titles in this act and ESEA and NCLB are available at the website for the National Education Association (NEA), www.nea.org.
5. See R. W. D. Wright and P. D. Wright, *Special Education Law*, 2nd ed. (Hartfield, VA: Harbor House Law Press, 2007) for an analysis of IDEA 2004 and commentary. I incorporated the authors' style of highlighting important words and phrases.
6. Positive behavioral interventions are not specifically defined in the statutes, although the Office of Special Education Programs (OSEP) provides a wealth of information and resources at the website for the Center on Positive Behavioral Interventions and Supports (PBIS), www.pbis.org. Positive Behavior Support (PBS), now included as law in IDEA, was first a prominent idea in special education philosophy and practice designed to protect from abuses. PBIS provides information, training, support, and guidance on addressing behavior problems in research-based and effective strategies.
7. Letter from Kenneth R. Warlick, American Music Therapy Association director of special education programs, to Andrea Farbman, American Music Therapy Association executive director, June 9, 2000: "If the IEP team determines that music therapy is an appropriate related service for a child, the team's determination must be reflected in the child's IEP, and the service must be provided at public expense and at no cost to the parents." This letter is reproduced in B. L. Wilson, ed., *Models of Music Therapy Interventions in School Settings* (Silver Spring, MD: American Music Therapy Association, 2002), 10–13. Music therapy as a related service first appeared in the language of the Senate Report in P.L. 94-142 (Senate Report No. 94-168, 1975, p. 13).

According to Warlick's letter, reference to music therapy was considered a "note" to the prior regulations and was removed, along with many other notes in the regulations, when the law was amended in 1997. This note and others are found in an accompanying document to the 1997 law entitled "Analysis of Comments and Changes."

8. To keep this section more reader-friendly, only main ideas of some amendments are presented, most without legal citations. Information about the laws and amendments is extensive and can be located easily online. I suggest you begin with the website for the US Deparment of Education at idea.ed.gov.
9. Sections of IDEA that relate to infants and toddlers are found in Part C, Infants and Toddlers with Disabilities, and sections that relate to children and youths from ages three through twenty-one are found in Part B, Assistance for Education of All Children with Disabilities.
10. If parents challenge the placement and request a due process hearing, the "Stay Put Rule" (IDEA 2004, Sections 615 and 615) requires that the student remain in the then-current educational placement, with two exceptions: when parents and the LEA agree to another placement or in a discipline context. The student remains in the interim alternative educational setting (IAES) pending the decision of the hearing officer or until expiration of the time period for the IAES, whichever occurs earlier.
11. LEAs are permitted to use a child's *response to* scientific, research-based *intervention* as part of the process to determine an SLD. Methods of intervention have come to be known as Response to Intervention (RTI). The term does not appear in the law. Essentially, RTI is an educational concept that describes scientific, research-based interventions that have the potential for identifying students who may be at risk for academic failure and who have not been evaluated as needing (but who may need) special education services under IDEA. Read more about RTI in "Ideas That Work" at the OSEP website, www.osepideasthatwork.org, and chapter 1 of this book.
12. This regulation suggests to me that appropriate aids and services should be made available for all school music activities, including those beyond the classroom such as field trips to concert halls.
13. The NIMAS is a technical standard that guides the production and electronic distribution of digital versions of textbooks and other instructional materials so they can be more easily converted to accessible formats, including braille and text-to-speech for students with reading disabilities. Read more about the NIMAS center at its website, aim.cast.org, and in chapter 4.
14. Universal design is included for the first time in IDEA 2004. IDEA states that its meaning "is consistent with the term used in the Assistive Technology Act of 1998." The AT Act defines universal design as "a concept or philosophy for designing and delivering products and services that are usable by people with the widest possible range of functional capabilities, which include products and services that are directly accessible (without requiring assistive technologies) and products and services that are interoperable with assistive technologies" (Assistive Technology Act of 1998, Section 3 [17]). Universal design has also inspired classroom applications, a topic discussed extensively in chapter 4.
15. The definition of "highly qualified teacher" in IDEA (U.S.C. § 1401) conforms to that given in Section 6319 of the No Child Left Behind Act. A highly qualified special education teacher in IDEA is one who has full state certification (no waivers), has a license to teach, and meets state requirements. A number of other requirements are specified for special education teachers who teach core academic subjects exclusively to children who are assessed against alternative academic achievement standards (e.g., children

with severe cognitive disabilities) and special education teachers who teach multiple subjects. These requirements are subject to change.

16. A useful site with the full text for the statute (20 U.S.C. 701, *et seq.*) can be found at the website for the US Department of Labor, www.dol.gov.
17. See the full text of Americans with Disabilities Act Amendments Act of 2008 (28 C.F.R. § 36.104) and other information on disability laws and standards for access at the ADA website, www, ada.gov.

INDEX

CPSIA information can be obtained
at www.ICGtesting.com
Printed in the USA
BVHW031242190720
584052BV00002B/5

9 780199 358779